Trade and Commercial Interactions in the Atlantic Basin: Present and Future Issues

Renato G. Flôres Jr. and Francine T. Martin
Editors

Co-funded by the
Erasmus+ Programme
of the European Union

Renato G. Flôres Jr. and Francine T. Martin, eds., *Trade and Commercial Interactions in the Atlantic Basin: Present and Future Issues*

Jean Monnet Network on Atlantic Studies, 2019.

Distributed and available via Brookings Institution Press
https://www.brookings.edu/press/

ISBN 978-1-7337339-3-9

Cover Photograph: AKaiser, shutterstock.com

Contents

Preface

We are pleased to present the book *Trade and Commercial Interactions in the Atlantic Basin: Present and Future Issues*, a collaboration among the institutions of the Jean Monnet Network on Atlantic Studies and the second text of this kind, resulting from the Network's research efforts.

The Jean Monnet Network on Atlantic Studies is an initiative across the four Atlantic continents by ten leading centres—many with Jean Monnet professorships and in countries identified by the EU as key strategic partners—aimed at the interdisciplinary exploration of three major Atlantic themes of particular relevance to the EU: energy, commercial interactions and challenges to human security.

The objective of the project is to create and develop a pan-Atlantic research network, to contribute to an emerging epistemic community on 'New Atlantic Studies', and to offer strategic perspectives for the design of energy, trade and security policies in the Atlantic world. The Jean Monnet Project is also supported and co-funded by the Erasmus+ Programme of the European Union.

The institutions involved in the Network or consortium are each vibrant centres of EU-related studies in their respective regions. Most have collaborated—recently as part of the FP 7 project ''Atlantic Future''—on themes related to Atlantic issues and the role of the EU as a conspicuous actor in this space.

Fundação Getulio Vargas, through its International Intelligence Unit, FGV IIU, based in Rio de Janeiro, leads the consortium whose members are:

- Fundação Getulio Vargas, International Intelligence Unit – FGV IIU, Brazil

- Johns Hopkins University, School of Advanced International Studies - SAIS (Center for Transatlantic Relations, CTR), United States

- University of Pretoria, South Africa

- Universidade Nova de Lisboa, Instituto Português de Relações Internacionais - IPRI, Portugal

- CIDE, Mexico

- Roskilde University, Denmark

- Orkestra - Basque Institute for Competitiveness, University of Deusto, Spain

- CIDOB, Barcelona, Spain

- Universidad Autónoma de Madrid, Spain

- OCP Policy Centre (OCP Foundation), Morocco

The Center for Transatlantic Relations of Johns Hopkins University SAIS led the first year's agenda on energy, focusing on the nexus between energy and transportation. On July 20-21, 2017, the Network´s first research conference (Energy and Transportation in the Atlantic Basin) took place at the Paul H. Nitze School of Advanced International Studies – SAIS, John Hopkins University, in Washington, D.C. Together with work leading up to and following it, the conference catalysed the research and insights that have produced the first book.

At the headquarters of Fundação Getulio Vargas, in Rio de Janeiro, the second conference took place during March 21–23, 2018, dealing with trade and commercial issues. The main contributions and discussions, including a final Round Table with trade experts from different backgrounds, and the closing speech by the EU Ambassador to Brazil, are the content of this second book.

As usual, the Project members wish to show their appreciation to the European Commission, that provided the funds which made this research and the related book publication possible. Though especially grateful to the team at the leading institution, in Rio, the Network partners have also participated, in a way or other, in the preparations and efforts that allowed the conference and the book come true.

It is our hope that the present work will continue to successfully propel this Jean Monnet Project, increasing its visibility and widespread impact. The next and final annual cycle will deal with defence and security aspects of relevance for the region.

The Network continues to pursue its goals to be a go-to resource on the contemporary role of the EU in the wider Atlantic space, advancing the comparative knowledge of integration processes in Europe and other Atlantic regions.

Renato G. Flôres Jr.

FGV IIU

in the name of all members of the Jean Monnet Atlantic Network

Contributors

Mark Aspinwall is Professor of International Studies (and currently Chair of the División de Estudios Internacionales) at the CIDE in Mexico City. He is also an Honorary Professorial Fellow at the University of Edinburgh, Scotland. Mark's research interests are in rule of law, comparative governance in environmental and labour sectors, and the impact of regional organisations on domestic politics in North America and the EU. His latest book on Mexican governance under NAFTA's labour and environmental agreements was published by Stanford University Press in 2013.

Macarena Larrea Basterra, Professor, Orkestra, University of Deusto, Bilbao, holds a PhD from the University of the Basque Country, with a thesis on cost aspects of electricity production. Her research is centred on energy and climate issues. She has participated in projects on future challenges for energy policies, especially in the area of elcctricity, the energy taxation system and the reform of electricity in Spain. She was awarded a Professional Qualification grant in the areas of European Matters and Inter-regional Cooperation from the Basque Country General Secretariat of External Action.

Renato Baumann is Deputy-Secretary, International Affairs, Ministry of Planning, Brazil, and Professor, Department of Economics, Universidade de Brasília. He holds a DPhil in Economics, Oxford University, and previously served as Director, UN/ECLAC Office in Brazil, 1995-2010; and Director, International Affairs, IPEA, 2011-2015.

Rim Berahab joined the OCP Policy Centre, a think tank based in Rabat, as a researcher in 2014. She works on issues related to international trade and regional integration in Africa. Her research focusses also on energy, economic growth and gender inequalities. Rim was a visitor at the IMF Research Department, in 2017. She holds an engineering degree from the National Institute for Statistics and Applied Economics, Morocco.

Daniele Bianchi is Advisor-Senior Legal Expert at the EC, Brussels, Contracting Professor of Food Law at Sorbonne University in Paris, lecturer in

Tours and Pisa Universities, as well as author of several books and articles on agricultural and food law.

Carlos Mariani Bittencourt is Chairman of the Board of Participações Industriais do Nordeste (PIN) and the Petrochemical PIN, as well as Vice-President of the Federação das Industrias do Estado do Rio de Janeiro. He was President of the Board of Directors of the Brazilian Chemical Industry Association, is Co-President of the Mercosul-EU Business Forum, Co-Chair of the Brazil-Japan Notables (Wise Men) Group and member of the Brazilian Business Coalition. He holds a degree in Engineering, Economic Engineering and Industrial Administration from the (nowadays) Federal University of Rio de Janeiro.

João Cravinho, EU Ambassador to the Federal Republic of Brazil, holds a PhD from the University of Oxford, with a Bachelor's and Master's degree from the LSE, London. He was Professor of International Relations at the University of Coimbra, Guest Professor at ISCTE and at the Law School, Universidade Nova de Lisboa. Between March 2005 and June 2011 was Secretary of State for Foreign Affairs and Co-operation in the Portuguese Government.

Roberto Fendt is Executive Secretary of the Brazil-China Business Council. He was professor of economics at the Foundation for Economic Research at USP and Professor and Deputy Director at the Brazilian Institute of Economics at FGV. He was Director of CACEX and Secretary of the Ministry of Finance, directed the Centre for Foreign Trade Studies Foundation and, later, the Brazilian Centre for International Relations. He holds a Master and PhD in Economics from the University of Chicago, United States.

Renato Flôres is Professor at the Graduate School of Economics and Director of the International Intelligence Unit, both at FGV, Rio de Janeiro, as well as co-ordinator of the Jean Monnet Project on Atlantic Studies. He was President of the Steering Committee of programme PEP (Poverty and Economic Policy), and President of the Brazilian chapter of the European Community Studies Association. He held top positions in the Brazilian government, at the federal (Ministry of Planning) and state (Rio de Janeiro) levels.

Daniel S. Hamilton is the Austrian Marshall Plan Foundation Professor and Senior Fellow at the Foreign Policy Institute of Johns Hopkins University's School of Advanced International Studies, where he co-leads the School's program on "The United States, Europe, and World Order." He also serves as Director of the Atlantic Basin Initiative, a group of eminent persons and research institutions examining connections among the four Atlantic continents. He is an award-winning author on the transatlantic economy. He served as U.S. Deputy Assistant Secretary of State and Associate Director of the Policy Planning Staff for two U.S. Secretaries of State.

Kirstyn Inglis is Visiting Professor at the Institute for International Relations, USP, São Paulo. She first qualified as a Solicitor and practiced in Scotland, London and Brussels, before joining Ghent University in 1998, from where she holds a PhD in EU external relations law, focus on food and environmental law. She has worked in development assistance and academic projects in Turkey, Central and Eastern Europe, for scientific communities seeking to participate in EU projects and for the European Academies Science Advisory Council.

Valdemar Carneiro Leão (Ambassador, CEBRI, Brazil), a career diplomat, was Brazil's ambassador to China until 2015. A specialist in trade issues, he was Deputy Secretary for Economic Affairs of the Ministry for Foreign Affairs; Brazilian Sherpa at the G20 and Head of Delegation at several bilateral and multilateral economic meetings, including the WTO, OECD and BRICS.

Francine Martin is an International Intelligence Analyst at FGV IIU, Rio de Janeiro. She holds a degree in International Relations from Estácio de Sá University and a master course in Foreign Trade and International Negotiations at FGV. Francine previously worked in multinational companies dedicated to Foreign Trade and International Business.

Frank Mattheis is Senior Researcher at the Centre for the Study of Governance Innovation at the University of Pretoria, South Africa and currently visiting researcher at the Institut d'Etudes Européennes at the Université Libre de Bruxelles, Belgium.

Kimberly A. Nolan García is currently at FLACSO Mexico. At CIDE, Mexico, she was assistant professor of International Relations. She is the author of more than 20 academic articles and policy papers on the linkage of labour rights guarantees to trade agreements and provides policy recommendations on the design of labour clauses for the ILO, the European Commission, and the Mexican Senate.

Eloy Álvarez Pelegry is a member of the Spanish Royal Academy of Engineering. He was the Director of the Energy Chair at Orkestra, the Basque Institute of Competitiveness. He holds a bachelor's Degree in Economics and Business from the Complutense University, Madrid, a Diploma in Business Studies from the LSE, London, and a PhD in Mining from the Higher Technical School for Mining, Madrid.

Lorena Ruano's research has focused on European integration and relations between Europe and Latin America. She has been Professor at CIDE, Mexico City, since 2003, and formerly Chair of its Department of International Studies. She graduated from El Colegio de México and has a D.Phil. from Oxford University, UK. She was Jean Monnet Fellow at the Robert Schuman Centre, Florence, and, in 2007, was awarded a Jean Monnet Chair. She was the scientific coordinator of CIDE's participation in the Atlantic Future Project, and also a Senior Associate Analyst at the EU Institute for Security Studies in Paris.

Introduction

The Jean Monnet Network on Atlantic Studies, conceived under the auspices of the EU, tries to position the Atlantic community within the fast-evolving international scenario. It pursues innovative ways to strengthen partnerships across both margins of the Atlantic, always bearing in mind the constructive role that the EU can play in the transatlantic space.

After having exploited the fundamental theme of energy, out of which a successful publication has already been produced,[1] the Network dedicated the whole next year to the encompassing area of trade and related commercial exchanges.

The qualification 'encompassing' is important because developments inside and among the major centres of power, together with ever renewed advances in technology, logistics and regulations as well, are transforming the patterns and issues relevant in the trade narrative.

The papers in this book reflect this transition period; they were presented and discussed during the second project seminar, which took place from March 21 to 23, at the FGV headquarters, in Rio de Janeiro.

The first chapter by Eloy Álvarez Pelegry and Macarena Larrea, active contributors to the Project, establishes a bridge between the two themes, discussing LNG trade in the Atlantic Basin. It is followed by a solid and classic piece by Rim Berahab, on the constraints and opportunities for the integration of West African states, evaluated through an augmented gravity model.

The always important idea of trade integration is then the subject of a sequence of four papers. It is important to notice how emphasis has shifted from standard, cookbook proposals of integration to a diversity of views and considerations that treat with much more care the difficult process leading to a trade and economic union.

---

1. *Energy and Transportation in the Atlantic Basin*, P. Isbell and E. Álvarez Pelegry, eds., Washington, DC: Center for Transatlantic Relations; distributed and available through Brookings Institution Press.

Frank Mattheis opens the sequence with a sober analysis of inter-regionalism in the South Atlantic. The EU–Latin America trade relations are then taken by Lorena Ruano, while Kimberly Nolan Garcia and Mark Aspinwall deal with modern questions associated to trade agreements. The former addresses the diffusion of fundamental rights through the EU trade policy, and the latter analyses the fascinating and unfortunately sometimes overlooked public attitudes to regional integration in the Atlantic Latin America.

Two additional papers tackle specific areas still close to the trade issue. The key question of nutritional information in the EU relations, by Daniele Bianchi, and that of EU values in EU external relations, by Kirstyn Inglis. Both give a special focus to Brazil, after introducing the broad questions.

A set of three less standard contributions end the volume; the transcripts of two live discussions part of the Rio meeting, and the closing speech of the March 22 sessions day, delivered by the EU Ambassador to Brazil.

Ambassador Valdemar Carneiro Leão, a senior diplomat specialised in international trade, who served as Brazilian Ambassador in China, introduced this major and unavoidable country into the context of the seminar. The other transcript reproduces a Round Table that concluded the meeting, in which an informal and lively debate on The Future Prospects and Shape of Trade Agreements in the Atlantic Region raised a series of issues that remain both unsolved and relevant.

Both transcripts, together with the bonus chapter, with the very full text of the speech by His Excellency João Cravinho, serve as a valuable record of the views and expectations at the time. Their contrast with the nowadays realities gives additional food for thought on the fast dynamics and changes governing the themes discussed in this second year of the Jean Monnet Project.

We firmly believe that all these contributions, in their diversity and open approach to the galaxy of trade problems, offer an attractive glimpse on the never-ending possibilities and maybe unanticipated evolutions of the trade and commercial relations within the Atlantic region.

Renato G. Flôres Jr.

Francine T. Martin

Chapter One

LNG trade in the Atlantic Basin:
Situation and Perspectives

Eloy Álvarez Pelegry and Macarena Larrea Basterra

Object and scope

In 1959, the first Liquefied Natural Gas (LNG) cargo was shipped from Lake Charles, Louisiana (US) to Canvey Island in the UK.[1] This can be considered the beginning of the development of the sector. However, it is not until 1964 when the first commercial cargo of LNG was shipped from Arzew (Algeria) to Canvey Island (UK) (BG Group, 2014). Since then natural gas trade has made enormous progress in terms of volume of transport.

Worldwide the total volume of traded gas has grown from 4.4% of production in 1970 to nearly 30% in 2015. LNG has increased continuously its share in the volume of total traded gas, from 5.9% in 1970 to 21.4% in 1999 and to 31.1% in 2015, as well as its share of total gas production from practically nonexistent in 1970 to 9% currently.

Curiously, as mentioned LNG trade began in the Atlantic Basin, but later this area lost importance in global terms. However nowadays the dramatic increase in shale gas production in the US and the increasing needs of gas imports in Europe have revitalized trade and commerce in the Atlantic Basin, especially in the North.

In this sense, in February 2016, US LNG exports started with the first cargo from Sabine Pass liquefaction plant (Cheniere) to Brazil. Four other liquefaction plants are currently under construction in the US that in 2020 could become the third largest exporter in the world after Australia and Qatar (Cornot-Gandolphe, 2016). Furthermore, the production and LNG exports from Africa (mainly from the Gulf of Guinea) and the Caribbean (Trinidad and Tobago) and the regasification projects with the corresponding gas imports in Latin America (Colombia and Brazil with floating stor-

---

1. The world's first LNG tanker, The Methane Pioneer, a converted World War II liberty freighter built in 1945, carried 5,000 cubic meters of LNG in five 7,000 bbl aluminum prismatic tanks (BG Group, 2014).

1

age and regasification units [FSRU] and Argentina) have also made significant contributions to the trade in the Atlantic Basin. All these elements stress the increasing role of the Atlantic Basin.

The following maps show the differences of natural gas and LNG trade flows in 2002 and 2016. Trade has interconnected the Atlantic Basin from coast to coast (principally South America, Europe and Africa) and at the same time "inter-basin" flows (Atlantic Basin vs. Pacific Basin) have appeared thanks to LNG growth, setting the basis of a globalized LNG market, in terms of developments of infrastructures (liquefaction and regasification plants), LNG vessels, as well as of spot traded volumes and prices (different among regions).

Looking to the medium term regarding the infrastructures, it is expected that LNG exports and as a consequence also LNG regasification terminals shall increase their capacity. The LNG fleet is forecasted to increase as well.

This chapter will deal with LNG trade in the Atlantic Basin. After a description of the main infrastructures of the LNG supply chain, next this chapter will focus on LNG trade continuing with contracts and prices and costs of LNG to finalize with an examination of the perspectives of LNG trade in the future and the relevance of the Atlantic Basin.

The Atlantic Basin. A brief review of concepts

It is worth referring to the Atlantic Basin concept. It can be considered from two main perspectives (Isbell, 2013).

The first could be called the 'broad Atlantic Basin'. This more political conception of the Atlantic Basin incorporates all four coastal continents of the Atlantic Ocean in their entirety, including those countries with no Atlantic coastline (ie, Peru and Chile, Tanzania and Kenya, etc.) along with those countries of the Mediterranean Basin (i.e. Algeria and Egypt). The second, more geographically 'narrow' conception could be called the 'geo-economic' Atlantic Basin or 'narrow Atlantic Basin'. This more specific regional scaling would embrace only those countries with an Atlantic coastline and those landlocked countries directly linked to (or integrated with) the Atlantic Basin, such as Paraguay. Most of the references made to the Atlantic Basin in this chapter will be from the point of view of the 'broad Atlantic Basin'.

Map 1. Major trade movements of natural gas and LNG (2002 and 2016)

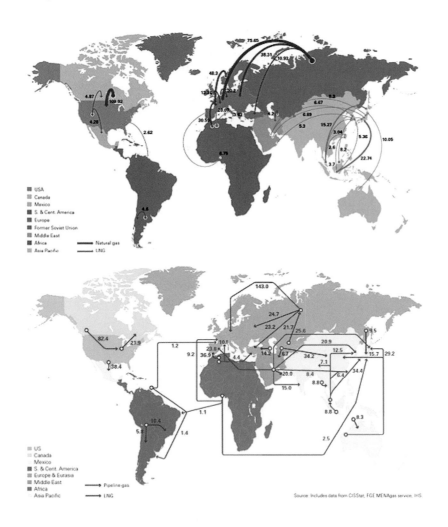

Source: (BP, 2003; BP, 2017).

One of the main challenges that the Atlantic Basin must face is the fact that relations are still established principally within each of its constituent regions instead of between them (Ayuso, A., & Viilup, E., 2013). In this regard, Africa is the place where intra-regional exports and cooperation are less developed. In contrast, in Europe, most trade is taking place inside the territory. However, Central and South America are more dependent on Atlantic exports than any other Atlantic territory.

LNG in the Atlantic Basin: Reserves and main infrastructures

Natural gas is the Earth´s cleanest burning hydrocarbon, whose combustion does not produce ash residues or sulphur oxides but only nitrogen oxides. Natural gas is found throughout the world alone or together with crude oil, under dry land or beneath the ocean floor. Methane is the primary component of natural gas, and prior to entering the market it undergoes processing (IGU, 2017b).

Natural gas can be transported in two main ways: as gas by pipeline and as liquid shipped in LNG cargoes. In the first case, an extensive network of high- and low-pressure pipelines lets transportation of natural gas from production places to demand points (IGU, 2017b).

In the second case, natural gas is shipped over long distances as a liquid, known as liquefied natural gas or LNG. In order to transform gas into liquid, it has to be cooled. This will lead the reduction of the gas volume by 600 times, and makes it possible to transport very large energy content in specially-designed ocean tankers and trucks[2]. Once the LNG tanker reaches its destination at the receiving terminal, it will be re-heated and converted back to a gas via a process known as regasification. Then it will be sent through pipelines to be delivered to end-users (IGU, 2017b).

Reserves are relevant in LNG trade situation and perspectives, together with liquefaction, transport and regasification, therefore next we will deal with these elements of the natural gas value chain.

Reserves

In 1990, the Atlantic Basin held around 22-23% of world total reserves of natural gas. In 2015, even if there were more reserves than in 1990, the Atlantic Basin lost weight to 18-19% according to estimations. In spite of the increase in reserves in OECD Americas (US) in the period 1990-2015, the Atlantic Basin decreased its percentage of worldwide reserves as although, the Atlantic Basin increased 24-39% its reserves, the world increased them by 50-65% according both to Cedigaz and *Oil & Gas Journal*.

---

2.   In this chapter we will deal especially with LNG transported in ships.

Table 1. World reserves of natural gas (billion cubic meters, bcm)

	Cedigaz			Oil & Gas Journal		
	End 1990	End 2015	Variation	End 1990	End 2015	Variation
Atlantic Basin	28,091	34,836	24%	26,846	37,402	39%
Total World	130,361	196,228	51%	118,807	196,363	65%
Total OECD	16,705	18,696	12%	15,302	17,244	13%
Non-OECD Europe/ Eurasia	55,150	66,212	20%	45,413	61,823	36%
Middle East	37,833	78,986	109%	37,478	79,530	112%
Africa	8,413	12,619	50%	8,070	17,129	112%
Asia	7,497	12,092	61%	7,864	12,969	65%
Non-OECD Americas	4,763	7,622	60%	4,680	7,668	64%

Note: The International Energy Agency defines Reserves as the portion of energy resources that can be recovered economically by using current technologies and for which a project has been defined.
Source: own elaboration from (IEA, 2017c).

In 2017, worldwide proved natural gas reserves grew according to the *Oil & Gas Journal*'s annual survey of reserves. In this regard, the latest estimates of natural gas reserves establishes them in 196,802 bcm. The newest estimates of non-OPEC countries show an increase of gas reserves. The main changes can be observed in the following table.

In the Atlantic Basin, only Venezuela and Argentina have shown a positive variation of reserves in 2017. The US, Canada, Mexico, Western Europe, Norway, UK and Brazil showed a decrease of their reserves.

Liquefaction capacity

Around 43% of the capacity of the first liquefaction projects of the period from 1964 to 1979 was installed in the broad Atlantic Basin (mainly the Mediterranean, 90.7%). However in the 1990s only 17.8% of total new liquefaction projects were developed in this Basin (Trinidad and Tobago and Nigeria). The new century brought a new and big wave of liquefaction projects (159.5 million tons compared to 55 million tons in 1991-2000 and 32.6 million tons in 1964-1979) (BG Group, 2014). In this period, the

Table 2. Geographical area and natural gas reserves variation from 2016 to 2017

Geographical area	Variation	Geographical area	Variation	Geographical area	Variation
Asia-Pacific	+3%	OPEC	0.033 tcf	Western Europe	-3,6%
India	+2 tcf	Venezuela	+1.34 tcf	Norway	-4%
Indonesia	+3%	US	-61 tcf	UK	-1,1 tcf
Thailand	-6,5%	Canada	-6%	Argentina	+6.4%
China	+4%	Mexico	-18%	Brazil	-12.2%

Note: shaded squares represent the areas of the broad Atlantic Basin.

Source: own elaboration from (Xu & Bell, 2017).

weight of the broad Atlantic Basin grew to 37.6% (60 million tons). Nevertheless, the Atlantic Basin had already lost its initial market share.

By the end of 2016, global LNG export capacity reached 451.8 bcm, increasing 7.4% relative to the previous year, when 30 billion cubic metres (bcm) of LNG liquefaction capacity were added and only two new final investment decisions (FIDs) were taken to expand existing or build new LNG facilities. In 2017, 159 bcm equivalent to 32.6% of total liquefaction capacity was located in the broad Atlantic Basin. Considering the "narrow" Atlantic Basin this figure would decrease to 17%. Average utilization of global liquefaction capacity was around 86.73%. The United States, Nigeria and Norway utilization were above this average (Stadnicka & Janiszewska-Kiewra, 2018).

As the above table shows, global natural gas markets are in the midst of a second big wave of expansion in the supply of LNG. It is expected that global capacity will grow from 487 bcm in 2017 to 650 bcm in 2022. In this period, from 2017 to 2022, 73.3% of the LNG projects under construction (139.4 bcm/y) are in the broad Atlantic Basin (102.3 bcm/y), more than half in the US (78.2 bcm/y)[3].

In August 2017, total US gas liquefaction capacity in the Lower 48 states increased following the completion of the fourth train unit at the Sabine Pass LNG terminal in Louisiana. A fifth train at Sabine Pass and five new projects (Cove Point, Cameron, Elba Island, Freeport and Corpus

---

3. For information about LNG projects under construction see annex 1.

Table 3. LNG liquefaction capacity operating and under construction as of June 2017 (bcm/year)

Region	Operation	Construction
Broad Atlantic Basin	159	102
Total	487	139
OECD Asia Oceania (Australia)	89	29
Non-OECD Asia	104	8
OECD Europe (Norway)	6	-
FS/non-OECD Europe (Russia)	15	22
Middle East	136	-
Africa (Algeria, Angola, Cameroon, Egypt, Equatorial Guinea, Nigeria)	97	2
OECD Americas (United States)	14	78
Latin America (Peru and Trinidad and Tobago)	27	-

Note: shaded squares represent the areas of the broad Atlantic Basin.

Source: Own elaboration from (IEA, 2017a).

Christi) will increase total US liquefaction capacity by the end of 2019 (Xu & Bell, 2018).

According to the International Energy Agency (IEA), Sabine Pass Train 6 and Corpus Christi Train 3 in United States, Fortuna FLNG[4] project in Equatorial Guinea, and Sakhalin II Train 3 in Russia, might take FID in time for a production start-up within the period till 2022. Three of these projects will be expansions of existing facilities with relatively low costs, and one will be FLNG.

There is a trend towards incorporating floating liquefaction projects and smaller LNG capacities. As a consequence, new independent players apart from national and multinational oil companies will be participating in LNG liquefaction projects.

It is expected that by the end of 2022 Australia will have the largest LNG export nameplate capacity, 117.8 bcm per year, and the United States will become the second largest exporter with 106.7 bcm per year (located

---

4. Floating liquefied natural gas (FLNG) refers to water-based LNG operations, employing technologies designed to enable the development of offshore natural gas resources. Floating above an offshore natural gas field, the FLNG facility produces, liquefies, stores and transfers LNG at sea before carriers ship it directly to markets.

in the Atlantic Basin), slightly above Qatar (104.9 bcm per year). These three big LNG export countries will make up half of the global total LNG export capacity by the end of 2022. The relevance of the LNG export capacity expected in the USA will lead to destination flexibility (IEA, 2017a) and will contribute to the role of the Atlantic Basin in LNG export.

Globally this expansion in supply will exceed expected growth in LNG demand (IEA, 2017b). Well-supplied markets will keep downward pressure on prices and discourage new investments in LNG liquefaction facilities. As a consequence of low LNG prices, only one final investment decision for new liquefaction facilities was taken in 2017, and demand, while growing robustly, is not keeping pace with the addition of supply. LNG capacity increase will slow from 2020 onwards.

Regasification capacity

Regasification facilities increased their capacity in 2016 by 34.2 bcm including expansions (IEA, 2017a), among them Escobar floating and storage regasification unit (FSRU) in Argentina (1 bcm), the Cartagena FRSU in Colombia (5.1 bcm) and the small scale Possi LNG in Finland (0.16 bcm).

In 2017 there were 1,116 bcm of regasification capacity operating and 118 bcm under construction. 42% of the total regasification capacity was located in the broad Atlantic Basin. After OECD Asia, Europe has the highest regasification capacity. In America, the regasification capacity is also significant and diversified.

In the Atlantic Basin there are 23.1 bcm/year under development, thus the great developments will not take place in this Basin, but mainly in China, India and Middle East. Finland-Manga LNG (0.5 bcm) and Uruguay with a significant regasification capacity of 5.5 bcm in LNG FSRU, are important to note, particularly as Uruguay is joining the list of LNG importing countries.[5]

Similar to the case of liquefaction capacity, there is a slight trend that instead of LNG having to be delivered into large import terminals before distribution to final consumers, it can now be delivered to individual plants and customers. Nearly every country that does not currently import LNG seems to have plans to build LNG receiving terminals (BG Group, 2014).

---

5. For information about regasification, projects under construction see annex 2.

Table 4. LNG regasification capacity operating and under construction as of June 2017 (bcm/year)

Region	Operation	Construction	Region	Operation	Construction
Broad Atlantic Basin	471	23.1			
Total	1.116	118			
OECD Asia Oceania (Japan and Korea)	438	3	FSU/non-OECD Europe	5	-
Non-OECD Asia (excluding China)	97	67	Lithuania	4	-
China	76	12	Malta	1	-
OECD Europe	228	3	Middle East and Africa	39	19
Belgium	9	-	Bahrain	-	8
Finland	0,1	1	Jordan	5	-
France	34	-	Kuwait	8	-
Greece	5	2	United Arab Emirates	13	-
Israel	3	-	Egypt	13	-
Italy	15	-	Ghana	-	5
Netherlands	12	-	Namibia	-	6
Poland	5	-	OECD Americas	197	-
Portugal	8	-	Canada	12	-
Spain	67	-	Chile	8	-
Sweden	1	1	Mexico	23	-
Turkey	20	-	United States	153	-
United Kingdom	49	-	Latin America	37	14

Note: shaded squares represent LNG regasification projects in the countries/ regions of the broad Atlantic Basin.

Source: own elaboration from (IEA, 2017a).

In this regard, FSRUs have opened the door to LNG for a range of additional markets recently, which import LNG to meet short-term gas demand when the LNG price is competitive with other fuels. FSRUs have been attractive for these markets because of lower initial investment cost, shorter installation period (around 18 months for FSRU versus more than 5 years for onshore conventional regasification terminals) and more flexibility in length of commitment than onshore regasification facilities. The most recent countries to invest in FSRU are Lithuania in 2014, Egypt and Jordan in 2015, and the United Arab Emirates in 2016 (IEA, 2017b).

Since the world's first FSRU starting operation in the United States in 2005, 24 FSRUs are now in operation. Globally, FSRUs account for 18.5% of the total number of regasification terminals and 10% of regasification capacity.

LNG trade in the Atlantic Basin

At a global level, around 30% of gas produced is traded internationally via pipeline and LNG, and around 70% is consumed in the country where it was produced. In 2000, 23% of all internationally traded gas volumes consisted of LNG. In 2016 this figure was around 33%, and by 2022, LNG share in the international trade is supposed to increase to approximately 38% according to the IEA.

Due to the flexibility of LNG cargoes to be diverted in response to price signals, gas markets are becoming increasingly integrated, with movements in global gas prices becoming more synchronized (BP energy economics, 2018). Moreover, in the last years there has been an increase in the number of nations involved in LNG trade. However, cross-border pipelines will remain the fixed arteries of natural gas international trade (IEA, 2017a).

In 2016, the shortest voyage length was in the Broad Atlantic Basin: Algeria to Spain (130 nautical miles, nm), and the longest one was from Norway to China (12,280 nm) (IGU, 2017b).

In the Atlantic Basin, in terms of gas production, the US play a relevant role, with clear implications on LNG exports and on the increase of LNG trade. European production decrease has also an impact on global LNG trade, and therefore this territory will probably need to increase LNG imports.

Even if it is not dealt with in this chapter, it is important not to forget that trade agreements can play a relevant role in this market. For instance, changes in the North America Free Trade Agreement (NAFTA) could complicate trade between the USA and Mexico (Wood A., Viscidi, & Fargo, 2018).

Map 2. Major LNG Shipping Routes (2016)

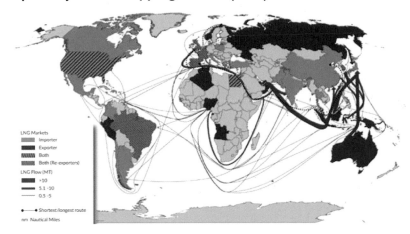

Source: (IGU, 2017b).

Global gas production

Global gas production is expected to increase by 1.6% per annum in the period from 2016 to 2022, continuing the growth trend of the prior six years.

The US will be the largest gas producer, representing around one-fifth of total gas production by 2022. Gas production in Mexico is declining, however the country expects to increase its gas use for power generation by

Table 5. Global gas supply growth by region, 2004-2010; 2010-2016 and 2016-2022 (bcm)

	OECD Ameri-cas	Latin Amer-ica	OECD Europe	Middle East	FSU/ non-OECD Europe	Africa	China	Non-OECD Asia	OECD Asia Ocea-nia	Global growth
2004-2010	63	25	-19	189	46	53	54	64	20	496
2010-2016	142	18	-54	120	23	-8	41	4	45	332
2016-2022	141	3	-36	67	83	35	64	-24	37	371

Note: shaded squares represent the areas of the broad Atlantic Basin.

Source: own elaboration from (IEA, 2017a).

Table 6. Global demand growth by region 2004-2010, 2010-2016 and 2016-2022

	OECD Americas	Latin America	OECD Europe	Middle East	FSU/ non-OECD Europe	Africa	China	Non-OECD Asia	OECD Asia Oceania	Global growth
2004-2010	64	26	44	135	33	28	65	81	43	519
2010-2016	117	24	-68	103	-26	21	99	23	26	319
2016-2022	55	13	-2	71	8	26	134	63	-12	357

Notes: Negative figures have a decreasing meaning. Shaded squares represent the areas of the broad Atlantic Basin.

Source: own elaboration from (IEA, 2017a).

almost 50% between 2016 and 2020, and therefore Mexico´s gas pipeline network is undergoing a major expansion (Xu & Bell, 2018). Thanks to the OECD Americas, the Atlantic Basin has now a relevant role in gas supply.

Production from FSU/non-OECD Europe will probably increase in 2022, mainly driven by the increasing exports from Russia and the Caspian region to China and to the OECD Europe. The Middle East will contribute almost 20% of global incremental growth in gas production in the period from 2016 to 2022. China will also show robust growth at an annual average of 6.6%, adding almost 65 bcm to the global gas output (IEA, 2017a).

Global gas demand

Global gas demand is projected to increase by 1.6% annually on average (around 60 bcm per year) over the period 2016-2022. With demand increasing by 10% over the period, total gas consumption is expected to amount to 3,986 bcm by 2022. By sector, natural gas demand growth will be led by industry and the power sector and supported by both continued industrialization in developing economies together with gas gaining share as some countries switch away from coal. The fastest rate of growth of gas demand is in the transport sector (in trucking and marine transport). Even though this increase is small in absolute terms (BP energy economics, 2018).

Table 7. Natural gas international exports evolution

	Total		Pipeline		LNG		% of LNG in exports
	bcm	% of pro-duction	bcm	% of pro-duction	bcm	% of pro-duction	
1970	45.68	4.4	42.93	4.1	2.69	0.3	5.9
1975	125.37	9.9	112.35	8.9	13.05	1	10.4
1980	200.98	13.2	169.64	11.1	31.34	2.1	15.6
1985	228.85	13.1	177.97	10.2	50.88	2.9	22.2
1990	307.43	15.4	235.29	11.8	72.14	3.6	23.5
1995	391.69	18.3	298.45	14	93.24	4.3	23.8
2000	652.3	26	505.7	19.9	146.06	5.75	22.4
2005	847.9	29.5	669.32	23.33	178.58	6.22	21.06
2010	983.73	30	684.37	20.85	299.36	9.12	30.43
2015	1,051.68	29.6	724.48	20.45	327.2	9.23	31.1

Source: own elaboration from IEA and (Álvarez Pelegry & Balbás Peláez, 2003).

US, Mexico and Canada demand will surpass 1,000 bcm by 2022, meaning that one quarter of the global gas will be used in North America, the only developed region where gas demand is growing (IEA, 2017a).

Europe demand will probably decrease while Middle East and Asia as a whole will see a considerable increase of gas demand. Indeed, demand for natural gas in the Middle East is expected to surpass demand in OECD Europe. Asia is expected to account the vast majority of the demand increase by 2040 (BP energy economics, 2018).

Therefore, the US is again the main driver in the future LNG demand of the Atlantic Basin, led by growth in industry, together with Latin America and Africa in the South Atlantic.

LNG exports

As mentioned, gas and LNG exports have increased over time. In 2016, top LNG exporters were Qatar (100.4 bcm) and Australia (57.6 bcm)[6]. The Atlantic Basin represented 17.7% of total exports.

---

6. Other relevant exporters were: Malaysia (32.5 bcm), Nigeria (24.2 bcm), Indonesia (21.6 bcm), Algeria (15 bcm), Russia (14 bcm), Trinidad and Tobago (13.8 bcm), Oman (10.5 bcm) and Papua New Guinea (9.6 bcm).

Graph 1. World LNG exports by region, 2016-2022

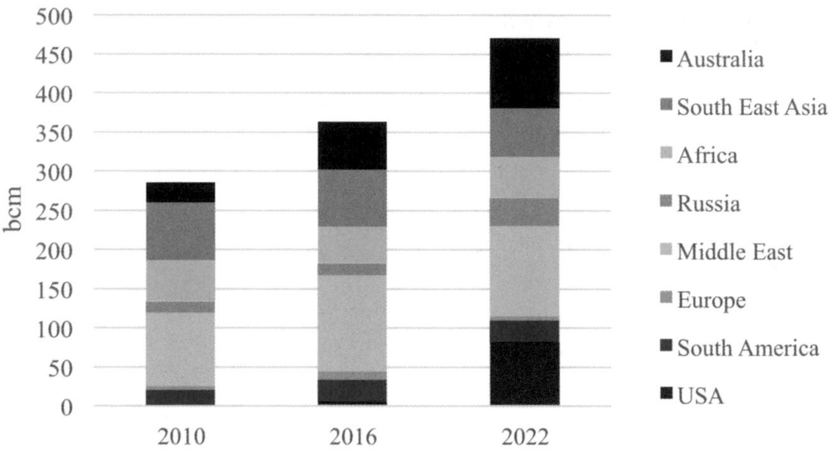

Source: own elaboration from (IEA, 2017b).

Traditionally LNG exports have come predominantly from non-OECD countries. However the new role of Australia and the US together with the stagnation of LNG export capacity in non-OECD countries will result in a more balanced picture as can be observed in next graph.

Australia has been the game changer, with an exported volume that more than doubled from 2011 to 2016 (IEA, 2017a).

OECD Americas will see a huge increase of LNG exports coming mainly from the US as a result of the shale gas boom. In this regard, the US has been a net gas exporter for 2017 and is expected to continue to export more natural gas than it imports throughout 2018 as exports of natural gas by pipeline to Mexico and of LNG will increase. Imports from Canada will decline (Xu & Bell, 2018) as gas from the Appalachian basin and other northern US producing areas is displacing US imports from Canada.

Latin America (particularly Trinidad and Tobago), Middle East and OECD Europe (Norway) will experience a slight decrease in LNG exports by the end of 2022, falling by around 6% from 2016 (IEA, 2017a). The highest decrease in LNG exports will be coming from non-OECD Asia region.

In Africa, LNG exports from Nigeria and Equatorial Guinea will remain relatively flat, and LNG exports from Angola and Cameroon will be concentrated in the period from 2019 to 2022. LNG exports from Algeria are expected to decrease due in part to the expiration of long-term contracts. This happens precisely when the market faces the largest glut, and it may struggle to sell uncontracted LNG in the market.

In spite of the evolution of Trinidad and Tobago and the EU, the increases in LNG exports from OECD Americas will imply a greater weight of the Atlantic Basin in the LNG future trade. However Qatar will continue to provide over 25% of LNG globally and Australia will be the second biggest individual exporter with 24% growth (Stadnicka & Janiszewska-Kiewra, 2018).

LNG imports

Global LNG imports are expected to grow until 2022. By 2022 some buyers will move their position towards a higher share of LNG in their natural gas supply, and new countries are expected to enter the LNG market (such as Bahrain, Bangladesh, Ghana, Haiti, Namibia, Panama, Philippines and Uruguay, four of them located in the narrow Atlantic Basin, and five in the broader one).

Even if OECD countries have traditionally been the largest source of global LNG demand, LNG import volumes of these countries have decreased and this tendency will probably continue (IEA, 2017a). By contrast, LNG demand of non-OECD countries has increased rapidly. In this regard, top LNG importers in 2016 were Japan (108.3 bcm), South Korea (43.8 bcm) and China (34.8 bcm)[7] (IGU, 2017b). Especially China and India increased their importance as importers in the period from 2011 to 2016, where China will probably be the main driver of the global LNG demand growth[8] and India is seen as an emerging LNG importer, capable of generating a meaningful demand increase.

In 2017, the Asia-Pacific Basin was the most relevant in terms of LNG imports. It will probably keep this relevance as next graph shows even if it is expected that Japan's and Korea's imports will probably decline in the near future.

---

7. Other countries with relevant regasification capacity are India (25 bcm), Taiwan (19.5 bcm), Spain (12.9 bcm), UK (9.6 bcm), Egypt (9.5 bcm), France (7.3 bcm), Turkey (7.3 bcm).
8. Relatively new importers will also show large increases in LNG demand. Bangladesh, Indonesia and the Philippines are supposed to join the LNG import list of countries and to start importing LNG before 2020 (IEA, 2017a).

Graph 2. World LNG imports by region, 2012-2022

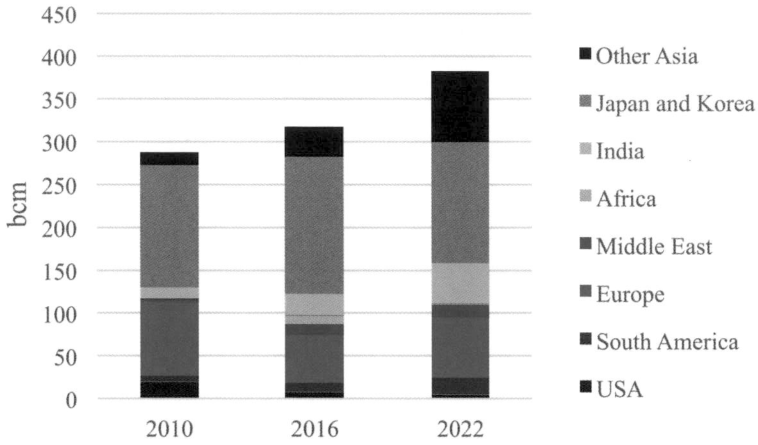

Source: own elaboration from (IEA, 2017a).

In 2016 the Atlantic Basin represented 24.7% of total imports. UK and Spain lost relevance and the principal changes in this basin were related to flows from the Persian Gulf and the Gulf of Guinea (Nigeria) to Europe and the US.

Stagnating demand and decreasing production will increase Europe's import needs. However it is expected that LNG contracted volumes in Europe will decrease by 2022, despite the fact that Finland, Lithuania, Malta, Poland and Sweden recently joined, as Uruguay, the list of LNG importers in Europe (IEA, 2017a). Europe's LNG demand has been and will be lower than the contracted LNG volumes, mainly because of weak gas demand and competition from pipeline gas. In this regard, Russia's Gazprom announced recently that the sea part of TurkStream first segment across the Black Sea had already been finished. For this country both the TurkStream and the North Stream 2 pipelines are vital to increase its presence in the European market (Energy Market Price, 2018).

In any case, Europe will remain a key market, both as a potential market of last demand for surplus LNG cargos and as a key hub of gas-on-gas competition between LNG and pipeline gas (BP energy economics, 2018).

Latin America will see some LNG demand increase with the addition of Colombia, Haiti, Panama and Uruguay. However, Canada, the US and

Graph 3. Global LNG flows (%) and major energy flows

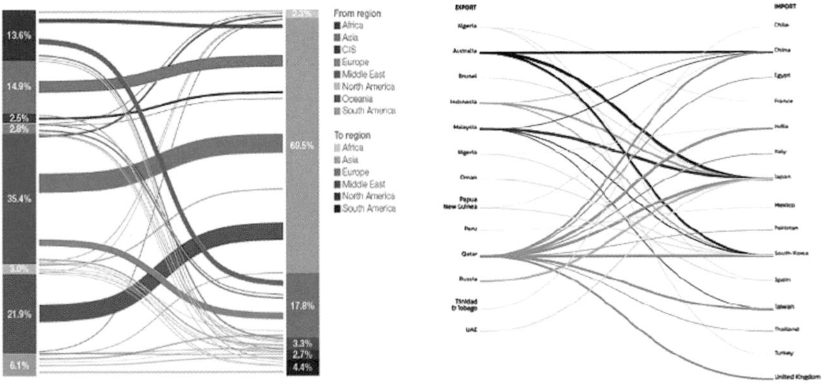

Source: (Stadnicka & Janiszewska-Kiewra, 2018) (GIIGNL, 2017).

Mexico will lose relevance due to the competition with pipeline gas in the region and the emergence of US as an LNG exporter.

Though Ghana and Namibia, both in the Southern Atlantic, are assumed to start importing LNG in the coming years, overall African LNG demand in 2022 will be around 2 bcm, one fifth of the 2016 level, mainly because Egypt (in the broad Atlantic Basin) is expected to benefit from domestic production of its new gas fields and ease its existing importing needs substantially.

Graph 3 shows the main LNG trade flows.

LNG contracts

LNG contracted sales can be split in between short term (less than two years), medium term (between two years and five years) and long term (more than five years).

Another classification is made between flexible destinations, referring to short-, medium- or long-term contracts that are either taken free on board (FOB) at the liquefaction plant or where the buyer has flexibility in destination[9]. On the other hand, fixed destination refers to contracts with delivered ex ship (DES) terms and/or with a destination clause.

Spot or uncontracted may be referred to sales that are not sold under short-, medium- and long-term contracts. By being "uncontracted", these volumes are fully flexible (i.e. no destination clauses) and can be directed to the most profitable markets. As contracts remain the essential link between LNG supply and demand, the evolution of contractual terms has to be closely monitored to properly understand ongoing market changes.

Long term gas supply purchase agreements (GSPA)

Long term contracts have been the most usual way of contracting gas in the past and continue to be quite usual. Long term means here that the term of the contract is 15-25 years. This period has changed decreasing in the last years but continue to be significant of long-term contracts.

The following table registers the long-term contracts that export countries located in the Atlantic Basin had in 2016. The total contracted capacity in terms of millions of tons of LNG per annum is 78,759 MTPA, which represents 10.28% of total long and medium-term contracts. 94% of these contracts have a European buyer. Considering the contract end date, it can be said that in Europe the expiration of LNG contracts in the coming years will allow to rebalance long positions.

It is interesting to note the average duration of the contracts (around 20 years) and also that quite a number of these contracts began the supply before 2000-2002, and most before 2005-2006. Taking into account this consideration it may be assumed that at least in the initial contracts, gas prices were basically linked to oil prices or oil products as will be described later[10].

LNG contract flexibility

There is nowadays an interesting trend to improve flexibility in terms of the annual contract quantity and the development of short/medium term

9. Flexibility can also be considered from the point of view of the contracted volume. That is to say the percentage of 'take-or-pay' in relation to the annual contract quantity. Flexibility increases as 'take-or-pay' decreases the possibilities of make up or carry forward increase the flexibility of contracts.

10. For more information in this respect see chapter 6 of Álvarez Pelegry, E.; Balbas Pelaez, J. (2003). El gas natural. Del yacimiento al consumidor. Aprovisionamientos y cadena del gas natural licuado. S.L. CIE Inversiones editoriales Dossat-2000. ISBN: 9788489656451.

Table 8. Some long-term and medium-term contracts in force in 2016-2017 in the Atlantic Basin

Export country	Seller	Annual Contract Quantity (MTPA)	Earlier initial date	Late contract end date	Average duration	Type of contract
Algeria	Sonatrach	14.9	1972	2022	26	DES, CIF and FOB
Egypt	SEGAS	4.3	2005	2030	22,5	FOB
	ELNG T1	3.6	2005	2025	20	FOB
	ELNG T2	3.6	2006	2026	20	FOB
Equatorial Guinea	EGLNG	3.3	2006	2023	17	FOB
Nigeria	Nigeria LNG T1 &2	5.1	1999	2022	22	DES
	Nigeria LNG T3	2.7	2002	2024	21	DES
	Nigeria LNG T4 & 5	7.4	2006	2026	20	DES
	Nigeria LNG T6	4	2008	2027	19	DES
Norway	ENGIE	0.5	2007	Depletion	-	FOB
	Statoil	2.98	2006	Depletion	-	DES, FOB
	Total	0.7	2007	Depletion	-	FOB
Trinidad and Tobago	Atlantic LNG T1	2.66	1999	2018	19	FOB
	ENGIE	0.6	2000	2020	20	DES
	Atlantic T2 & 3	6.69	2002	2026	20	DES, FOB
	BP	0.75	2003	2023	20	DES
	Atlantic LNG T4	6	2006	2027	17	FOB
USA	Cheniere	9 + exceso de Sabine Pass	2016	2036	20	FOB

Notes: 1 MTPA ~ 1.3 bcm/year. Since March 2018 Statoil new name is Equinor.

Source: own elaboration from (GIIGNL, 2017).

Graph 4. LNG export contract volumes by destination flexibility, 2012-22

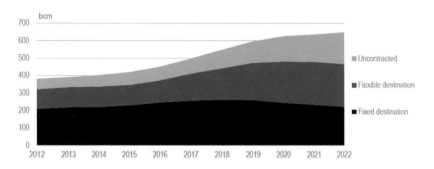

Source: (IEA, 2017b).

contracts (i.e. less than four years). The desire for flexibility both on supply and demand side is a key driver for understanding markets changes and how these changes might affect security of supply.

Over the next few years, opportunities for more flexibility would hence come from the contracts themselves. In fact, a greater proportion of new contracts have flexible terms, encouraged by both the innovative business models of the US suppliers and policies in the consuming countries and territories. It is expected that US LNG exports will, so to speak, revolutionize international LNG trade. Their contract structure (linked to the US gas spot price, no destination clauses and the use of tolling agreements) and the projected volumes will enable greater flexibility in the international LNG market and facilitate price convergence between regional markets (Cornot-Gandolphe, 2016).

Expiration of long-term contracts would also provide an opportunity to renegotiate terms towards more flexibility[11] (IEA, 2017b).

In the period from 2012 to 2017 the evolution observed in new signed contracts shows that the share of LNG contracted volumes without destination clauses in total trade has hardly changed being 34% in 2016. However, it should increase dramatically to 53% by 2022. By this year, flexible

---

11. The two regions from where most of the contracts (fixed and flexible) are expiring over the coming years are the Middle East and Africa. The two countries seeing the most contracts expiring in the 2016-22 period are Malaysia (all fixed) and Algeria (-13 bcm/y fixed and -2bcm/y flexible).

Graph 5. LNG export contract volumes with fixed and flexible destination by region and country

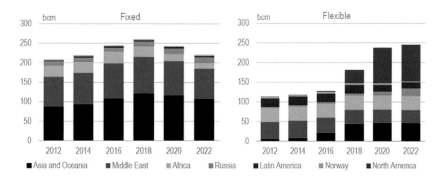

Source: (IEA, 2017b).

Graph 6. LNG import contract volumes with fixed and flexible destination by region, 2012-2022

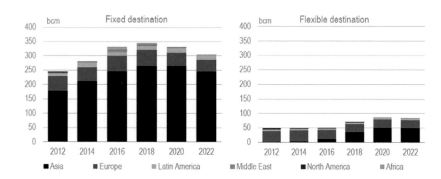

Source: (IEA, 2017b).

volumes would double, led by North America and mostly the US (IEA, 2017b).

Asian exporters appeared to be the least flexible (12%), while US volumes will be fully flexible as can be observed in next graph.

From the importers/customers' perspective, the share of flexible contracts at 13% in 2016, is less than half that of exporters. Although the volume of flexible destination contracts will almost double between 2016

Graph 7. Spot natural gas and LNG prices (US$/MMBtu)

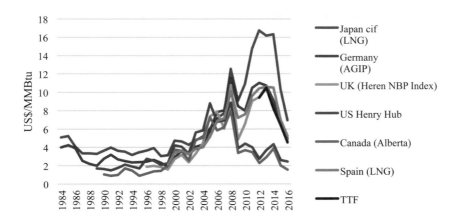

Source: own elaboration from datacomex, my.Elexys.be and Platts in (BP, 2017).

and 2022, it would still account for a minority of currently known import contracts for 2022, with a share of 22% in terms of volume (bcm) (IEA, 2017b).

Inflexible volumes are expected to decrease both in Asia and Europe. This will be among others due to the abovementioned expiry of legacy contracts and development of flexible US contracts. For instance the contracts between US operators and European buyers, who saw an opportunity of diversifying and lowering the price of their LNG supplies, do not include destination clauses and the LNG can be sold on any market (Cornot-Gandolphe, 2016).

Other importing regions such as Africa, Latin America and the Middle East are currently relying on short-term and spot supplies, which are expected to prevail in the near future.

Flexibility can also be seen from the point of view of quantities that are not committed on take or pay or also as the spot and short-term LNG sales quantities which accounted for 29% of the market in 2015. In this regard, Russia, Algeria, the United Arab Emirates and Qatar should increase spare capacity, uncommitted to term contracts. Hence, they should be a reliable source of production flexibility in case demand or supply shocks occur (IEA, 2017b).

Gas prices and LNG supply chain costs

From the previous sections it should be clear that there have been dramatic changes in the last 15 years, not only because the volume of trade increased, but what is more important because the pattern of flows have changed very significantly. In this regard, gas prices and costs are key elements to explain trade, and particularly trade in the Atlantic Basin.

Gas prices

In 2013 there was a huge price divergence between regions, when prices in Japan were around four times US wholesale prices. Since 2015 convergence on prices was observed particularly between gas prices in Far East (i.e. China, Japan) and Europe (i.e. Spain, U.K), mainly due to the over-supply and the decline in the price of oil that have brought down natural gas prices in some regions.

Ample availability of LNG is putting pressure on traditional ways of pricing and marketing natural gas. As a consequence, in 2016 these differences had already decreased, more than expected and prices converged into lower levels than those forecasted. The Henry Hub natural gas price

Map 3. National natural gas market overview. World LNG estimated landed prices. January 2018

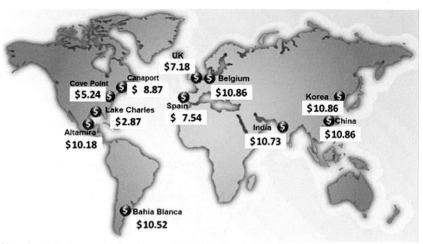

Note: landed prices are defined as received at the terminal, and are based on a netback calculation.
Source: (FERC, 2018).

Graph 8. Natural gas prices by region in the scenario of new policies (US$/MMBtu [2013])

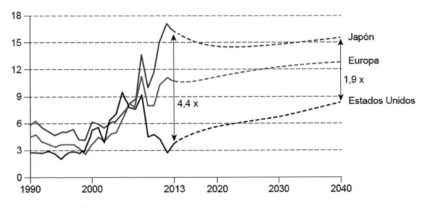

Source: (OECD/IEA, 2014).

averaged US$ 2.27/MMBbtu from April 1 to July 25 th, 2016, compared with US$ 3.03/MMbtu during the same period in 2017 (Xu & Bell, 2018).

According to the IEA differences on prices by regions were going to be maintained in the long run, even if in 2014, for instance, projections showed a reduction of price differential from 4.4 to 1.9 by 2040. In any case, Japan would still have the highest prices and the United States the lowest ones.

Changes in trade flows described before are expected to lead to a more competitive international supply environment where some of the pricing and contractual rigidities that characterized long-distance gas trade in the past would be loosened. This change will be further accelerated by the expansion of US exports that have already been mentioned, which are not tied to any particular destination and so will play a major role in increasing the liquidity and flexibility of LNG trade.

As the growth of US export capacity is gradual, the consequences on gas markets will probably be felt from 2018 (Cornot-Gandolphe, 2016), with the corresponding implications for the relevance of the Atlantic Basin in global LNG trade where market flexibility is increasing (Barnes, 2018a).

Moreover, it is considered that with the launch of American LNG exports, Henry Hub pricing has emerged '*as a new international touchstone*'

Table 9. World gas price formation 2016

Region	OPE	GOG	BIM	Total gas consumption
North America	0.0	130.5	0.0	130.5
Europe	152.1	265.7	0.0	417.8
Asia	91.4	12.1	0.0	103.5
Asia Pacific	190.5	25.8	0.0	216.4
Latin America	20.9	8.8	1.0	30.7
FSU	21.7	0.0	29.7	51.4
Africa	4.5	9.6	3.8	17.9
Middle East	13.5	4.6	17.3	35.4
Total	494.6	457.2	51.7	1,003.6
%	49%	46%	5%	100%

Note: In terms of the allocation between different price formation mechanisms, the general rule is that the wholesale price at the "point of first sale" in the country is the one to be considered. For example, if gas enters a country under an OPE contract and is then re-traded at a hub it is still considered to be in the OPE category.

Source: (IGU, 2017c).

(Barnes, 2018b). Therefore, in a more globalized LNG market, the Henry Hub price could play a key role in determining future prices (Cornort-Gandolphe, 2018).

Gas price formation mechanisms

There are several price formation mechanisms that differ mainly from region to region as can be observed in next table, and that have influence on the pattern of trade. The main mechanisms are pricing based on oil price escalation or indexation (OPE), the gas-on-gas competition (GOG) and the bilateral monopoly (BIM).[12]

In the countries that make up the Atlantic Basin coexist different pricing mechanisms. In Europe there are two main ways of price formation. In the Northwest Europe from 2005 to 2016 there has been an evolution from OPE to GOG, but on the contrary, in the Mediterranean area the OPE formation of gas prices is still quite relevant (IGU, 2017c). This is clear for example in the case of Spain (in the Mediterranean area) which in 2016 imported 37.29 bcm of gas, of which 15.68 bcm of LNG. The relationship

---

12. For more information on price formation and regions see the Annex.

Graph 9. Comparison of the average price of NG+LNG in Spain and the Brent with lag

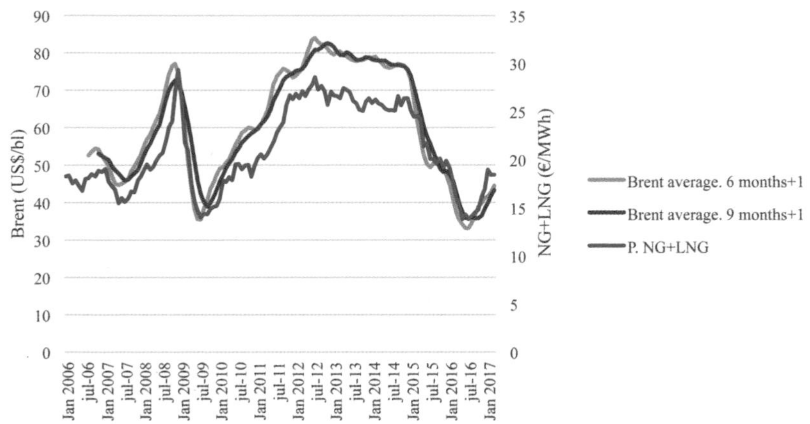

Source: own elaboration based on indexmundi and (CNMC, 2017).

between the price of imported LNG and oil is quite clear in the period from 2006 to 2016.

However, in North America, the mechanism employed is the GOG while Latin America and Africa are more diversified, as most of all the different mechanisms coexist, even though in Latin America OPE has a considerable weight.

The principal consequence of the existence of several pricing mechanisms is the difference on prices levels. This together with the various degrees of developments of internal wholesale gas markets (i.e. Henry hub in the US, Title Transfer Facility [TTF] in central Europe) explain, at least partially the prices differences. As can be seen in next graph during the period 2005-2016 gas prices have differed substantially depending on the mechanisms of price formation, and lower prices have been shown in those more developed wholesale markets.

Since 2009, the OPE mechanism results in the highest gas prices with the highest volatility and correlation with oil prices. The above graph shows the gas prices convergence of most of the mechanisms.

Nowadays it is particularly relevant for the Atlantic Basin the US LNG exports price formation. The trend towards shortening prices differences

Graph 10. Wholesale price levels 2005 to 2016 by price formation mechanism

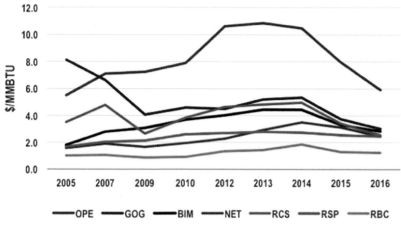

Source: (IGU, 2017c).

among regions will be further accelerated by the expansion of US exports, which are not tied to any particular destination and are not oil indexed, as seen before (IEA, 2017a).

The cost of the LNG supply chain

This section deals with the several components of the LNG supply chain: gas prices in the export countries, the liquefaction cost, the LNG transport cost and the regasification cost. Thus the cost at the importing location/ importing country will be the outcome of adding these four components. This cost is related to prices, although these are determined whether by the fundamentals of supply and demand and/or by the bilateral contractual negotiations.

Gas price in exporting countries

In relation to gas price in exporting countries, there are notably differences among regions. For instance US LNG exports index their prices to the Henry Hub (HH) gas spot price, which among other advantages supposes a diversification from OPE contracts. Furthermore, most buyers signed tolling agreements for 15-20 years or a use-or-pay basis (Cornot-Gandolphe, 2016), so if the buyer decide not to take the LNG, they will only have to pay a fixed fee (2.25-3 US$) instead of the full cost of the LNG in traditional contracts containing take-or-pay clauses.

In the US the gas-on-gas competition has made of the Henry Hub price a clear reference that has been incorporated to the CIF prices of some derivatives. So a formula of the type:

$$P_{LNG} = 1.15 \times HH + B$$

was proposed by Cheniere and has been mentioned by (Kuhn, 2013), where HH is the Henry Hub gas price and B represents a coefficient.

Other references such as the Gulf of Guinea are related to a basic price (P_0) plus an escalation referred to gas oil and fuel oil for different qualities in some ports of destination, such as Rotterdam. Likewise the analysis can be done from the cost of gas in origin side[13]. In this respect it must be taken into account that in some countries prices are determined by the national oil or national gas companies or by international oil/gas companies based on complex relations with the production sharing contracts or agreements.

Liquefaction cost

Liquefaction cost is a very important component, as it is the most expensive part of the LNG supply chain (Wood A. et al., 2018). Plant costs vary widely and depend on location, capacity and liquefaction process, the number of storage tanks, the access to skilled labour and the regulatory and permitting costs.

Estimations established this cost for 2000 on the calculation of agents debt of 20/80 and 60/40 of US$/MMBtu 1.4-1.0, assuming capital costs (CAPEX) of US$ 1,100-1,400 (Álvarez Pelegry & Balbás Peláez, 2003). At the time, the cost of the CAPEX was around 200 US$/tpa as can be seen in next graph.

However, this importance is now greater as there has been a dramatic increase of liquefaction cost as next graph shows. The increases have resulted in liquefaction costs, for instance, of 2.25-3.5 US$/MMBtu for Sabine Pass and Corpus Christi (Ripple, 2016).

---

13. In this respect some references can be found in (Álvarez Pelegry & Balbás Peláez, 2003).

Graph 11. Evolution of liquefaction costs (US$/tpa)

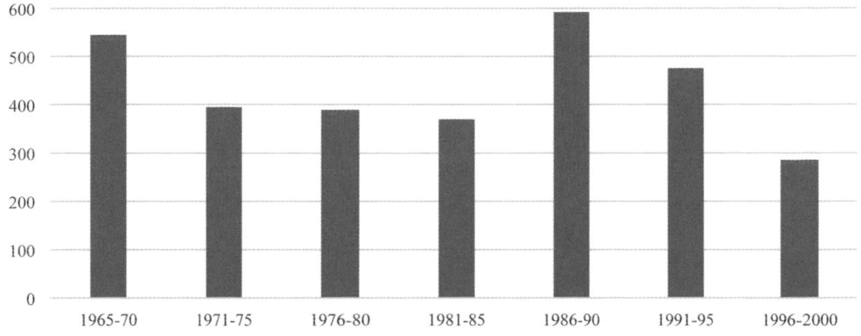

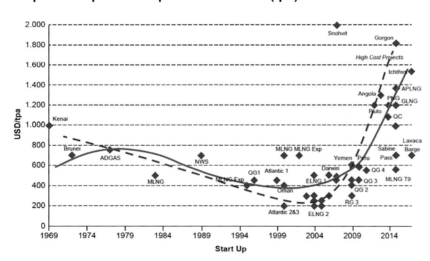

Source: (Álvarez Pelegry & Balbás Peláez, 2003) from Global Octane and Merrill Lynch.

Graph 12. Liquefaction plant metric cost (tpa)

Source: (Songhurst, 2014).

The costs escalation has occurred worldwide, and not only in the Atlantic Basin, where the costs rose from US$461 in the period 2000-2008 to US$1,221 in 2009-2016. Projects in the Atlantic and Pacific Basin have experienced higher costs during 2009-2016 relative to 2000-2008 (IGU, 2017a).

Nowadays, the low price environment, reduces the margin for US LNG trade. Consequently, buyers that own capacity at the US export terminals have tried to renegotiate prices (Wood A. et al., 2018).

Shipping costs

Shipping costs are also a relevant part of the final costs for the LNG chain. Their share in the total cost of liquefied natural gas ranges between 10 to 35% of the final price paid for the natural gas. This component is more dynamic than other components of LNG price and include rental costs of methane carriers (charter rates in US$/day), fuel costs and operation and maintenance costs, harbour fees and charges related with freight by sea (i.e. crossing channels' fees) and insurance (Zajdler, 2015).

Assuming a given route, prices change mainly with the time charter rate. Short term rates rose dramatically in the early 2010 and later fell from US$/day 155,000 to 24,500 in 2015. Throughout 2017 short term charter rates increased from US$/day 25,000 to US$/day 47,000-78,000 depending mainly on the type of vessel (ST = Steam Turbine; DFDE = Dual Fuel Diesel Electric, more expensive) (Howard, 2018).

These differences in time charter rates, make for a same route (i.e. US Gulf Coast to UK) a transportation cost increase or decrease. Longer distances imply greater differences (Howard, 2018). That is to say that it is not the same the distances between US Gulf, the North African gas suppliers (mainly Algeria and to a less extent Libya and Egypt), Nigeria or the Persian Gulf (Qatar, Oman, Abu Dhabi) to Europe.

The above figures give an idea of the differences in transport prices or costs from the same origin. This discussion allows to introduce the matter of arbitrage. If gas prices on the Far East were higher enough than the European ones, gas sales (short term or spot) may finally go from the USA or Trinidad and Tobago in the Atlantic Basin to regasification plants in China instead to regasification plants in Europe. Then as long as gas price differentials increase the flows in the Atlantic Basin may decrease.

Table 10. Shipping (one-way) distances between Sabine Pass and destination ports, voyage days, time charter rates and transport cost (US$/MMbtu)

Loading Port	Discharge Port	Nautical Miles	Voyage days	Time charter rates	Time charter rates/MMbtu
Sabine Pass (US)	Isle of Grain (UK)	4,897	10.7	504,735	0.1336
	Gateway (NL)	5,002	11.0	515,557	0.1365
	Tokyo	15,762	34.6	1,624,592	0.4303
	Tokyo (via Panama Canal)	9,209	20.2	949,173	0.2514
	Tokyo (via Suez Canal)	14,521	31.8	1,496,682	0.3964
	Shangai	15,098	33.1	1,556,154	0.4122
	Shangai (via Panama Canal)	10,081	22.1	1,038,700	0.2751
	Shangai (via Suez Canal)	13,854	30.4	1,427,934	0.3782

Notes: 19 nautical miles per hour; 160.000 m3 of LNG, time charter rate = 47,000 US$. This table does not include the fuel´s cost.

Source: own elaboration from (Howard, 2018).

As mentioned, fuel costs are also relevant, especially in those vessels that use part of the cargo to feed the propulsion. In this regard, when unloading cargo in the final port of discharge, the shipper retains a part of it to serve as fuel gas on the way back to the load port. This results in a reduced amount of delivered LNG. In consequence, the exporters stipulate the prices for the amounts actually delivered to import terminals. The price of the LNG intended to be used as propulsion engine fuel reduces transportation costs (Stanivuk, Tokic, & Soskic, 2013).

Regasification costs

Global LNG regasification capacity has increased following the demand. Over the past few years, new markets have been able to complete regasification projects fairly quickly using FSRU whose capital costs are lower than those of traditional regasification facilities as shown in next graph. However, operational costs (OPEX) of the floating facilities are higher.

Graph 13.Regasification costs based on Project Start dates (2005-2016) (US$/tonne)

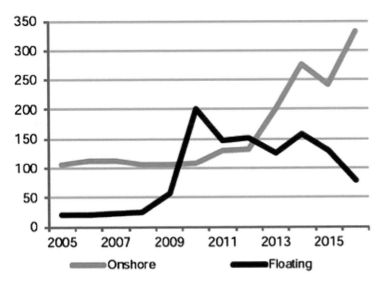

Source: (IGU, 2017a).

In 2016, the average capital costs of new onshore LNG import capacity was US$/tonne 334, which is significantly higher than the average of 2015 (US$/tonne 242). New onshore terminals with smaller storage units were expected to reduce overall CAPEX costs to US$/tonne 212 in 2017 and US$/tonne 285 in 2018. New floating terminals' CAPEX remained roughly steady declining from US$/tonne 158 in 2014 to US$/tonne 78 in 2016.

US LNG deliveries started in late February 2016. They were headed by the countries offering the highest margin after deducing from the landed LNG price. Europe where the LNG is in competition with pipeline gas imports, is at a disadvantage compared to other areas where competition occurs among LNG exporters, because the regasification cost has to be added.

The total cost of LNG

(Howard, 2018) estimated the breakdown cost of recent or new LNG projects, considering the cost components that have been mentioned until now. Gas costs range from 5 to 10 US$/MMbtu; US Greenfield to Europe is around 7 US$/MMBtu, with no much difference with US to Asia. In

Graph14. Estimated breakeven costs of recent or new LNG projects

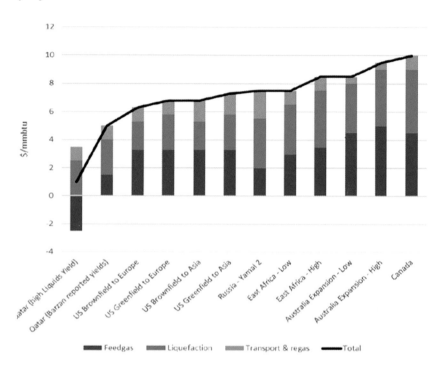

Source: (Stern, 2017).

terms of costs there is potential in the Far East as time charter rates are not high, given the cost advantage of suppliers in the Atlantic Basin in comparison with the new higher cost projects in Australia.

It is interesting to note the price differentials with Asia, due mainly to transportation costs (US$/MMbtu 1.5) and regasification costs (i.e. in Japan LNG do not compete with gas by pipeline, as it is the case in Europe and therefore, regasification costs are not considered in the comparison as all the gas imported in Japan comes by sea).

In this regard for instance, since 2014, the premium paid by Asia has fallen and even disappeared in 2016. As a consequence, the reduction of prices in Asia has result in the improvement of the attractiveness of the European area for LNG exporters in the Atlantic Basin and in eliminating the economic incentive to reroute cargoes to Asia (Cornot-Gandolphe, 2016).

Table 11. Margins from the Cheniere export project (US$)

Delivered price to (MMBtu)	Europe	Asia
Gas	2.6	2.6
Transportation	1	2.5
Regasification	0.4	0
Total cost	4	5.1
Landed price	5 (TTF)	6.9 (JKM)
Margin	1	1.8

Note: the authors consider that in this table Europe represents Northern Europe and not the Mediterranean where OPE in the main pricing mechanism employed.

Source: (Abiteboul).

As seen, liquefaction costs together with gas price in export countries are the most relevant components of the total cost of LNG and have increased during the last years. However in terms of trade, transportation costs also play a relevant role. The balance of these elements will influence the final decision of where to sell the LNG.

Indeed, because LNG can be transported to markets in different parts of the world. LNG supplied under a long-term contract may be sold and delivered to customers in different destinations to those established in the contracts. This is due to the differences in gas prices between markets that create arbitrage opportunities. Flexibility will probably bring changes in this regard.

Perspectives of LNG in the Atlantic Basin

The Atlantic Basin has a significant role in global LNG trade. Gas reserves in the basin have increased from 1990 to 2015 by 24-35% (depending on the origin of the data). This increase although very significant is lower than the increase of reserves worldwide.

43% of liquefaction capacity was installed in the Atlantic Basin from 1964 to 1979, and in 2017 nearly one third of total liquefaction capacity and more than 40% of total regasification capacity was in this basin. 73% of LNG projects under construction were in the Atlantic Basin, and more than half in the United States. However, 20% of the regasification projects under construction are in the Atlantic.

In the context of global gas production and demand expected to increase annually in the period from 2016 to 2022, LNG exports have increased substantially in recent years and are expected to be around 450 bcm in 2022, from around 350 bcm in 2016, mainly driven by the US and Australia. LNG imports are also expected to grow. The Atlantic Basin represented nearly 18% of LNG exports and 25% of LNG imports.

The volume and diversity of LNG trade flows are increasing rapidly with the appearance of new exporting and importing countries that add new LNG capacity to a market where demand is declining in some of the large, traditional LNG importing countries.

In the Atlantic Basin the US will grow dramatically its gas demand as well as its LNG exports. Europe will play mainly as importer of gas from Russia and in the future from the Caspian region. The US LNG could be for Europe an instrument to reduce the continent´s current dependence on Russian gas. In any case, it is important for the EU to be an attractive market for LNG exporters and as a consequence, the development of the internal gas market is a necessity to achieve a correct security of supply.

The South Atlantic will increase its relevance. Latin America and Africa will probably increase demand and play a more active role in LNG trade; however, these territories will need considerable investments and the development of their own domestic markets. These territories also face other challenges such as accessing finance or the need of regulatory stability. In the meanwhile, exports from Western Africa will increase.

Besides the situation and perspectives of infrastructures (liquefaction and regasification plants, shipping vessels and pipelines) which set the physical basis for LNG trade as well as the fundamental economics of LNG supply and demand, three other factors shall influence the volumes and patterns of trade flows in the Atlantic Basin. Namely the type of contractual supply agreement, the pricing mechanisms and the cost of the LNG supply chain.

So first, in terms of capacities worldwide there is a global situation which will imply pressure for lower LNG prices. Technologies such as FRSU, FU and small liquefaction plants will mean more variety, more flexibility and more possibilities of LNG trade. However, the ability to increase LNG exports will also be driven by market conditions.

In relation to the contractual supply agreements the existence of long term contracts, with gas price formulas, in most of the cases presumably linked to oil and oil products and with a great part of the volume contracted related to "take or pay" clauses will probably evolve to contracts gas-on-gas pricing, shorter term contracts, and more flexibility. In this sense, the US and Northern Europe are relevant.

Regarding the pricing mechanisms on both sides of the North Atlantic Basin different mechanisms are taking place GOG competition in North America and Northern Europe and OPE in the Mediterranean. Nevertheless, these mechanisms are evolving through a GOG in South Europe and towards considering the HH price as a reference on imports from the US.

This situation shall create dynamics of sales at different terms (from long, medium and short to spot) related not only to the fundamentals of gas supply and demand but also for oil and oil derivatives.

The third factor with influence over the volumes and patterns of trade in the Atlantic Basin is the costs of the LNG supply chain. The increasing costs of liquefaction plants and the variations in time charter rates, together with the cost of shipping depending on the routes (i.e. US-Europe vs. US-Far East) will also affect the dynamics of LNG trade. On the one hand bringing a certain floor price given the marginal cost of the supply chain, on the other by the arbitrage that may take place because of the price gaps between the Far East (Japan and South Korea) and the Atlantic Europe.

As a consequence, LNG prices, price indexation and flexibility mechanisms will shape the patterns of trade flows in the Atlantic Basin together with the gas exports from the US that will imply a clear advantage in cost that shall be translated into a competitive advantage. All in all, LNG markets shall be more interrelated and interconnected in terms of flows, volumes and prices.

Looking at the future, gas should play a key role in the transition towards a low carbon economy. Global demand and supply for gas and international trade, including a growing role of LNG, will increase in the medium term (2017-2022).

To conclude, one of the main challenges that the Atlantic Basin must face in terms of LNG trade is the fact that relations are still established principally within each of its constituent regions instead of between them. Perhaps shale gas in US will imply more interrelationship within North America (Canada, US, Mexico). This, together with the decrease of gas production in Europe and its increase in gas demand, shall shape an LNG dynamic area in the North Atlantic Basin. However, new dynamics should be developed in the future in order to include the South Atlantic and achieve a more unified Atlantic Basin.

References

Abiteboul, J.In IFRI (Ed.), *US LNG supply & impact on EU security of supply.* Retrieved from https://www.ifri.org/sites/default/files/atoms/files/presentation_j._abiteboul.pdf

Álvarez Pelegry, E., & Balbás Peláez, E. (Eds.). (2003). *El gas natural. Del yacimiento al consumidor. Aprovisionamientos y cadena del gas natural licuado.* Madrid: Dossat.

Ayuso, A., & Viilup, E. (2013). Introducción: una nueva mirada al Atlántico. *Revista CIDOB d´Afers Internacionals,* (102-103), 7.

Barnes, B. (2018a, March 2018). Forward intelligence. Europe primed to benefit from US exports. *Petroleum Economist*, 26.

Barnes, B. (2018b, March 2018). Forward intelligence. Global LNG hubs. *Petroleum Economist*, 22.

BG Group. (2014). In British Chamber of Commerce (Ed.), *LNG 50. A celebration of the first commercial shipment of LNG.* Singapore: Retrieved from http://www.britcham.org.sg/files/event_document/6/6LNG%20A5%20Booklet-FINAL.compressed.pdf

BP. (2003). *BP statistical review 2002 of world energy* Retrieved from https://www.griequity.com/resources/industryandissues/Energy/bp2002statisticalreview.pdf

BP. (2017). *BP statistical review 2017* Retrieved from www.bp.com

BP energy economics. (2018). *BP energy outlook. 2018 edition* Retrieved from https://www.bp.com/content/dam/bp/en/corporate/pdf/energy-economics/energy-outlook/bp-energy-outlook-2018.pdf

CNMC. (2017). *Informe de supervisión del mercado mayorista y aprovisionamiento de gas. Periodo de marzo de 2017.* Madrid: Retrieved from www.cnmc.es

Cornort-Gandolphe, S. (2018). In IFRI (Ed.), *Le gaz dans la transition énergétique européenne: enjeux et opportunités.* Paris: Retrieved from https://www.ifri.org/fr/publications/etudes-de-lifri/gaz-transition-energetique-europeenne-enjeux-opportunites

Cornot-Gandolphe, S. (2016). *The US natural gas exports. New rules on the European gas landscape.* Paris: IFRI. Retrieved from https://www.ifri.org/sites/default/files/atoms/files/etude_cornot_gaz_naturel_en_europe_en_okdb_complet-reduit_ok.pdf

Energy Market Price. (2018). Russia´s Gazprom announced on Monday it had finalized the sea portion of the first segment of the TurkStream offshore gas pipeline across the black sea. Retrieved from www.energymarketprice.com

FERC. (2018). *World LNG estimated landed prices. National natural gas market overview: World LNG landed prices*. Retrieved from www.ferc.gov/oversight

GIIGNL. (2017). *The LNG industry. GIIGNL annual report 2017*. France: Retrieved from www.giignl.org

Howard, R. (2018). *The LNG shipping forecast: Costs rebounding, outlook uncertain* The Oxford Institute for Energy Studies. Retrieved from https://www.oxfordenergy.org/publications/lng-shipping-forecast-costs-rebounding-outlook-uncertain/

IEA. (2017a). *Gas 2017. Analysis and forecasts to 2022* Retrieved from www.iea.org

IEA. (2017b). *Global gas security review. How is LNG market flexibility evolving?* Paris: Retrieved from www.iea.org

IEA. (2017c). *Natural gas information. 2017 edition*. Paris: Retrieved from www.iea.org

IGU. (2017a). *2017 world LNG report*. Barcelona: Retrieved from https://www.igu.org/news/igu-releases-2017-world-lng-report

IGU. (2017b). Natural gas facts & figures. Retrieved from https://www.igu.org/resources-data

IGU. (2017c). *Wholesale gas price survey. 2017 edition. A global review of price formation mechanisms. 2005 to 2016*. Barcelona: Retrieved from www.igu.org

Isbell, P. (2013). La energía en el Atlántico y el horizonte estratégico. *Revista CIDOB d´Afers Internacionals, 102-103*, 73.

Kuhn, M. (2013). *Presentation given at the 2nd annual UGOS gas & oil summit 2013*. London:

OECD/IEA. (2014). *Gas medium-term market report*. Paris: Retrieved from https://www.iea.org/publications/

Ripple, R. D. (2016). In IAEE Energy Forum (Ed.), *U.S. natural gas (LNG) exports: Opportunities and challenges* Retrieved from https://www.iaee.org/en/publications/newsletterdl.aspx?id=341

Songhurst, B. (2014). *LNG plant cost escalation* The Oxford Institute for Energy Studies. Retrieved from LNG Plant cost escalation

Stadnicka, M., & Janiszewska-Kiewra, E. (2018). In McKinsey (Ed.), *The 2017 LNG market in 10 charts* (Energy Insights ed.) Retrieved from https://www.mckinseyenergyinsights.com/insights/the-2017-lng-market-in-10-charts/

Stanivuk, T., Tokic, T., & Soskic, S. (2013). *Transport costs affecting LNG delivery by moss tyoe carriers* doi:10.7225/toms.v02.n01.005 Retrieved from https://hrcak.srce.hr/file/148135

Stern, J. (2017). *Challenges to the future of gas: Unburnable or unaffordable?* (OIES PAPER: NG 125. ed.) The Oxford Institute for Energy Studies. doi:ISBN 978-1-78467-099-3. Retrieved from https://www.oxfordenergy.org/publications/challenges-future-gas-unburnable-unaffordable/

Wood A., Viscidi, L., & Fargo, J. (2018). In The dialogue (Ed.), *LNG in the Americas. How commercial, technological and policy trends are shaping regional trade* Retrieved from https://www.thedialogue.org/wp-content/uploads/2018/04/LNG-in-the-Americas.pdf

Xu, C., & Bell, L. (2017). Worldwide oil, natural gas reserves inch higher in 2017. *Oil&Gas Journal, December 2017*, 18.

Xu, C., & Bell, L. (2018). Production restraint by OPEC, other key to oil-market balance this year. [Oil&Gas Journal], 16.

Zajdler, R. (2015). In Zajdler Energy Lawyers (Ed.). *The importance of LNG transport costs* Retrieved from http://www.zajdler.eu/raporty/show_pdf.php?ID=9

Annex: Types of price formation mechanisms

Mechanism	Observations
Oil price escalation (OPE)	The price is linked, usually through a base price and an escalation clause, to competing fuels, typically crude oil, gas oil and/or fuel oil. In some cases coal prices can be used as can electricity prices.
Gas-on-gas competition (GOG)	The price is determined by the interplay of supply and demand – gas-on-gas competition – and is traded over a variety of different periods (daily, monthly, annually or other periods). Trading takes place at physical hubs (e.g. Henry Hub) or notional hubs (e.g. NBP in the UK). There are likely to be developed futures markets (NYMEX or ICE). Not all gas is bought and sold on a short term fixed price basis and there will be longer term contracts but these will use gas price indices to determine the monthly price, for example, rather than competing fuel indices. Also included in this category is spot LNG, any pricing which is linked to hub or spot prices and also bilateral agreements in markets where there are multiple buyers and sellers.
Bilateral monopoly (BIM)	The price is determined by bilateral discussions and agreements between a large seller and a large buyer, with the price being fixed for a period of time – typically one year. There may be a written contract in place but often the arrangement is at the Government or state-owned company level. Typically there would be a single dominant buyer or seller on at least one side of the transaction, to distinguish this category from GOG, where there would be multiple buyers and sellers trading bilaterally.

Netback from final product (NET)	The price received by the gas supplier is a function of the price received by the buyer for the final product the buyer produces. This may occur where the gas is used as a feedstock in chemical plants, such as ammonia or methanol, and is the major variable cost in producing the product.
Regulation cost of service (RCS)	The price is determined, or approved, formally by a regulatory authority, or possibly a Ministry, but the level is set to cover the "cost of service", including the recovery of investment and a reasonable rate of return.
Regulation: social and political (RSP)	The price is set, on an irregular basis, probably by a Ministry, on a political/social basis, in response to the need to cover increasing costs, or possibly as a revenue raising exercise – a hybrid between RCS and RBC.
Regulation below cost (RBC)	The price is knowingly set below the average cost of producing and transporting the gas often as a form of state subsidy to the population.
No price (NP)	The gas produced is either provided free to the population and industry, possibly as a feedstock for chemical and fertilizer plants, or in refinery processes and enhanced oil recovery. The gas produced maybe associated with oil and/or liquids and treated as a by-product.
Not known (NK)	No data or evidence.

Source: (IGU, 2017c)

Chapter Two

Trade integration in the Economic Community of West African States: Assessing Constraints and Opportunities Using an Augmented Gravity Model

Rim Berahab and Abdelaaziz Ait Ali

The proliferation of Regional Economic Communities (REC) in Africa underlines the importance of regional integration, which has become an essential priority for this region. Regional integration is seen as an important tool for the continent's development, since one third of its economies are landlocked and depend on their coastal neighbours for trade. In addition, domestic African markets are small, fragmented and below the critical size needed for companies to grow and achieve significant economies of scale.

Accounting for nearly 17% and 30% of Africa's surface area and population respectively, the Economic Community of West African States (ECOWAS) is one of the most densely populated areas on the continent. Despite its great potential in terms of human and natural resources, the ECOWAS still faces obstacles to achieve effective regional integration. Indeed, the performance of its intraregional trade remains very modest compared to other economic blocs of the world. Intra-regional trade is limited, in fact, to around 10% while, it exceeds 20% in the East African Community for instance and 25% in the Association of Southeast Asian Nations (ASEAN) in 2016. Therefore, it becomes crucial to investigate the existence of a potential for intra-regional trade in the ECOWAS as well as the constraints for its realization.

It is recognized that the potential of regional integration in Africa has been largely untapped (UNCTAD (2013) and ADB (2017)). Studies such as Geda & Seid (2015) and Ebaidalla & Yahia (2015) have shown how significant is this potential between African countries. Using a standard gravity model, they projected the intra-flow of trade and revealed the huge potential for trade expansion. The majority of African countries seems to operate well below the potential and are not reaping the benefits of the trade liberalization. These studies concluded, however, over the necessity to upgrade the quality of infrastructure and diversify their productive fabric to further economic integration. However, the structural poor performance of trade integration casts doubts over the fitness of standard empirical models and the deployed approach to estimate the trade potential. This calls for an innovative approach and methodology to tackle this issue. Thus, it is imperative to revive this old issue capitalizing on a new approach to assess whether Africa, in the case of ECOWAS, is likely to witness an improvement in its integration dynamic in the medium term.

This chapter contributes to the literature in three main ways. First, it estimates a gravity model to explain trade flows inside a REC with a Free Trade Area (FTA) to address the heterogeneity of trade policies adopted towards economic partners outside the REC. Second, it simulates trade potential inside the ECOWAS region, using coefficients estimated over a well-integrated region, such as ASEAN. If, otherwise, we perform the estimation over the ECOWAS region (with their economic partners in this case) and then simulate the potential, the simulation is likely to project the same dynamics and end up with trade potential around the observed data. Third, it deploys an augmented version of the gravity model that controls for the quality of infrastructure and the bilateral complementarity between economic partners and then compares simulations to those of a basic form of the gravity model.

Following this spirit, the chapter is organized as follows: a first section is dedicated to a brief overview of the trade structure of the ECOWAS countries and analyses some relevant trade indicators. A second section attempt to overview the literature on this issue. The third section describes the model and the data while the fourth section discusses the result estimation and the simulations output for the ECOWAS. By offering policy recommendations, section five concludes.

Economic Overview of the ECOWAS

The ECOWAS is a regional grouping of 15 West African states founded in 1975. It is a free trade area whose main objective is to foster regional cooperation and integration in all economic fields, with the intent of creating an economic union. Within the ECOWAS, eight member countries[1] form the West African Economic and Monetary Union (WAEMU), which became operational in 2000. The WAEMU is a custom union that uses the CFA franc as a common currency. The ECOWAS has witnessed a sustained economic growth—despite a drop in 2010 amid the economic and financial

---

1.   Benin, Burkina Faso, Cote d'Ivoire, Guinea Bissau, Mali, Niger, Senegal and Togo.

Figure 1. GDP growth (percentage) of ECOWAS and Sub-Saharan Africa during the period 2005-2018

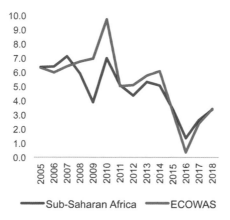

Figure 2. GDP growth average (2005-2017) and GDP per capita (2005) of ECOWAS countries[a,b,c]

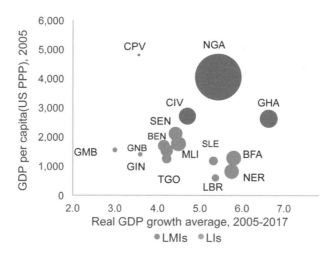

Source: International Monetary Fund.
a. Bubble size represents population
b. "Low-income economies (LIs) are defined as those with a GNI per capita, calculated using the World Bank Atlas method, of $1,005 or less in 2016; lower middle-income economies (LICs) are those with a GNI per capita between $1,006 and $3,955". Source: World Bank.
c. Benin (BEN), Burkina Faso (BFA), Cape Verde (CPV), Côte d'Ivoire (CIV), Gambia (GMB), Ghana (GHA), Guinea (GIN), Guinea-Bissau (GNB), Liberia (LBR), Mali (MLI), Niger (NER), Nigeria (NGA), Senegal (SEN), Sierra Leone (SLE), and Togo (TGO).

crisis—with rates ranging from 5 percent to 10 percent. In 2014, however, a sharp slowdown has been observed due to the decline in commodity prices in general and oil prices specifically, when GDP growth decreased from 6 percent in 2014 to 0.4 percent in 2016, given the negative performance of the biggest economy of the region Nigeria. In fact, Nigeria remains the largest contributor of wealth creation in the ECOWAS and the largest in terms of population. According to the latest estimations[2], GDP growth is likely to pick up in 2017 and 2018.

With the exceptions of Cape Verde, Nigeria, Ghana, and Côte d'Ivoire, all ECOWAS members are classified as Least Developed Countries.[5] Hence, their growth performances vary quite sharply, reflecting their diversity. Between 2005 and 2017, average growth rates of real GDP ranged from 3 percent in Gambia to 6.6 percent in Ghana. When taking into consideration population growth, real GDP per capita goes from -0.3 percent in Gambia to 4 percent in Ghana. Despite a slowdown in real GDP growth the latest years, Nigeria still accounts for 70 percent of this bloc's GDP with $395 billion for 2017, nearly ten times the GDP of the region's second largest economy, Ghana, which accounted for only 8 percent with $45 billion for the same year. Nigeria has also the second highest GDP per capita estimated at $5,402 behind that of Cape Verde estimated at $6,327 in 2017. In terms of economic structure, only a few member countries have developed relatively bigger manufacturing industries such as Benin, Côte d'Ivoire and Senegal whose share of manufacturing in their GDP vary between 13 percent and 14 percent in 2015, while most others, notably Sierra Leone, Gambia and Mali depend primarily on agriculture as shown in figure 3.

Efforts to reduce trade barriers within the ECOWAS have not yielded effective results since intra-trade remains low. The share of exports from ECOWAS countries sold within the bloc has stayed relatively steady 1995 to 2016, around 10 percent. As it can be seen in Figure 4, Nigeria and Côte d'Ivoire, given their size, dominate trade within the ECOWAS by supplying the highest volume of merchandises. Their share in total intra-regional exports to the ECOWAS is estimated at 35.6 percent and 28.9 on average between 2005 and 2016 respectively. Yet, Nigeria's exports to ECOWAS represents only a small percentage—around 4 percent—of its total exports to the world, while this share reaches 24 percent for Côte d'Ivoire. This means that Nigeria relies less on ECOWAS partners in terms of its trade relations. During the same period, Senegal, (which is the next most import-

---

2. IMF. 2017. *Fiscal Adjustment and Economic Diversification. Sub-Saharan Africa Regional Economic Outlook.*

Figure 3. Size and Economic structure of ECOWAS Members in 2015[a,b]

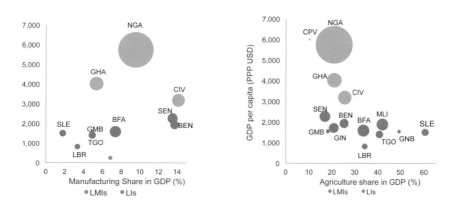

Source: World Development Indicators, *World Economic Outlook*.
a. Bubble size represents population.
b. Data regarding the share of manufacturing in GDP is not available for Cabo Verde, Guinea, Guinea Bissau, Mali and Niger.

ant exporter to the region) Togo and Gambia account for 9.3 percent, 5.4 percent and 0.1 percent of the total exports to ECOWAS partners respectively, yet they rely heavily on ECOWAS. Indeed, their exports account for 37 percent, 47 percent and 26 percent of their total exports to the world respectively.

The same observation can be drawn for imports. Between 2005 and 2016, Côte d'Ivoire, Ghana and to a lesser extent Mali and Nigeria imported high volume of merchandises from the ECOWAS, ranging from $984 million to $2.0 billion. Nevertheless, imports' share of Ghana and Nigeria from ECOWAS make up a relatively low percentage. This point stands out the most for Nigeria in particular; whose import from ECOWAS partners represents only 2 percent of its total imports from the world. Unlike Nigeria, other countries, namely Burkina Faso, Sierra Leone, Niger, Gambia and Guinea Bissau, are heavily supplied by the ECOWAS. Therefore, even though intra-regional trade in ECOWAS remains low, particularly for large economies, compared to other developing economic blocs of the world, few countries rely on it for a large portion of their trade.

The range of products traded within the ECOWAS has not been submitted to significant changes. As shown in Table 1, during the period 2005-

Figure 4. Intra ECOWAS export and imports, average 2005-2016, by country.

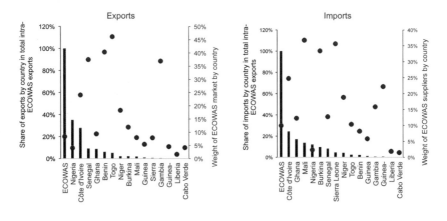

Source: UNCTAD

Table 1. Top 10 products traded by the ECOWAS (in value, average 2005-2016)

Top 10 intra-regional Trade in the ECOWAS		Top 10 ECOWAS EXPORTS to the World		Top 10 ECOWAS IMPORTS from the World	
Fuels	54%	Fuels	72%	Machinery and Electrics	20%
Chemicals	7%	Food Products	7%	Fuels	15%
Food Products	7%	Stone And Glass	6%	Transportation	13%
Vegetable	5%	Plastic OR Rubber	3%	Vegetable	9%
Transportation	4%	Vegetable	3%	Chemicals	8%
Minerals	4%	Transportation	2%	Metals	8%
Plastic OR Rubber	4%	Minerals	1%	Food Products	6%
Animal	3%	Textiles and Clothing	1%	Plastic OR Rubber	6%
Metals	3%	Chemicals	1%	Animal	4%
Wood	3%	Wood	1%	Textiles and Clothing	2%

Source: World Integrated Trade Solution (WITS).

Figure 5. Evolution of ECOWAS imports structure by country

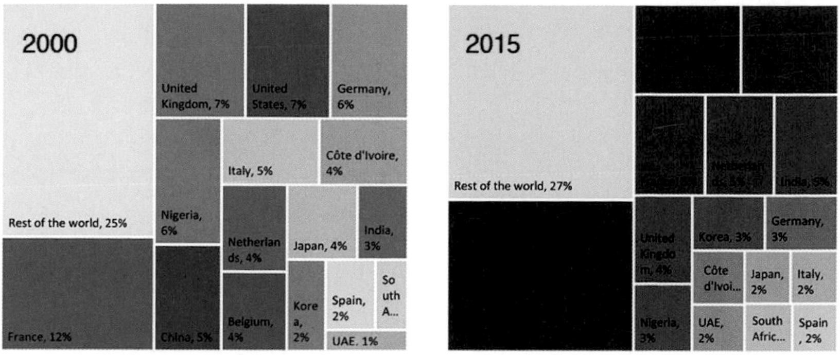

Source: UNCTAD.

2016, trade concerns mainly fuel products (oil), which accounted for 54 percent of intra-regional trade in the ECOWAS, followed by chemicals and food products. It is important to note however, that official intra-regional trade volumes data are underestimated since it does not include informal trade, which accounts for a large share of trade between ECOWAS countries.[3] In addition, misreporting and inconsistencies in data results in the difference between volumes in monetary units of intra-regional export and intra-regional import. Regarding trade with the world, exports of the ECOWAS are concentrated in fuels, followed by food products, stone, and glass, whereas imports of the ECOWAS concern machinery and electrics, followed by fuel and transportation.

When it comes to imports structure by economic partner, the figures above indicate how the Chinese economy is positioning itself as a major supplier of ECOWAS's market, as it captures around 21 percent of total imports. It is worth mentioning that in 2000, Chinese products was representing only 5 percent of total imported goods, below United Kingdom and France with respectively 7 percent and 12 percent. The Indian economy is being considered as a major economic partner of the ECOWAS, with a positive dynamic since 2000, suppling around 5 percent of total imported goods in 2015 after 3 percent in 2000. The favourable dynamics of Asian economies, especially China and India, was achieved to the detriment of European economies that have witnessed a shrink in their market share in

---

3. European Centre for Development Policy Management, "Overview of trade barriers to trade in West Africa: Insights in political economy dynamics, with particular focus on agricultural and food trade". DP No. 195, July 2016.

the last two decades. France and United Kingdom and Germany have been in 2000 at the top of economic partners of the ECOWAS, while in 2015 they have been overtaken by China and United States. For instance, the prominence of France, given historical and cultural links especially with francophone countries, made it one of the most important partners in the beginning of the 21th century. This relationship has lost momentum during this century, with France being in fourth position. In the European Union, Belgium could be considered as an exception, with a stronger market presence. Its share has, thus, increased from 4 to 6 percent. For the United States of America, it has been able to maintain its share in the ECOWAS market, at around 7 percent.

Trade complementarity index

Another way to evaluate intra-regional trade within the ECOWAS is to look at the trade complementarity index, which measures the potential trade between two partners. It illustrates to what extent the export profile of ECOWAS members corresponds the import profile of other ECOWAS members. It is constructed as follows:

$$TC_{j,k} = 100 * \left[1 - \frac{\sum |X_{i,j} - M_{i,k}|}{2} \right]$$

Where $X_{i,}$ is the share of good i in global exports of country j and $M_{i,}$ is the share of good i in all imports of country k. Values close to 100 indicate a great match between country j's export structure and country k's import structure and values close to 0 indicate a low correspondence in their export and import pattern. Countries with a high index suggest a gain from trade expansion.

Results for ECOWAS are shown in Table 2. Trade complementarity index varies considerably across countries of ECOWAS and does not exceed 50 percent. Senegal, as an exporter, displays relatively high levels of bilateral complementarity with almost all ECOWAS members except with Côte d'Ivoire and Liberia. Interestingly enough, Côte d'Ivoire as an exporter has a relatively high bilateral complementarity index with Senegal. This indicates that the exports structure of Côte d'Ivoire match with the imports structure of Senegal, whereas the exports structure of Senegal does not match with the imports structure of Côte d'Ivoire. Benin has also a high complementarity index with a number of ECOWAS countries, namely Burkina Faso, Cabo Verde, Guinea-Bissau and Senegal, and Togo with Burkina Faso, Ghana, Guinea-Bissau and Mali. The lowest level of

Table 2. Trade complementarities index in ECOWAS, 2013*

	BEN	BFA	CPV	CIV	GMB	GHA	GIN	GNB	LBR	MLI	NER	NGA	SEN	SLE	TGO
BEN	_	31	30	17	21	23	30	31	11	27	21	23	35	29	25
BFA	16	_	16	10	14	15	17	16	9	17	13	17	19	16	16
CPV	10	9	_	12	8	12	10	9	4	9	9	11	9	7	10
CIV	29	30	29	_	22	25	29	32	13	30	20	26	41	27	29
GMB	15	11	14	11	_	13	12	12	5	11	12	12	13	12	11
GHA	10	11	12	30	11	_	10	11	8	11	12	11	22	10	9
GIN	4	5	6	26	3	5	_	4	2	4	4	6	15	4	3
GNB	2	1	2	4	1	1	1	_	1	1	1	2	4	2	1
LBR	5	7	7	10	5	6	6	5	_	6	6	8	8	6	5
MLI	10	12	10	10	9	11	10	9	7	_	10	11	11	9	9
NER	20	30	32	8	14	14	28	23	8	22	_	17	23	42	41
NGA	9	9	10	25	8	9	8	10	7	8	6	_	21	9	8
SEN	34	43	43	28	33	33	43	44	13	43	33	35	_	35	34
SLE	5	4	5	5	4	5	4	3	4	4	4	6	4	_	4
TGO	26	30	27	22	29	32	26	32	14	31	27	28	28	24	_

*Latest year available.

Source: UNCTAD

bilateral complementarity is recorded between Guinea-Bissau and several ECOWAS countries, namely Burkina Faso, Gambia, Ghana, Guinea, Liberia, Mali, Niger and Togo.

Empirical Literature

Intra-regional trade in Africa has been the focus of many empirical and theoretical studies since the creation of regional economic communities in the continent, the proliferation of free trade zones and custom unions. Scholars have indeed argued that intra-regional trade holds a great potential for raising the level of welfare of Africans by promoting regional economic development and improving the living standards of their population (Longo and Sekkat, 2001; Geda and Kibret, 2008).

However, the unsatisfactory performance of Africa in boosting intra-regional trade has led to a growing interest for studies that assesses not only the trade patterns, but most importantly the potential of intra-regional trade in several African Regional Economic Communities using gravity models. The latter are commonly used as an ex post analytical framework in empirical studies of bilateral trade flows. They can also be used to address the issue of regionalism by simulating trade potentials between any groupings of countries.

Tinbergen (1962) analysed the determinants of bilateral trade patterns and the effect of regional trading arrangements (RTAs). He applied a gravity model on 42 countries. His findings demonstrate the positive impact of the Gross Domestic Product (GDP) of both the exporting and importing country on trade flows on the one hand and the negative impact of distance on trade on the other hand. Following on Tinbergen (1962), Eichengreen and Irwin (1995) introduced historical variables to a dynamic gravity model to analyse whether countries with a history of trading continue to trade with each other. They found that the exclusion of historical factors exaggerates the impact of trading blocs. Further studies have expanded the gravity model and used variables like contiguity, common colonizer, common language, tariffs, exchange rates etc. (Hacker and Einarsson, 2003; Cardamonc, 2006; Adekunle and Gitau, 2011).

With particular emphasis to the Sub-Saharan Africa (SSA), Foroutan and Pritchett (1993) applied the traditional gravity model for 19 SSA countries based on proximity, economy size and other characteristics. They used the Tobit maximum likelihood estimation method to correct censoring bias produced by the Ordinary Least Square (OLS) method. They compared actual trade data with the prediction of the model. Despite the low intra-African trade, Foroutan and Pritchett (1993) found that the reported intra-trade is higher than the potential predicted by the model. The actual share of SSA's trade was an average of 8.1 percent whereas the gravity model estimated a slightly lower mean of 7.5 percent.

Cassim (2001) conducted an empirical study on the determinants of intra-regional trade in Southern African countries employing the gravity model with a Tobit maximum likelihood estimation method. He found that intra-regional trade in the South African Development Community (SADC)[4] is actually in line with international standards, meaning that this region's trade is beyond its potential. He confirmed that fundamental economic factors like economic and geographic size of the trading partners measured by GDP and land areas have significant impact on trade flows, while transport costs adversely affect the bilateral trade. However, this result is biased by the high volumes of exports from South Africa to the rest of the members. In fact, the model uses by Cassim (2001) shows that intra-SADC trade excluding South Africa is low, indicating the existence of a potential for increased exports.

---

4. SADC includes Angola, Botswana, Dem. Rep. Of the Congo, Lesotho, Madagascar, Malawi, Mauritius, Mozambique, Namibia, Seychelles, South Africa, Swaziland, United Republic of Tanzania, Zambia, Zimbabwe.

Alemayehu and Haile (2008) replicated the gravity model using a Tobit formulation to test the determinants of bilateral trade flows and assess the outlooks and challenges of regional integration in the Common Market for Eastern and Southern Africa (COMESA).[5] The findings demonstrate that the standard gravity model variables such as the GDP of both the exporting and partner countries, bilateral distance and contiguity have the expected signs except for the common language variable. This strengthen the hypothesis that trade between similar countries tend to be higher. However, the coefficient of regional integration dummy was negative and non-significant, meaning that regional trading blocs in Africa fail to promote intra-regional trade.

Alemayehu and Edris (2015) re-examined the potential for intra-Africa trade with the objective of advancing regional economic integration by trade. They used a variety of gravity models to two groups of countries- a group characterized by an advanced level of integration (West and Central Africa) and a group that comprises the rest of the continent (North, East and Southern Africa). They estimated the model using the Pseudo Poisson Maximum Likelihood (PPML) technique. A simulation exercise was conducted afterwards to analyse the potential of intra-Africa trade for each group of countries, given the parameters of the model. This was then compared with actual trade of each country. The results showed the existence of significant potential for intra-Africa trade, which is however dampened by lack of complementarities of exports and imports, weak infrastructure as well as the relative competitive position of African potential export suppliers.

Regarding the ECOWAS specifically, Luqman et al. (2015) analyse bilateral trade patterns and the openness level of ECOWAS through a gravity model using three techniques: the PPML, the fully modified ordinary least squares (FMOLS) and canonical cointegrating regression (CCR), for the period 1981-2003. Trade openness was negatively significant under PPML, whereas financial openness was negatively significant under FMOLS and CCR. Contiguity (common border) and distance had a strong effect on ECOWAS trade, while there is a negative effect of trade flow among ECOWAS members.

---

5. The COMESA includes Burundi, Comoros, Dem. Rep. Of the Congo, Djibouti, Egypt, Eritrea, Ethiopia, Kenya, Libya, Madagascar, Malawi, Mauritius, Rwanda, Seychelles, Sudan, Swaziland, Uganda, Zambia, Zimbabwe.

Recent studies introduce infrastructure variables to the gravity models in order to capture their impact on bilateral trade in Africa, especially given the fact that the continent faces an important deficit in terms of infrastructure provision, which in turn act as a barrier to the entire process of regional integration. Deen-Swarray et al. (2011) investigate the effect of infrastructure development on intra-regional flows of member countries of the ECOWAS employing a modified gravity model and using both a time series and a cross-sectional analysis for the period 1990-2008. They developed an index for different kind of infrastructure (road, rail, airport etc.) to analyze how they individually influence trade. Deen Swarray et al. (2011) used three estimation methods, namely a pooled model, a fixed effect model and random effects model. The found that GDP, language, common currency and distance variables have a significant and the expected effect on total trade in ECOWAS, whereas infrastructure index variable have a puzzling negative impact on total trade.

Akpan (2014) examines the effect of improving the quality of a regional road infrastructure within ECOWAS if it was at the level of roads in South Africa. He uses a traditional gravity model that includes variables for contiguity, common language and road quality as well as the positive difference in per capita GDP between exporting and partner countries. Akpan (2014) used a Tobit estimation and found that improvement in road infrastructure lead to an increase in intra-regional trade relative to the 2012 level of 5.3 percent.

With regards to another economic grouping, Zarzoro and Lehmann (2003) used the gravity model with fixed effects to evaluate the trade potential between Southern Common Market (MERCOSUL) members and the European Union (EU) following the agreements established between the two blocs. The model includes 20 countries (4 members of MERCOSUL in addition to Chile and 15 members of the EU). The authors fund that variables such as infrastructure, income differences and exchange rates have important determinants of bilateral trade flows.

Methodology: specification and the estimation technique

The gravity model has been derived initially from Newton's Law of Universal Gravitation. Tinbergen (1962) introduced this physical law in the area of international trade. According to the model, the intensity of bilateral trade between two economies, like the gravitational force between two objects, depends positively on their respective 'masses' (in economics, nominal GDP is often used as a proxy) and inversely on the distance separating them. The distance per se is not the key element, but in fact it captures the cost of transportation or cost of trade in general. Therefore, the distribution of goods or factors across space is determined by gravity forces conditional on the size of economic activities at each location. The equation translates a supply (GDP of the exporting country) and demand (GDP of the importing country) mechanism. The gravity equation can be expressed in its non-linear form as:

$$Trade_{ijt} = \alpha . \frac{GDP_{it} {}^\circ GDP_{jt}}{Distance_{ij}} .$$

The equation has been often transformed into the following linear form:

$$\log Trade_{ijt} = \alpha + \varrho \log GDP_{it} + \beta \log GDP_{jt} + \mu \log Distance_{ij} + \mu_{ijt}$$

Since then, international trade economists have been referring to this equation whenever they study the determinants of international bilateral trade flows (WTO (2016)). Besides, economists have enriched the equation with other characteristics that might hamper/foster trade, such as a free trade agreement, or other types of bilateral costs, usually referred to as bilateral trade resistance. The success of this equation in literature owes it to the ease of estimation and handling. In addition, gravity models enjoy fit of between 60 and 90 percent with aggregate data as well as with sectoral data (WTO (2016)). However, despite being extensively used in empirical literature, the gravity model was lacking solid theoretical microeconomic foundations. Anderson (1979) and Anderson and van Wincoop (2003) derive the gravity equation starting from the assumptions that goods are differentiated by place of origin (Armington, (1969)) and CES utility function in which preferences are homothetic and identical across countries.

Moreover, Anderson and van Wincoop (2003) highlighted that trade intensity between any pair countries depends not only on factors affecting the two economies themselves but also on how difficult it is for each of them to trade with the world, the so-called "multilateral resistance term". Baldwin and Taglioni (2006) generalized Anderson-Van Wincoop's concept to fit panel data estimation and suggested to add systematically time-varying exporter and importer dummies. WTO (2016) pointed out that these dummies will control for the unobservable multilateral resistances, and potentially for any other observable and unobservable characteristics that vary over time for each exporter and importer.

Regarding the estimation technique, Silva and Tenreyro (2006) demonstrated in a pioneer paper how biased the coefficients are when the gravity model is estimated in its log-log form by Ordinary Least Squares (OLS). The heteroscedasticity, which often plagues trade, hampers the consistency of the OLS estimates. In addition, the censored nature of such trade data implies that the log-linearized form disregard zero trade flows. They suggested a Pseudo Poisson Maximum Likelihood (PPML) estimator for gravity models that address all caveats associated with OLS, estimating the function over the exports in monetary units instead of the logarithm of exports.

Several studies have confirmed the advantages of using such technique. WTO (2016) recommended the use of this estimator when dealing with gravity models. Besides, the estimation technique produces robust coefficients that address heteroscedasticity issues. Silva and Tenreyro (2006) pointed out the need to perform a test to assess the specification of the model. Ramsey Reset test is the most recommended one, Silva and Tenreyro (2006) and WTO (2016). The null hypothesis (H0) states that the model is correctly specified, while the hypothesis (H1) states that the model suffers misspecification or omitted variables.

In this paper and in line with these novelties, the following two gravity equations are estimated over bilateral trade flows between the ten members of the ASEAN, covering the period 2007-2014:

Standard basic gravity model:

$$Trade_{ijt} = \alpha + \varrho \log GDP_{it} + \beta \log GDP_{jt} + \mu \log Distance_{ij} + \gamma\ Contiguity_{ij} + \mu_{ijt}$$

Augmented version of the gravity model:

$$Trade_{ijt} = \alpha + \varrho \log GDP_{it} + \beta \log GDP_{jt} + \mu \log Distance_{ij} + \gamma\ Contiguity_{ij} + infrastructure_{it-1} + infrastructure_{jt-1} + Complementarity\_index_{ijt-1} + \mu_{ijt}$$

Where $Trade_{ijt}$ is bilateral trade between pair of countries, contiguity is a dummy variable equals to 1 if a pair country shares borders and 0 if not. Infrastructure is an index that captures the quality and the availability of infrastructure. Regarding the complementarity index, "it measures to what extent the export profile of country i to the world matches the import profile of country j from the world. The index values range from 0 to 1 with 0 indicating that there is no correspondence between country i's export structure and country j's import structure and 1 indicating a perfect match in their export/import pattern" (UNCTAD). A higher indicator, ceteris paribus, implies a chance to increase trade, as the demand fits the supply.

The two models are estimated using the PPML approach, suggested by Silva and Tenreyro (2006), considering the multilateral resistance term captured through time-varying exporter and importer dummies. Following, Donaubauer, Glas & Nunnenkamp (2015) we attempt to evaluate the impact of infrastructure on the performance of bilateral trade. We tried to address endogeneity by integrating the lagged observation of infrastructure index and complementarity index. This latter is included in the equation to address the productive structure and matching issue between the supply side and the demand side. For example, this indicator is expected to bring down the potential between two economies such as Angola and Algeria. Being two of the biggest economies of the continent, the standard gravity equation must expect huge potential of bilateral trade. However, the structure of the two economies is heavily concentrated on energy products and their exports are likely similar.

The estimation of the two models aims to generate two version of the trade potential. (*Estimated trade*$_{ijt}$) and compare it to the observed trade. In case, the ratio is above 100%, we conclude that trade potential between two pair economies has reached a threshold, fully exploited and is hardly expected to grow in the medium term and vice-versa.

Estimation and simulations: results

According to the model presented in Table 3, an estimation has been performed using the PPML technique. Results estimations shows that all variables[6] in the two version of the model are significant and have the expected economic sign. In an alternative version of the specification (not reported in the paper), variables such as being landlocked has enriched the model specification. However, they were not significant and their sign was not following the economic intuition. The same conclusion comes out of the impact analysis of cultural variables, such as common spoken language or colonial links. They do not enrich significantly the model. One explanation is that REC generally gather countries that have already shared history and cultural links.

---

6. For data description, refer to Annex 1.

Table 3. Intra-trade between ASEAN members (2007-2015): PPML estimation

Variables	Standard version	Augmented version
Ln (GDP-exporting)	1.2 ***	3.1 ***
Ln (GDP-importing)	1.1 ***	0.8 ***
Ln (bilateral Distance)	-1.1 ***	-1.4 ***
Contiguity	0.35 *	0.34 *
Lagged Infrastructure index exporting	-	2.9 **
Interaction term between distance and infrastructure-exporting	-	0.12 *
Lagged Infrastructure index- importing	-	0.15 ***
Lagged Complementarity index	-	2***
Constant	-10,6***	-41.8***
Time varying exporting fixed- effect	Yes	Yes
Time varying importing fixed-effect	Yes	Yes
R^2	0.95	0.98
RESET P-value	0.0001	0.23

Standard errors in all estimations are clustered by trading pair in order to account for any intra-cluster correlations. The estimates of the time varying fixed effects for exporting or importing countries are omitted for brevity. ***,**,* significance at 1%, 5% and 10%. For the case of contiguity and the Interaction term, the significance is at 14 percent.

In the standard version of the model, all the elasticities are close to the unity, suggesting for example that an increase in the size of the exporting or the importing countries by 1 percent foster exports by the same scale. For the case of contiguity variable, sharing borders in fact increases trade by 4.1 percent.[7]

For the augmented version of the gravity model, except for the elasticity of the exporting GDP that has increased, the scale of the coefficients did not dramatically change after the addition of the infrastructure and complementary indexes. These explanatory variables have the expected economic sign showing how important is it to have an upgraded infrastructure whether for the exporting or the importing country in order to foster trade. Besides, when comparing the scale of the coefficients related to infrastructure, it is worth mentioning that what matters the most is the infrastructure qual-

---

7. The semi-elasticity exp (0.35)-1.

ity of the exporting country rather than that of the importing one.[8] This result is in line with the finding of Donaubauer, Glas & Nunnenkamp (2015). The role of infrastructure especially of the reporting country goes beyond. In fact, we have integrated an interaction term between the distance and the infrastructure variable and the coefficient reveals that the quality of infrastructure tends to attenuate the impact of the distance separating a pair of a country. In other words, the infrastructure base for the exporting country mitigate the role of distance and transportation cost and in fine broaden the international market for domestic suppliers. These results confirm the finding of Bougheas et al (1999) who showed that transportation cost depends not only on the distance but also on the stock of infrastructure. Regarding the significance of the infrastructure indicator in the importing country, our results might have some important implications for policy makers, at least in the ASEAN or in any REC. In fact, the availability and the quality of infrastructure could be considered as an *international public good* that serve foreign companies to penetrate domestic markets.

Regarding the complementarity index, it plays an important role in determining the intensity of bilateral trade with a statistically significant coefficient at the 1 percent level. Economies in which demand and supply seems to match, are expected to have higher bilateral trade, while those who do not enjoy this quality, could not leverage uniquely on their size or the infrastructure to foster their trade cooperation. The specification we choose, once infrastructure and complementarity are considered, passes the misspecification test. We could not reject the null hypothesis of the correct specification.

The next step is to "borrow the dynamics" observed in the ASEAN countries and try to replicate them over the ECOWAS region in order to predict the theoretical exports per country to the community itself. Then a ratio of actual exports to potential exports is calculated for the two version of the model. Given the coefficients estimated for the standard model, the potential for all countries is significantly above the actual level. As expected, the well-known regional integration in the ASEAN is translated into a higher potential in the ECOWAS region than the actual level.

However, the potential for the intra-trade is revised downward, given the structure of the production and the infrastructure. With no exception, the potential is lower for all the countries (see Table 4). In fact, the simu-

---

8.   The *T*-test confirms that the coefficient related the exporting country is statistically higher than coefficient of the importing country.

Table 4. Intra-trade potential in the ECOWAS*

Countries	Standard	Ratio of Actual trade to Potential in (%) Augmented version	Intra- trade 2015 (%)	Nominal GDP billions of current $ (2015)
Sierra Leone	Below 1%	<500	8.9	4
Liberia	Below 1%	<500	1.7	2
Guinea	Below 1%	<500	4.7	9
Gambia	Below 1%	<500	36.1	1
Burkina Faso	Below 1%	<500	11.9	8
Benin	Below 1%	[200-300]	44.2	10
Senegal	Below 1%	[100-200]	38.3	14
Cabo Verde	Below 1%	[50 - 100]	3.0	2
Mali	Below 1%	[20 - 50]	8.7	13
Côte D'Ivoire	Below 1%	[0 - 5]	24.8	33
Ghana	Below 1%	[0 - 5]	10.0	38
Nigeria	Below 1%	[0 - 5]	4.0	481

*Calculated ratios are presented in Annex 2.

lations show that actual trade is largely above the potential especially for Sierra Leone, Liberia and Guinea and it happens to be that these economies are small and their intra-trade is relatively low and below the 10 percent average. The prospects for furthering their integration in the economy is conditional on the effectiveness of policy actions aimed to stimulate economic diversification and large-scale infrastructure investments. In the opposite way, large economies as Ghana and Nigeria still seem to enjoy a scope for improvement in their integration rate, as the actual trade is significantly below the estimated potential. For the largest economy in the ECOWAS and in Africa, Nigeria have greater policy leeway in terms of promoting its integration and reaping the benefits of the trade liberalization process in the REC, as it has the lowest ratio of actual trade to theoretical exports. However, this result needs to be interpreted with caution. The simulation analysis has been conducted over nominal variables (GDP and Trade) and this period witnessed a surge in Oil prices amplified by the rebasing of Nigerian GDP in 2013 that leads to over 70 percent increase. The simulation analysis is likely to translate this expansion in the economic size as an unseized opportunity to export. In fact, the ratio of actual trade to potential

Table 5. Intra-trade potential in the ECOWAS by economic partner

Exporter/ Importer	Benin	Burkina Faso	Côte D'Ivoire	Cabo Verde	Ghana	Guinea	Gambia	Liberia	Mali	Nigeria	Senegal	Sierra Leone	Total Opportunities per exporter
Benin		■	■	■	▲	▲	▲	■	■	▲	■	■	4/11
Burkina Faso	■		■	▲	■	■	■	■	■	▲	■	▲	3/11
Côte D'Ivoire	▲	▲		▲	▲	▲	▲	▲	▲	▲	▲	▲	11/11
Cabo Verde	■	▲	■		■	■	▲	▲	▲	▲	▲	▲	7/11
Ghana	▲	▲	▲	▲		▲	▲	▲	▲	▲	▲	▲	11/11
Guinea	■	■	■	■	■		■	■	■	■	■	■	0/11
Gambia	■	▲	▲	▲	▲	■		■	■	■	■	▲	5/11
Liberia	■	■	▲	■	▲	■	■		■	■	■	■	2/11
Mali	▲	▲	▲	▲	▲	▲	▲	▲		▲	▲	■	10/11
Nigeria	▲	▲	▲	▲	▲	▲	▲	▲	▲		▲	■	10/11
Senegal	▲	■	▲	▲	▲	▲	▲	■	■	▲		■	7/11
Sierra Leone	■	■	■	■	■	■	■	■	■	■	▲		1/11
Total Opportunities per market	5/11	7/11	4/11	5/11	6/11	8/11	6/11	5/11	5/11	8/11	5/11	7/11	

*Not Concerned. ■ = Above; ▲ = Below potential.

is slowing down over time. For Cote d'Ivoire, despite the importance of ECOWAS market as it represents 25 percent of total exports, the room for improvement is still important.

The simulation exercise per partner shows significant divergence across economies. It appears that most of the untapped potential for each of the ECOWAS members is related to their bilateral trade with the Nigerian economy. As explained above, the increased size of the Nigerian Economy opened great opportunities for domestic economies to expand their supply. In addition, potential intra-trade expansion is in favour of large economies or is likely to occur within major economies, namely Nigeria, Ghana, Cote d'Ivoire and Senegal. However, the scope for regional integration is likely to be constrained within smaller economies. For example, Côte d'Ivoire, Ghana and Nigeria could witness an expansion of their trade with almost all the ECOWAS members.

Overall, translating the observed dynamics in the ASEAN on the ECOWAS does not end up systematically with higher opportunities of regional integration, once the stock of infrastructure and the matching system between supply and demand is considered. International organizations, such as ADB (2017) and World Bank, pointed out the high level of transaction cost between African countries that challenge policy makers' ambition to further their integration. The regional integration does not respond mechanically to tariffs eliminations. Issues ranging from complex administrative procedures to regulatory barriers raise transaction costs and depress trade integration. The quality of -infrastructure poses also serious issues on the capacity of African economies to meet the challenge. Indeed, the infrastructure index as computed by the World Economic Forum shown Table 6 highlights the weak state of overall infrastructure in countries of the ECOWAS in particular. The necessity to scale up intra-trade-oriented infrastructure investment is imperative to contribute to trade facilitation. According to ADB assessment, the estimated financing requirement to close Africa's infrastructure deficit amounts around 100 billion annually until 2020. ADB (2017) indicated that transportation and communication infrastructure for intra-African trade is less developed than those that connect Africa to the rest of the world.

Referring to the trade cost indicator provided by the World Bank[9], a simple comparison of the average trade cost between the ECOWAS, the

---

9. "This indicator provides estimates of bilateral trade costs. It is built on trade and production data collected in 178 countries. Symmetric bilateral trade costs are computed

Figure 6. Trade costs (2006-2015 average) and distance in Complementarity index.

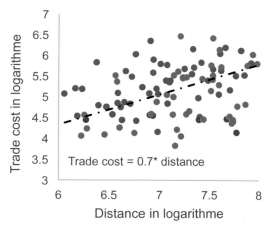

Green, blue and red marks relate to ECOWAS, ASEAN and MER COSUL members respectively.

Figure 7: Trade cost elasticity to distance and the ECOWAS, ASEAN and MERCOSUL.

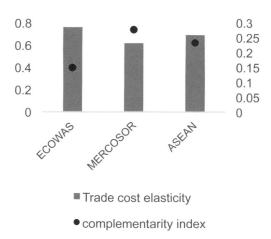

The latest data available are for 2013.

using the Inverse Gravity Framework (Novy 2009), which estimates trade costs fo^{...}
country pair using bilateral trade and gross national output". (World Bank)

Table 6. Infrastructure Index for ECOWAS member countries

	2006	2007	2008	2009	2010	2011	2012	2013	2014	2015	2016
Benin	2.3	2.2	2.3	_	2.4	2.6	2.7	2.7	2.6	2.6	2.4
Burkina Faso	_	_	_	2.0	2.1	2.2	2.1	2.1	2.6	2.6	2.4
Côte D'Ivoire	3.5	3.4	3.3	3.1	2.8	2.8	2.9	2.8	_	_	_
Cabo Verde	_	3.6	3.6	3.4	3.1	3.1	3.0	3.1	3.5	3.3	_
Ghana	3.6	3.4	3.3	3.3	3.4	3.6	3.7	3.8	4.0	3.7	3.1
Guinea	3.3	2.9	2.7	3.0	3.0	2.9	2.8	2.9	3.1	3.0	_
Gambia	2.4	_	1.8	1.8	1.7	1.9	_	_	_	_	_
Liberia	2.4	2.6	2.6		2.4	2.8	_	_	_	_	_
Mali	2.8	2.9	3.1	3.2	3.0	3.0	2.8	2.6	2.7	2.6	2.6
Nigeria	2.0	2.1	2.1	2.1	2.3	2.3	2.2	2.0	2.3	2.2	2.2
Senegal	3.1	3.0	3.0	2.9	2.8	2.5	2.6	2.7	3.3	3.0	2.6
Sierra Leone	2.6	2.3	2.1	2.1	2.1	2.1	_	_	_	_	_

Source: World Economic Forum
1 = extremely underdeveloped, among the worst in the world; 7 = extensive and efficient, among the best in the world.

ASEAN and the MERCOSUL, shows how far is it higher in Africa compared to the other regions. It is 2.7 and 1.3 times higher in the ECOWAS, than MERCUSOR and ASEAN. Figure 7 presents how elastic is the cost of trade, as it is provided by the World Bank, to the distance separating a pair of countries. While the average elasticity is around 0.7, suggesting that any increases in the distance by 1 percent would rise trade cost by 0.7 percent. However, 74 percent of the ECOWAS of each pair of ECOWAS members are located above the fitted trend curve, while this number is around 40 percent for ASEAN members. Regarding the matching issue between supply and demand in each of these RECs, the prevailing fact is that ECOWAS is lacking considerably complementarity between the structures of production and demand of each of its members, with an index around 15 percent. For the MERCOSUL and ASEAN, the index is well above that level.

Supply Side Constraints:
the Revealed Comparative Advantage index analysis

The analysis of trade potential within the ECOWAS, once controlling for the quality of infrastructure and the production structure has shown how observed trade is close to its theoretical level, especially for small economies unlike what was widely accepted regarding the huge potential. Having said that, trade dynamics are much more complicated and depend on several factors ranging from short-term variables, such as macroeconomic policy or structural aspects dealing with trade facilitation initiatives or doing business climate in general. In addition, expanding trade between ECOWAS members is expected to come at the expense, at least in the short term, of classic suppliers of these countries, such as China or the US. The competitiveness of local products is a central element that determines how far ECOWAS's products can substitute for foreign products. That is why we are referring in the next section of what might be a proxy for competitiveness in ECOWAS' export fabric, such as Revealed Comparative Advantage index.

This indicator "illustrates whether a country is in the process of extending the products in which it has a trade potential, as opposed to situations in which the number of products that can be competitively exported is static. It can also provide useful information about potential trade prospects with new partners" (WITS, Trade Indicators). Therefore, countries displaying comparable RCA within the same category of product tend to trade less, whereas countries with different RCA tend to trade more. Within a regional economic community such as the ECOWAS, a country with a RCA similar to the world average will benefit more from integration in the sense that it can become the supplier of these goods instead of the world market. However, there is a risk of trade diversion since these goods are likely to be more expensive that those exported by the world market since they are not expected to be produced as efficiently as in the world market (Venables, 1998). RCA is calculated as follows:

$$RCAi,j = (Xi,j/Xi,t)/(Xw,j/Xw,t)$$

Where $X_{i,}$ and $X_{w,}$ represents the values of export of country i of product j and values of export the world of the same product, and where $X_{i,}$ and $X_{w,}$ refer to the total exports of country i and the world. A value greater than one indicates that the country i displays a revealed comparative advantage in the product j, while a value less than one entails that the country i has a revealed comparative disadvantage in the product j.

Table 7 shows that revealed comparative advantages remain clustered among Food and Animal products and commodity exports (Minerals and Fuels), with the exception of Textiles and Clothing and Stone and Glass. The range of comparative advantages is relatively less concentrated for

Table 7. Revealed Comparative Advantage of ECOWAS members China and the United States with the world, 2015[a]

HS Classification	BEN	BFA	CPV	CIV	GMB	GHA	GIN	MLI	NER	NGA	SEN	TGO	Total	USA	CHN
Animal	0.4	0.2	0.1	11.9	0.2	0.4	6.3	2.0	0.5	0.2	5.9	1.9	5/11	0.9	0.4
Vegetable	6.0	4.8	3.2	0.1	0.6	0.8	10.5	0.5	2.6	0.5	2.6	2.6	7/11	1.4	0.3
Food Products	0.6	0.2	14.6	5.1	6.8	0.4	3.5	0.2	1.4	0.6	3.6	3.1	7/11	0.9	0.4
Minerals	5.1	0.2	0.2	0.0	1.3	31.4	0.0	0.0	43.6	0.0	11.9	18.4	6/11	0.5	0.1
Fuels	0.4	0.0	1.7	3.6	0.0	0.0	0.3	0.1	1.8	5.8	1.4	0.1	5/11	0.7	0.1
Chemicals	0.1	0.1	0.3	0.0	0.1	0.0	0.4	0.2	0.0	0.1	1.1	1.1	2/11	1.2	0.5
Plastic or Rubber	0.1	0.0	1.3	0.1	0.5	0.6	0.5	0.1	0.0	0.3	0.4	2.9	2/11	1.1	0.9
Hides And Skins	0.0	0.0	0.0	0.0	0.0	0.0	0.0	0.7	0.0	5.9	1.0	0.1	1/11	0.5	2.2
Wood	0.9	0.0	0.9	0.0	1.7	3.3	1.4	0.1	0.0	0.1	0.4	1.1	4/11	1.1	0.8
Textiles and Clothing	9.3	3.0	0.6	0.6	0.1	0.1	6.2	2.0	0.6	0.2	0.4	2.6	5/11	0.4	2.6
Footwear	0.0	0.0	0.5	1.8	0.0	0.0	0.3	0.0	0.0	0.5	1.6	3.5	3/11	0.1	3.1
Stone and Glass	0.5	12.7	1.3	0.0	17.2	8.3	0.0	21.2	1.1	0.0	2.1	0.8	7/11	1.0	0.8
Metals	1.0	0.5	0.1	0.1	0.4	0.0	0.2	0.1	0.0	0.1	0.5	0.6	0/11	0.7	1.2
Machinery &Electrics	0.1	0.1	0.1	0.2	0.0	0.1	0.1	0.1	0.0	0.0	0.1	0.1	0/11	0.9	1.6
Transportation	0.8	0.1	0.2	1.1	0.0	0.6	0.1	0.0	0.6	0.1	0.1	0.3	1/11	0.9	0.5

Source: World Integrated Trade Solution (WITS).

a. Latest data for Gambia is 2014, for Ghana and Mali is 2012 and for Nigeria is 2010. No data available for Guinea-Bissau, Liberia and Sierra Leone.

Figure 8. Revealed Comparative Advantages of top 10 products imported by the ECOWAS

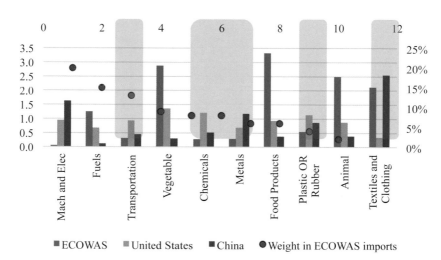

Source: World Integrated Trade Solution (WITS).

Togo and Senegal, who display RCAs for nine and eight group of products respectively, ranging from Vegetable, Food Products, and Chemicals to Textile and Clothing. Regarding, Guinea and Niger, they have the strongest RCAs for Minerals with indexes ranging from 31.4 to 43.6. None of ECOWAS members has RCAs in Metals and Machinery and Electrics and only one country (Côte d'Ivoire) has a RCA in Transportation. As a result, aside from fuel products and other primary commodities like vegetables, ECOWAS's main imports such as Machinery and Electrics, Transportation, Chemicals and Metals (as shown in Table 1) originate from other countries of the world such as China and the United States. In fact, 60 percent of the top 10 products imported by the ECOWAS during the considered period come from countries outside the region who display stronger RCAs for these products.

Conclusion

The process of regional economic integration in the ECOWAS has not reached its full potential yet, as intra-regional trade remains low compared to other developing regions of the world. Stemming from empirical literature, this chapter aims to analyse the potential for intra-regional trade in the ECOWAS. Two gravity models have been estimated using the PPML approach and controlling for multilateral resistance term through time-varying exporter and importer dummies. The estimation has been conducted over the ASEAN community, which display high trade integration across its members.

Using the coefficients of these models, a simulation has been performed on the ECOWAS region in order to predict the theoretical intra-regional exports per country and hence calculate the trade potential of these countries. Although the results imply the existence of a potential for intraregional trade in the ECOWAS, it remains unlike what is widely agreed. Moreover, achieving this potential in order to eventually foster regional integration is confronted to several obstacles, which lie, as demonstrated, in the deficit in infrastructure stock and the lack of complementarity between ECOWAS members.

Policy measures to advance regional economic integration of the ECOWAS through intra-regional trade should hence focus on the challenges regarding the lack of infrastructure on one hand and the lack of diversification and competitiveness of ECOWAS exports on the other hand. Therefore, improving and investing in adequate infrastructure between member countries of the ECOWAS is crucial, since improved stock of infrastructure can mitigate the distance and the high transportation costs between two partners, which leads to a greater level of not only intra-regional but also international integration, through increased levels of trade.

Furthermore, developing trade complementarities between members of the ECOWAS is found to play a crucial role in determining the intensity of bilateral trade. Indeed, economies in which demand and supply seem to match are likely to increase their trade. In addition, supply side factors related to the extent to which ECOWAS economies are likely to substitute for already foreign products pose serious challenges to the capacity of these countries to increase their integration. Revealed comparative advantage indexes display how specialized and concentrated are ECOWAS countries.

References

Adekunle, B. and Gitau, M., 2011. "Illusion or Reality: Understanding the Trade Flow between China and Sub-Saharan Africa".

African Development Bank, (2017) "Trade policies and regional integration in Africa" *African Economic Outlook.*

Akpan, U. S., 2014. "Impact of Regional Road Infrastructure Improvement on Intraregional Trade in ECOWAS". *African Development Review.*

Alemayehu G. and Haile K., 2008. "Regional Economic Integration in Africa: A Review of Problems and Prospects with a Case Study of COMESA". *Journal of African Economies.*

Alemayehu, G., and Edris, H-S., 2015. "The potential for internal trade and regional integration in Africa". *Journal of African Trade.*

Anderson, J. E., and Wincoop E. V., (2003). "Gravity with Gravitas: A Solution to the Border Puzzle." *American Economic Review.*

Armington, P.S., (1969). "A Theory of Demand for Products Distinguished by Place of Production." *International Monetary Fund.*

Baldwin, R.E., and Taglioni D. (2006). "Gravity for Dummies and Dummies for Gravity Equations." NBER Working Paper No. 12516.

Bougheas S. et al. (1999). "Infrastructure, Transport Costs and Trade" *Journal of International Economics.*

Cardamone, P., 2006. "A Survey of Assessments of the Effectiveness of Preferential Trade Arrangements Using Gravity Models"; Working Paper University of Calabria, Italy Trade Preference.

Cassim, R., 2001. "The determinants of intra-regional trade in Southern Africa with Specific reference to Southern Africa and the rest of the Region". DPRU Working Paper, University of Cape Town.

Deen-Swarray, M., Adekunle, B., Odularu, G., 2011. "The Impact of Infrastructural Development on Intra-Regional Trade: The Case of the Economic Community of West African States (ECOWAS)".

Donaubauer J., Glas A., Nunnenkamp P., (2016) "Infrastructure and Trade: A Gravity Analysis for Major Trade Categories Using a New Index of Infrastructure" Kiel Institute for the World Economy.

Ebaidalla M. and Yahia A. M., (2015), "Performance of Intra-COMESA Trade Integration: A Comparative Study with ASEAN's Trade Integration", *African Development Review.*

Eichengreen, B., Irwin, D. A., 1995. "Trade blocs, currency blocs and the reorientation of world trade in the 1930s". *Journal of International Economics.*

European Centre for Development Policy Management (ECDPM), 2016. "Overview of trade barriers to trade in West Africa: Insights in political economy dynamics, with particular focus on agricultural and food trade". Discussion Paper.

Foroutan, F. and Pritchett, L., 1993. "Intra-Sub-Saharan African Trade: is it too little?" *Journal of African Economies*.

Geda, A., Kibret, H., 2008. "Regional integration in Africa: a review of problems and prospects with a case study of COMESA". *J. Afr. Econ.*

Hacker, R.S and Einarsson, H., 2003. "The Pattern, Pull and Potential of Baltic Sea Trade", *Annals of Regional Science*.

International Monetary Fund (IMF). 2017. "Fiscal Adjustment and Economic Diversification". *Sub-Saharan Africa Regional Economic Outlook*, October.

Longo, R., Sekkat, K., (2001). "Obstacles to expanding intra-African trade. OECD Technical Paper.

Luqman A. O., Bakar N. A. A., Izraf A. A. M., (2016). "The Gravity Model Approach: An Application of the ECOWAS Trade Bloc". *South East European Journal of Economics and Business*.

Martinez-Zarzoro I, Nowak-Lehmann F., (2003). "Augmented Gravity Model: An Empirical Application to MERCOSUL-European Union Trade Flow". *Journal of Applied Economics*.

Piermartini, R. and Yotov Y. V. (2016). "Estimating Trade Policy Effects with Structural Gravity", World Trade Organization, Working Paper.

Santos Silva, J.M.C., and Silvana Tenreyro, (2006). "The Log of Gravity." *Review of Economics and Statistics*, 88(4): 641–658.

Santos Silva, J.M.C., and S. Tenreyro, (2011). "Further Simulation Evidence on the Performance of the Poisson Pseudo-Maximum Likelihood Estimator." *Economics Letters*.

Tinbergen, J., (1962). "Shaping the World Economy: Suggestions for an International Economic Policy". *The Economic Journal*.

United Nations Conference on Trade and Development, (2013) "Economic Development in Africa Intra-African trade: Unlocking private sector dynamism".

United States Agency International Development, (2015). "EADS Analytical Brief on Trade in West Africa".

Venables, A. J. (1999). "Regional Integration Agreements: A force for convergence or divergence?" Annual Bank Conference on Development Economics, The World Bank.

Annex: Data Description

The bilateral trade data, just as the bilateral complementarity index are taken from the UNCTAD database, while nominal GDP is extracted from the World Bank Database (World Development Indicators). The infrastructure index refers to the infrastructure quality index published by the World Economic Forum (WEF) within The Global Competitiveness Report. It contains assessment of the quality and availability of transport, electricity and communication infrastructures. In fact, a survey is conducted among business leaders around the world to captures their opinions on the quality and availability of infrastructure, from which an aggregated indicator is constructed (WEF). A higher indicator means higher quality of infrastructure. The contiguity and the distance are taken from Centre d'Etudes Prospectives et d'Informations Internationales (CEPII).

The countries used in the gravity estimation as well as the simulation:

Table A-1. Member countries of ASEAN and ECOWAS used in the gravity model and simulation

ASEAN members (model estimation)	ECOWAS members (simulation)
Brunei Darussalam	Benin
Cambodia	Burkina Faso
Indonesia	Cabo Verde
Laos	Côte D'Ivoire
Malaysia	Gambia
Myanmar	Ghana
Philippines	Guinea
Singapore	Liberia
Thailand	Mali
Vietnam	Nigeria
	Senegal
	Sierra Leone

For a detailed description of the data, see CEPII website. Infrastructure data are not available for Guinea Bissau, Niger and Togo. They were excluded out of the simulation analysis.

Table A-2. Annex 2- Intra-trade potential in the ECOWAS

Country	Potential/Observed Trade in (%)
Benin	204.6
Burkina Faso	586.2
Côte D'Ivoire	5.1
Cabo Verde	75.8
Ghana	1.7
Guinea	2118.1
Gambia	743.2
Liberia	2415.9
Mali	29.5
Nigeria	0.5
Senegal	140.8
Sierra Leone	12169.9

Chapter Three

Trade Interregionalism Between South America and Southern Africa

Frank Mattheis

The external relations of regional organisations tend to concentrate on the immediate neighbourhood and on other regional organisations with a strong sense of actorness, such as the European Union (EU). South-South inter-regionalism is a less prominent phenomenon giving the limited autonomy of regional institutions in the South, the absence of interregional development aid flows and the lack of economic complementarities. Consequently, this type of inter-regionalism warrants particular interest when it emerges (Lidsegård and Mattheis 2018). This chapter examines the first interregional trade agreement in the Global South, namely between the Common Market of the South (Mercosul) and the South African Customs Union (SACU).

The next section deals with the historic background for the emergence of inter-regionalism across the South Atlantic. After that, the three involved regionalisms, Mercosul, SACU and the Southern African Development Community (SADC) are analysed with respect to the interregional capacity and compared. Here the typology proposed by Gardini and Malamud (2018) based on Hurrell (1995) and Hänggi, Roloff and Rüland (2006) will be applied to categorise the form and function of inter-regionalism. The typology is applied to inter-regionalism as a consequence of the proliferation of regionalism across the world and thus goes behind the case of European external relations (Baert, Scaramagli and Söderbaum 2014). It proposes a distinction between five forms of inter-regionalism: pure inter-regionalism between regional groupings, trans-regionalism driven by individual member states, hybrid or quasi inter-regionalism between a regional power and a regional grouping, overlapping inter-regionalism between regional groupings within the same region, and stealth inter-regionalism with its imperial connotation. The last two forms of inter-regionalism are largely absent from Afro-Latin relations due to the lack of overlaps and imperial links. Trans-regionalism does exist—for instance in the form of ocean-based cooperation—but does not directly relate to existing regionalisms (Mattheis 2018). Although a direct relationship between inter-regionalism and regional actorness has been established (Mattheis and Wunderlich

2017) there is still relatively little knowledge about the extent of the reciprocal impact between regionalism and inter-regionalism.

Subsequently, this chapter will concentrate on the establishment of inter-regionalism between the three organisations Mercosul, SADC and SACU as an oscillation between hybrid and pure forms of inter-regionalism before concluding with remarks on the role of summitry in these types of inter-regionalism.

Historic background

Latin America's involvement in political relations with Africa was shaped by the crisis of the economic model of industrialisation through import substitution after World War II (Ffrench-Davis 1998). The notion of economic dependency established itself as a central discursive and theoretical model, first in Latin America and soon in the newly independent states of Africa (Prebisch 1950). Its blend of progress and emancipation was a fitting match for Pan-Africanism. This brought about a rapprochement of both continents under a common conception of obstacles to its own economic development. The UN provided the structure for formalised collaboration akin to trans-regionalism, most importantly the United Nations Conference on Trade and Development (UNCTAD) and the United Nations Economic Commissions for Africa (UNECA) as well as CEPAL.

There was no pure inter-regionalism between the regions but rather several trans-regional and global venues that facilitated interregional dialogue and learning. The nascent regional organisations in both regions related directly to this framework and directed their efforts at overcoming the structures of economic dependence. However, the common framework of reference did not deepen the relations between those organisations. Overcoming dependence was a global project but the regional organisations were designed to achieve it as dissociated entities. Thus, the coalition in global arenas did not result in a diversification of external partners but rather in a fragmentation. The UN represented a key meeting point, particularly its technical agencies dealing with the export of raw materials. Yet, the regional organisations were inward looking and generally did not provide for extra-regional relations. Economically, they followed a model of industrialisation that required selective isolation from world markets, at least until key industries would have matured. Politically, regional organisations primarily dealt with armed conflicts in their vicinity—chiefly with

Apartheid South Africa and in Central America—and from the mid-1980s on with political transitions in their precincts.

Bilateral relations between individual countries across the Atlantic rarely had sizable regional impacts. Most countries did not engage in bilateral collaboration in the first place and even if they did, it was very limited in time and scope. Specific interests triggered punctual activities without prolonged interaction best described as the phenomenon of "spasmodic relationship" (Lechini 2005: 320). The two major exceptions in terms of inter-regionalism were the Cuban mission in the war in Angola between 1975 and 1989 as well as the alliances between Apartheid South Africa and military dictatorships in South America. Both relationships qualify as hybrid inter-regionalism with Cuba and South Africa respectively engaging with the other region in a delineation that corresponds to their own interests.

1989 was a turning point for the various coalitions. They faced a major identity crisis since their rationale had been based on a sense of homogeneity within a bipolar world. National interests and the strategies to achieve them had to be reassessed individually in a multipolar world. Countries in South America and in Africa evidently displayed many commonalities that provided the grounds for a renewal of regional arrangements. All countries feared being once again marginalised in the upcoming world order. They underwent political transitions and they adopted the dominating neoliberal paradigm. The realignments under these paradigms led to the creation or re-creation of new regional organisations. A more outward-looking type of regionalism emerged in the early 1990s and was more prone to insertion into the global economic system. Consequently, extra-continental relations emerged as a valid component. Both Mercosul (1991) and SADC (1994) fell into this new period and enabled the emergence of pure inter-regionalism as a new element in relations between South America and Africa.

Mercosul and interregionalism

Mercosul has conducted external relations from its very beginning in 1991. Even though it had no legal personality until 1994, it had already started to reach out to third partners and was reciprocally perceived as a bloc by others (Gómez-Mera 2013). The primary outreach of the organisation was twofold.

The first pillar of external relations consisted of overlapping inter-regionalism and was directed towards Mercosul's neighbours to create a

South American region by means of expansion and interaction. Inter-regionalism materialised in associate membership for the countries of the Andean Pact and trough ALADI.

The second pillar was largely pure inter-regionalism that aimed at negotiating agreements with the U.S. and the EC. Africa was initially not a focus, as the ambition was fuelled by the fears of being left behind as the international political economy underwent major changes, which triggered an orientation towards the West. The technocratic elite in charge did not consider Mercosul to be a purpose on its own but rather a means to achieve larger economic benefits. Accordingly, Mercosul fulfilled the purpose of a stepping-stone that would help its members to a level where they could sign FTAs with the U.S., the EC or even both. Mercosul was contemplating the initiative by US President George H.W. Bush to form a Pan-American free trade zone. Pure inter-regionalism was considered the first step towards a new region. The creation of the NAFTA was a sign for the viability of such a path and the Mercosul states were not keen to be left behind. At the same time, Europe was still the main trading partner and the consolidation of the EU increased the attractiveness of a pure interregional agreement (Bulmer-Thomas 2006).

In sum, Mercosul's external relations were torn between trying to establish and consolidate South America as a region as well as seeking close partnership with the US and the EC at the same time. The twofold aims have resulted in a very flexible structure within the institution. It combines seemingly opposing elements of regional governance and would provide the framework for all interregional interactions to come, including those with Africa.

In principle, external relations are guided by a fundamental supranational element. The power to negotiate and sign international agreements is vested into the leading body of Mercosul, the CMC. Concerning trade, which initially constituted the core area of Mercosul, individual states cannot sign individual treaties. In practice however, the competence over international agreements is delegated to an intergovernmental organ, the Group of the Common Market. This means that in fact, agreements are signed by representatives of the individual member countries and not by a common Mercosul body (Gardini 2010). The intergovernmental element is further reflected in the negotiations where the delegations consist of national functionaries that remain part of their respective ministries. Negotiation groups can be set up ad hoc while long-term interests are institutionalised within de facto permanent structures. This institutional set-up suggests that the form of pure inter-regionalism contains strong functional elements of trans-regionalism.

This pattern stayed in place for most of the first decade of Mercosul's existence before undergoing two fundamental shifts that facilitated the emergence of Africa as an interregional partner. Firstly, the financial and economic crises that hit the region between 1998 and 2001 altered the foreign alignments. Chiefly, Argentina abruptly stopped being an acclaimed implementer of policies of the IMF. Debt cancellations and nationalisations obstructed relations with the global economic centres. The shift of paradigm brought socialist presidents into power in all Mercosul states. These presidents, in particular Brazil's Lula da Silva, put more emphasis in partnerships with other developing countries, notably in Africa. Taking advantage of the rotating presidency of the Mercosul, Brazil could push for opening negotiations with new partners. Secondly, the negotiations with the EU and the US did not move forward, neither interregionally nor in the WTO. The juxtaposed defensive and offensive interests in agriculture, industry and services did not allow any significant progress. The WTO negotiations effectively stalled in 2003 and severely encumbered pure inter-regionalism. Meanwhile, the Eastern enlargement and 9/11 imposed new priorities for the EU and the US. These shifts reshaped the structure of Mercosul's foreign outreach and paved the way for interregional cooperation with Africa.

The first pillar of overlapping inter-regionalism expanded and solidified with the geopolitical shifts in the region. Mercosul turned into the unrivalled regional organisation in South America and consolidated its expansion with the full membership of Venezuela. Though the Andean Pact did not entirely vanish, it was notably consumed by the interregional relationship. The stand-alone position of Mercosul allowed the organisation to speak on behalf of its region vis-à-vis external partners

The second pillar of pure inter-regionalism with the EU and the US experienced a breakdown (Gratius 2008). The Mercosul had turned into a vehicle that served its new leaders to emancipate themselves against the US. The plans for a FTAA effectively collapsed in 2005 due to the Mercosul opposition leading the US to pursue a bilateral approach within the region. Likewise, the negotiations with the EU got caught up in countless rounds trying to revive the process but these attempts could not overcome the evermore diverging economic interests and political priorities. At the same time both Mercosul and the EU had to deal with an increasing discrepancy within their region, which made a common position difficult to attain. The prospect of a meaningful agreement between the two regions continuously grew fainter.

The consolidation of Mercosul within South America enabled the organisation to expand hybrid and pure inter-regionalism in other fields. The substantial impediments to relations with the traditional partners in the North imposed an unprecedented diversification of those relations. The shifting world order had amplified the scope of potential economic partners and political allies and Mercosul was now on the verge of exploring new waters. The hitherto largely feeble links to other regions of the South did not allow for a grounded anticipation of where increased interaction could unfold. Therefore, Mercosul initiated talks with numerous potential partners. The result was the initiation of hybrid interregional dialogues with a variety of emerging countries such as India, Egypt and South Korea but also pure inter-regionalism with regional groupings such as the Gulf Cooperation Council (GCC) and SACU. The main commercial interest was to tap into new markets for Mercosul's competitive agricultural industry, such as the meat industry. In addition, there were opportunities for the automotive industry. Some dialogues turned into trade negotiations that led to actual agreements.

The governing structure of Mercosul is characterised by a temporary presidency that rotates twice a year. Negotiations with third parties are thus led and organised by the respective foreign office in charge. The imperative of a consensus notwithstanding, one country is thus able to specify the priorities during six months. This entails a lack of continuity that results in many pending negotiations that may pursue entirely different purposes reflecting specific national interests (Dabène 2009). Brazil under Lula da Silva took advantage of this position to open or accelerate negotiations with partners of strategic interest. Some negotiations had a clear economic focus, such as the promotion of agricultural exports that was very discernible with Egypt and Morocco. Others were mainly an expression of political will, such as the agreements with Israel and SACU.

Current political developments in the main Mercosul states Argentina and Brazil have brought governments into power that are less engaged in fostering relations with Africa and eager to pursue trade agreements with Western countries, specifically the EU. The South-South orientation is thus likely to stay on the back burner for the time being, although existing agreements with Africa are not being questioned.

In sum, the initial pillars focussing on overlapping regionalism and pure inter-regionalism with North America and Europe have been complemented and partly even replaced by pure and hybrid inter-regionalism with other parts of the world.

SADC and interregionalism

SADC had a similar initial external pattern as Mercosul although the logics at play were different. Legal personality had been established in 1992 with its creation. Like Mercosul, it engaged in external relations both with its neighbours and foreign powers from the beginning. Unlike Mercosul, SADC accredits foreign ambassadors and high commissioners, who are almost all African and European and thus reflect the twofold rational: a continental perspective of overlapping inter-regionalism and a donor-driven outreach of pure and stealth inter-regionalism.

Overlapping inter-regionalism within Africa essentially meant membership expansion to legitimise and establish the organisation. The internalisation of the Congo conflict with the accession of the DRC brought this strategy to its limits. In 1998, a war broke out in the country and the adjacent Great Lakes region. SADC members were divided over how the organisation should act in the DRC conflict. One group led by South Africa called for an international peacekeeping mission instead of a SADC intervention. Angola and Zimbabwe led the other group that had already proceeded to follow the DRC's President Kabila's call for intervention. To legitimise their national economic and security interests, they sought SADC's permission afterwards. Being faced with a *fait accompli*, South Africa quickly joined and even took the lead of the mission. The use of preponderant force brought about a military stalemate securing Kinshasa and the Congolese government (Francis 2006). The subsequent political negotiations accompanied by the deployment of UN troops further consolidated SADC in its respacing and distribution of power (Nathan 2012).

Europe was the other focus of inter-regionalism, as it constituted the main donor of development aid to build the organisation. The D in SADC does not only indicate the desire to development its own countries but also needs be understood as a commitment to the development idea of Northern donors (Tjønneland 2008). The EU has been very active from the start to provide financial and technical assistance to the organisation and this relationship has shaped most of SADC's extra-continental outreach (Mattheis 2010). The personnel at the secretariat are extensively engaged in interacting with the EU. Many functionaries devote much of their working time to attending training, reporting to donors or participating in official visits. The dependence on foreign aid fosters a form of stealth inter-regionalism that restricts the capacity and the interest to engage in external relations with non-donors.

On the commercial side, SADC has been concerned with establishing a free trade area among its members. This process has been characterised by a lack of performance due to the divergent trade interest of member states and the importance of tariff revenues for national budgets. External trade agreements have been hampered by the same constraints. The main inter-regional negotiations were the Economic Partnership Agreements with the EU and SADC proved to be incapable of negotiating as a full bloc. Only a smaller group of SADC members with vested interests signed an interregional trade agreement.

SACU and interregionalism

SACU overlaps with SADC but is a regional organisation in its own right. Contrary to SADC it is rarely covered in depth. It is usually praised as the oldest custom union in the world but seems to be known for little else (Jovanovíc 2006; Gibb and Treasure 2011). Even its 100-year anniversary in 2010 did not bring about any significant coverage or appraisal. Its core area is tariffs and all other regional issues such as development, security and energy are being dealt with in SADC. The latter also claims to be the sole representative for the integration architecture within the AU. High-level politics thus takes place within SADC while SACU is more specialised and dominated by ministerial technicians. SADC might be far away from a customs union but declarations do exist and should they be followed, SACU would become de facto redundant.

A customs union on a severely marginalised continent in the global economy did not generate much interest outside of the region. Private foreign businesses generally concentrated on the South African market and public donors had priorities that coincided with SADC's agenda.

In 2002, a reform of the SACU was concluded to even out some of the inequalities in the treaty in force that still dated from 1969 and reflected the geopolitical landscape of that era (Kirk and Stern 2005). After overcoming the bane of Apartheid, South Africa had regained credibility as an international partner and as such it was able to sign a comprehensive

Trade, Development and Cooperation Agreement (TDCA) with the EU in 1999 (Gantz 2009). Though this seems like a clear example of hybrid inter-regionalism the agreement had considerable effects on the grouping of SACU as a whole, specifically concerning tariff revenues and competition as goods from a third party start to enter free of duty. Such effects are exacerbated in the case of a large economic partner such as the EU. For the other SACU members, the TDCA corresponded to declining revenues and the increase in competitive EU imports to South Africa would make their way—often through informal channels—to the rest of the region. Though SACU was not party to the TDCA, it was affected by it as if it were pure inter-regionalism. Consequently, the other SACU members pushed for a reform to prevent further unilateral actions. Besides the creation of institutions and a recalculation of the revenue sharing, the member states were obliged to conduct negotiations with third parties as a bloc. South Africa was most affected by such a reform but agreed for three main reasons. The ANC government was eager to show benevolence with its neighbours in the aftermath of Apartheid. Additionally, there was less at stake for South Africa as it had just sealed the deal with its main trade partner, the EC (Council of the European Union 1999). Finally, and most importantly, South Africa made sure that it remained in a dominant if not hegemonic position.

On paper, SACU ceased to be a body administrated by the South African government. Nevertheless, the latter de facto did not give up any sovereignty concerning negotiations with third parties. South Africa as a hegemon determined the choice of interlocutors and remained in charge of conducting the talks and negotiations. The set-up might be intergovernmental, as it requires trade delegations to be composed of delegates from all member countries. However, hegemonic practices remained in place under the formally consensual umbrella (Mattheis 2014). As a result, inter-regionalism involving South Africa will invariably involve the SACU region as a whole.

Interregionalism compared

In both regions, member states have generally dismissed the introduction of supra-nationalism in their organisation. Institutionalisation has largely been limited to facilitate collaboration. Potential supranational bodies such as the regional parliaments or the secretariats have yet to be vested with substantial powers.

The structures for external relations have a high degree of institutional flexibility but follow the rationale of the main actors: behaving as a joint actor without conceding too much national sovereignty. The set-up is thus best described as target-oriented while its emergence corresponds to neo-functionalist logic. It is thus not clearly classifiable according to traditional divisions of supra-nationality and inter-governmentalism.

This is particularly visible in inter-regionalism. The desire to conduct external relations as a bloc established a consistent and progressing policy field. Albeit based on intergovernmental mechanisms, external ties have expanded considerably in scope as joint negotiation and working groups are fulfilling the role of main interlocutor in this area.

While not free from frictions, external relations still have less potential for conflict than internal issues such as common economic policy. Generally, the national benefits of common external negotiations are perceived as more substantial than the potential loss of sovereignty that consensus building entails. Even though the member states have not given up bilateral relations, negotiations via regional alliances are increasingly superseding in a range of commercial and security issues. Overlapping inter-regionalism is particularly relevant to position the regional organisations vis-à-vis its neighbourhood and project its ambitions. At the same time, pure inter-regionalism with other parts of the world, especially North America and Europe, remain of vital concern. The governing bodies of both organisations have the power to negotiate the full gamut of interregional agreements. Yet, any agreement is ultimately signed by the individual member countries and not by a common institution. Any interregional relationship thus carries an element of trans-regional inter-regionalism.

One major difference between SADC and Mercosul is the former's focus on development aid that enables a kind of stealth inter-regionalism less present in the latter. While both give special attention to the North in their extra-regional relations, their outreach follows a different pattern. SADC continues to heavily depend on foreign funds and even trade negotiations chiefly revolve around the issue of economic partnership agreements with the EU. The material contribution of the EU to Mercosul is comparatively limited. By contrast, SADC continues to primarily look at development agencies to the North as well as to the sub-continental organisations under the umbrella of the AU.

Inter-regionalism across the South Atlantic: Mercosul, SADC and SACU

The beginning of pure inter-regionalism between South America and Southern Africa was a consequence of Brazil's partial retreat from Africa in the 1990s. The own region and specifically Mercosul became the priority and the strategy to engage with the whole continent was abandoned in favour of identifying strategic partners, chiefly South Africa, Angola, Mozambique, and Nigeria. The rapprochement with SADC was thus mainly an expression of Brazil's interest to rationalise its main interests in the region.

Relations with South Africa had been reinstalled during the transition process from Apartheid and were improving at a fast pace on both political and economic terms. Relations with Angola and Mozambique were motivated by growing cultural and economic ties while Nigeria constituted an important source of oil and therefore the main trade partner in Africa. In addition, Namibia was considered as a potential new partner.

Since these countries except Nigeria were members of the SADC and Brazil was in the process of rationalising its relations with Africa, engaging in condensing interregional relations promised more efficiency. On the South American side, Mercosul already bound the member states to act commonly. From Brazil's perspective, negotiating a free trade agreement with SADC would be a first test whether Mercosul could effectively improve the position of its member countries in the global world order.

Starting in 1995 mutual high-level visits between Brazil and South Africa took place frequently and after identifying common interests various bilateral accords were signed, eventually giving way to a Joint Commission Agreement in 2000. During that time, Nelson Mandela also participated at a Mercosul summit in 1998 as the first President outside of the region.

Political commitment was thus clearly visible on both sides but engaging in pure inter-regionalism turned out to be complicated in practice. Firstly, the institutional setting did not facilitate interregional agreements. None of the secretariats had the capacity to conduct external relations on their own, let alone an external representation. South Americans officials were as rare to find in Gaborone as Africans in Montevideo. Secondly, trade between most countries was modest and concentrated in a few volatile natural resources dependent on world market prices. Lastly, except for South Africa SADC members simply did not have resources for such an endeavour.

The scarce personnel capable of negotiating such an agreement would have to be spared from the WTO rounds or SADC itself (Stahl 2000).

In contrast, relations with South Africa on its own looked more promising and the country by now offered an entry point into the whole region. In the 1990s, the increase of South Africa's trade with Argentina and Brazil was impressive and underpinned the economic opportunities of an agreement (Molate and van Ernst Seventer 2003). The private sectors of South Africa, Brazil and Argentina also manifested some interest and in particular the automotive industries formulated explicit demands (White 2003; Automotive Industry Export Council 2007).

Eventually, Mercosul opted to start negotiating a free trade agreement with South Africa in 2000. An expansion to SADC stayed desirable and relations between SADC and Mercosul were maintained over time but pure inter-regionalism was effectively given up in favour of hybrid inter-regionalism.

South Africa's interest in Mercosul can mainly be attributed to the priorities of the post-Apartheid government. On the global level, it strived to overcome the decades of isolation, particularly in multinational forums. Former opponents had turned into potential allies. South Africa's Department of Trade and Industry (DTI) developed the so-called "trade butterfly" strategy (Erwin 1999). In addition to the traditional ties with Africa, Europe and the US, South Africa should spread out its wings to Latin America and Asia. Mercosul being the most innovative and successful grouping on its continent at the time, it cropped up as the natural partner. South Africa was also interested in the experiences of South America in dealing with issues of reconciliation after the military dictatorships.

Brazil and South Africa both shared the idea of exploring possibilities for South-South agreements with potential allies. But while Mercosul formally constrained Brazil to negotiate trade agreements as a regional group, South Africa was able to start the negotiations on its own terms, as its regional framework was less constraining. SADC and SACU members were hitherto free to sign individual FTAs. After South Africa unilaterally completed a FTA with the EU in 1999, the SACU members, who would bear its consequences without having been involved in the negotiations, called for a revision of the rules. The subsequent reform in 2002 did not reverse the hegemonic structure for that matter but it changed enough to become relevant for the South Atlantic realm.

SACU members were now required to sign new trade agreements as a single entity—much like within Mercosul. The negotiations Mercosul had so far undertaken with South Africa were consequently being transformed into a SACU issue. Hybrid inter-regionalism transformed back into pure inter-regionalism, albeit with a different partner, namely SACU instead of SADC. Mercosul states feared having suddenly to negotiate with four additional countries, making a potential agreement more difficult to reach. However, Mercosul's fears were unfounded, as South Africa hegemonic role in SACU translated into the country being the sole negotiator. Though formally framed by pure inter-regionalism the negotiations in fact continued to be a hybrid inter-regionalism between South Africa and Mercosul.

Despite a profound economic crisis that hit Mercosul, conditions for inter-regionalism improved significantly between 2001 and 2003. Lula Da Silva became President of Brazil and not only continued to pursue the Brazilian interests in South-South relations initiated by his predecessor Cardoso but intensified concrete engagements. By extension the foreign policy of Mercosul adopted a similar logic as commercial linkages with less traditional partners were being sought after (Nutenko 2006). Mercosul was the natural channel to transform political South-South initiatives such as the India-Brazil-South-Africa Dialogue Forum (IBSA) into substantial economic agreements. In addition, the WTO negotiations experienced a collapse that led to a languishing of multilateral trade. A group of developing countries led among others by South Africa and Brazil brought the WTO talks to a standstill. Their interests in agricultural goods as well as services and investment were directly opposed to those of EU and the U.S. The adamant stance against the countries of the North was further pursued by Mercosul with the stalling of negotiations with the US on a Pan-American free trade zone as well as with the EU on a bilateral agreement. The rationale for Mercosul to persist as a vital trade bloc in the global economy was to use its capacities to extend to other Southern countries.

Consequently, Brazil firmly occupied the driver's seat of the SACU-Mercosul talks. This position corresponded to its idea of leading the emerging South-South relations that would overturn the international political economy to its favour. Mercosul's role by now went far beyond being an organisation focusing on internal economic integration. It became a convenient instrument for Brazil to gain influence and prestige in the world while ensuring the cohesion of its own regional grouping. Brazil thus engaged in convincing the other Mercosul countries to pursue a preferential trade agreement (PTA).

As a result, the SACU-Mercosul negotiations were as much about political strategy as they were about tariffs (Roberts 2004). At the end of the day technocrats still had to come up with categories, quotas and timelines. But the decision to conclude an agreement as well at its design arose from the political project of South-South cooperation. In doing so, both sides showed a considerable degree of flexibility. A perfect customs union with a common access to external goods was clearly not a priority. South Africa and Brazil acknowledged the internal asymmetries of their groupings and as a result different concessions were made to the smaller countries.

Within two years relations assumed a more formalised stage and a preferential trade agreement was agreed and signed by both parties in 2004. However, it was a very simple agreement that left central issues such as customs jurisdiction unresolved. It included about 1900 tariff lines but excluded most crucial export goods such as agricultural and automotive products. Due to its limitations, the PTA was not considered ripe for ratification and negotiations towards an improved trade agreement started. Eventually, after twelve lengthy rounds of negotiations concerned with technical details, a new PTA was signed in 2008 and 2009. About 300 tariff lines had been added and parts of the initial agreement were further developed but crucial parts such as the automotive sector were again postponed as they faced major opposition in South Africa. Overall substantial changes were lacking. The SACU countries enjoyed preferential trade schemes with the EU and the US proved and feared that competitive goods of the Mercosul would benefit on their expenses from free trade access (Maihold 2007).

The agreement was a disappointment, especially to the small countries that had been dragged into lengthy negotiations that occupied their scarce resources. Rounds of negotiations for over nine years (including four years of revising an initial agreement) were a considerable effort to be invested to achieve an agreement giving preferential access to a very limited amount of goods.

For South Africa and Brazil the immediate impact on trade was less relevant. Political elites in charge visibly gave priority to the South Atlantic negotiations even though substantial economic benefits are meagre. There is little evidence of active demand from the private sector or third parties. The PTA was not pushed as a pure trade agreement but as a political instrument for South-South cooperation that would include increased trade interdependence among other aspects. The PTA would serve larger goals as by paving the way for an upcoming IBSA-based cooperation and a trilateral trade agreement between SACU, Mercosul and India.

The negotiations do not reflect major economic interests as trade effects are expected to be rather low due to a lack of complementarities and protective industrialising interests in many countries. However, there has been a persistent political will to promote the agreement over many negotiation rounds, even though actual results might be limited. It has been one of the few agreements signed by Mercosul and the first one by SACU. As such, it enhances the strategic options of its members in dealing with the political and economic world order. This is particularly important for countries with an explicit global agenda, such as Brazil and South Africa. In sum, despite being an agreement of pure inter-regionalism, this undertaking resembled more to hybrid inter-regionalism on both ends. South Africa and Brazil were both constrained to include their neighbours into the regional power approach (Soares de Lima and Hirst 2006).

Conclusion: interregionalism and summitry

The inter-regionalism discussed in this chapter primarily refers to the relations between formalised organisations, namely Mercosul on the one side and SADC or SACU on the other one. These relations oscillate between hybrid and pure inter-regionalism, depending on whether the regional powers or the regional grouping carry more weight. Brazil and South Africa, the two hegemonic powers in the respective regions, thus play a central role in shaping inter-regionalism. Where their interests coincide—such as in the reform of the WTO, market access to Europe or technology exchange—they can act as facilitators or inter-regionalism but if similarities in their economic structures—such as commodities or manufactures—put them in a competing position, inter-regionalism will face severe obstacles.

Summitry is not the main modus operandi of this case. Though meetings of heads of state have been crucial in triggering inter-regionalism, the negotiations were carried out in continuation by task managers from various ministries. In this context, summits have a clear role to play, namely to provide a mandate and a sense of strategic priority to those actors. Negotiations can subsequently carry on autonomously for some time but summits again become necessary to resolve diverging agendas and to sustain commitment. Mercosul relations with SADC and SACU are not only about summitry but given the weak external actorness of these regional organisations inter-regionalism easily falls by the wayside without summitry. This was evident at the end of the PTA negotiations, when the agreement was not signed during a common ceremony of an interregional summit. Rather both regional groupings signed the agreement separately at one of their regular regional meetings.

Relations between Mercosul and SADC/SACU have not been sustained by summits, not least because more relevant venues have emerged. For instance, IBSA and BRICS summits have provided South Africa and Brazil with additional alternatives. On an interregional level, additional exist in the context of South Atlantic relations. The Zone of Peace and Cooperation in the South Atlantic (ZOPACAS) and the Africa-South America (ASA) summits represent the main venues for trans-regionalism and are primarily characterised by summitry in the form of supposedly regular meetings of ministers and heads of states (Abdenur, Mattheis and Seabra 2016). These summits are covering both sides of the Atlantic and thus encompass two regions but they have not had any relevant impact on the pure and hybrid inter-regionalisms between Mercosul and SADC/SACU.

References

Abdenur, Adriana, Frank Mattheis, and Pedro Seabra. 2016. "An ocean for the Global South: Brazil and the zone of peace and cooperation in the South Atlantic." *Cambridge Review of International Affairs* 29 (3): 1112–1131.

Automotive Industry Export Council. 2007. "*Automotive Export Manual 2007.*" Pretoria: Automotive Industry Export Council.

Baert, Francis, Tiziana Scaramagli, and Fredrik Söderbaum. 2014. "Introduction: Intersecting inter-regionalism." In *Intersecting inter-regionalism*, Edited by Francis Baert, Tiziana Scaramagli and Frederik Söderbaum, 12–23. New York: Springer.

Bulmer-Thomas, Victor. 2006. "Globalization and the New Economic Model in Latin America." In *The Cambridge Economic History of Latin America Vol. II: The long twentieth century*. Edited by Victor Bulmer-Thomas, John H. Coatsworth, and Roberto Cortés Conde, 135–68. Cambridge: Cambridge University Press.

Council of the European Union. 1999. "Agreement on Trade, Development and Cooperation between the European Community and its Member States, of the one part, and the Republic of South Africa, of the other part. 1999/753/EC. 42. *Official Journal of the European Communities*. Brussels: European Union.

Dabène, O. 2009. *The Politics of Regional Integration in Latin America*. New York: Palgrave MacMillan

Erwin, Alec. 1999. "Globalisation and Regionalism in the South in the 21st Century." In *Exploring South-South dialogue: Mercosul in Latin America and*

SADC in Southern Africa. Edited by Greg Mills and Claudia Mutschler, 15–21. Johannesburg: SAIIA.

Ffrench-Davis, Ricardo. 1998. "The Latin American economies, 1950-1990." In *Latin America: Economy and society since 1930*. Edited by Leslie Bethell. Cambridge: Cambridge University Press.

Francis, David J. 2006. *Uniting Africa: Building Regional Peace And Security Systems*. Aldershot: Ashgate.

Gantz, David A. 2009. *Regional trade agreements: Law, policy and practice*. Durham, NC: Carolina Academic Press.

Gardini, Gian Luca. 2010. *The origins of Mercosul: Democracy and regionalization in South America*. 1st ed. New York: Palgrave Macmillan.

Gardini, G. L. and A. Malamud. 2018. Debunking Inter-regionalism: Concepts, Types and Critique—With a Pan-Atlantic Focus, in *Inter-regionalism across the Atlantic space*, Edited by Frank Mattheis and Andréas Lidsegård, 15–32. Cham: Springer.

Gibb, Richard, and Karen Treasure. 2011. "SACU at centenary: theory and practice of democratising regionalism." *South African Journal of International Affairs* 18 (1): 1–21.

Gómez-Mera, Laura. 2013. *Power and regionalism in Latin America: The politics of Mercosul*. University of Notre Dame Press.

Gratius, Susanne (ed.). 2008. *MERCOSUL y NAFTA. Instituciones y Mecanismos de Decisión en Procesos de Integración Asimetricos*. Madrid: Iberoamericana

Hänggi, Heiner, Ralf Roloff, and Jürgen Rüland (2006). *Inter-regionalism and international relations*. London: Routledge.

Hurrell, A. 1995. "Explaining the resurgence of regionalism in world politics." *Review of International Studies* 21 (04): 331.

Jovanovíc, M. 2006. *The economics of international integration*. Cheltenham: Edward Elgar.

Kirk, Robert, and Matthew Stern. 2005. "The New Southern African Customs Union Agreement." *The World Economy* 28 (2): 169–90.

Lechini, Gladys. 2005. "Is South-South Co-operation still Possible? The Case of Brazil's Strategy and Argentina's Impulses Towards the New South Africa and Africa." In *Politics and social movements in a hegemony world: lessons from Africa, Asia and Latin America*. Edited by Borón, Atilio and Gladys Lechini, 319-346. Buenos Aires: CLACSO, Consejo Latinoamericano de Ciencias Sociales.

Lidesgård, Andréas and Frank Mattheis. 2018. "The Atlantic Space—A Region in the Making." In *Inter-regionalism across the Atlantic space*, Edited by Frank Mattheis and Andréas Lidsegård, 1–14. Cham: Springer.

Maihold, Günther. 2007. "Die brasilianische Afrikapolitik: Neues Engagement oder bewusster Pragmatismus?" In *Brasilien: Großmacht in Lateinamerika*. Edited by Bernd Rill, 73–91. Argumente und Materialien zum Zeitgeschehen 55.

Mattheis, Frank. 2010. "MERCOSUL - A child of the post-Cold War world order?" In *World orders revisited*. Edited by Ulf Engel and Matthias Middell, 193–206. Leipzig: Universitätsverlag Leipzig.

Mattheis, Frank. 2014. *New regionalism in the south: Mercosul and SADC in a comparative and interregional perspective*. Leipzig: Universitätsverlag Leipzig.

Mattheis, Frank. 2018. "Volatile Inter-regionalism: The Case of South Atlantic Relations." In *Inter-regionalism across the Atlantic space*, Edited by Frank Mattheis and Andréas Lidsegård, 33–50. Cham: Springer.

Mattheis, Frank, and Jens-Uwe Wunderlich. 2017. "Regional actorness and interregional relations: ASEAN, the EU and Mercosul." *Journal of European Integration* 39 (6): 723-738.

Molate, Carol, and Dirk van Ernst Seventer. 2003. "Bilateral Trade Between South Africa and Brazil." TIPS Focus on Data Series. Unpublished manuscript, last modified December 09, 2012.

Nathan, Laurie. 2012. *Community of Insecurity: SADC's Struggle for Peace and Security in Southern Africa*. Farnham: Ashgate.

Nutenko, Leonid. 2006. "MERCOSUL y los países de Asia y de África: Nueva etapa de interacción." *Iberoamérica (Trimestral desde Moscú)* (3): 103–12.

Prebisch, Raúl. 1950. *The economic Development of Latin America and its principal problems*. Lake Success, N.Y. U.N. Dep. of Economic Affairs.

Roberts, Simon. 2004. "Reflections on Approaching an FTA Negotiation with Mercosul: A Review of Key Issues." SAIIA Trade Policy Report 6.

Soares de Lima, Maria, and Monica Hirst. 2006. Brazil as an Intermediate State and Regional Power: Action, Choice and Responsibilities. *International Affairs* 82(1): 21–40.

Stahl, Heinz-Michael. 2000. *"Towards a South Atlantic Free Trade Area? The Business, Trade and Investment Dimensions."* Southern Africa and Mercosul/l: Reviewing the Relationship and Seeking Opportunities. Report of the Second Meeting between SADC and Mercosul. 83-92.

Tjønneland, Elling N. 2008. *From aid effectiveness to poverty reduction: Is foreign donor support to SADC improving?* FOPRISA report 4. Gaborone, Botswana: Published by Lightbooks on behalf of Botswana Institute for Development Policy Analysis.

White, Lyal. 2003. "Driving SACU - Mercosul: Trans-atlantic Co-operation in the Automotive Industry." SAIIA Reports 34.

Chapter Four

EU-LAC Trade Relations in a Post-Liberal Era

Lorena Ruano

This chapter explores the current situation, opportunities and challenges of trade between the European Union (EU) and Latin America and the Caribbean (LAC), at a time when the erosion of the liberal consensus about the benefits of free trade sweeps the globe. The recent wave of protectionism and nationalism that has taken over United States (US) trade policy constitutes a powerful incentive for Europe and some LAC countries to coalesce around the defence of rules-based trade. However, political polarization and economic instability on both sides of the Atlantic mean that the establishment of new agreements is far from straightforward.

The next section explores the current context of EU trade policy. It argues that the rise of populist governments and political polarisation in some member states does not seem to have affected thus far the liberal frame within which the EU conducts its trade policy, yet recently, the process of negotiation and ratification has become trickier. On the side of LAC, explored in the third section, two contextual trends are identified: first, their vulnerability to the change in US trade policy and the ebbing of the so called 'pink wave', which revived a more liberal approach to trade, but which remains fragile and is not generalized across the region.

The fourth section provides an overview of EU-LAC trade in the past decade, noting their asymmetries and concentration in a few markets, as well as the effect of the end of the commodities boom and the importance of European investment for LAC today. The fifth section explores the current state of regionalism and explains that polarisation among the governments of LAC has undermined their capacity to act as a group or even sub-groups. The FTAs that the EU has sought to establish with LAC regional groups (MERCOSUL and the Andean Community) have not come to fruition. Instead, trade negotiations have been easier with those individual countries, like Mexico and Chile, Colombia and Peru, which have displayed a more durable commitment to openness, and EU attention has moved to the Pacific Alliance, a new outward looking group recently set up.

The final section is devoted to current trade negotiations between the EU and LAC. The 'Trump effect' was visible in the speeding up of the negotiations between the EU and Mexico and with Chile to modernize their existing Association Agreements during 2017-2018. The reactivation of long dormant negotiations with MERCOSUL in 2017 can also be attributed to that effect, as well as the more liberal outlook of the governments of Brazil and Argentina. Yet, their conclusion cannot be taken for granted.

The current context of EU trade policy

Being the oldest and most integrated policy of the EU, trade policy constitutes a key element of the EU's role in the international arena. Given the size of its market, export capacity, the relatively high level of income of its consumers, and also, its influence in setting up rules at the multilateral level and in bilateral negotiations, the EU has been described as "powerful *in* trade [and] *through* trade".[1] In relation with LAC, trade policy has played a central role of the EU strategy towards that part of the world since the 1990s, with which it has sought to establish Free Trade Agreements (FTAs) with individual countries and regional groupings. So far it has created such frameworks with Mexico, Chile, Central America, Colombia, Peru and Ecuador.

EU trade policy has been relatively insulated from the vagaries of national politics in the member states, because, since the Treaty of Rome, the decision to create a customs union led to a high degree of delegation of competences to supranational institutions, with the Commission as single negotiator with outside partners, while the Council decides on its negotiating mandate by qualified majority voting.[2] The Treaty of Lisbon (2009) included new trade issues under EU competence, such as investment, environmental protection, government procurement and intellectual property. It is probably due to this institutional setting that the EU has kept the liberal frame of mind in its approach to trade negotiations, despite the Great Depression,[3] and the increased challenges to the liberal credo that have arisen in a number of member states. Thus, the EU has recently concluded FTA negotiations with Vietnam (2015), Canada (known as CETA –Comprehensive Economic and Trade Agreement- 2016), Japan (2017), and Singapore

1. Sophie Meunier and Kalypso Nicolaïdis, 2006, 'The European Union as a conflicted trade power', *Journal of European Public Policy*, vol. 13, n. 6, pp. 907.
2. Alasdair R Young and John Peterson, 2014, *Global parochial Europe: 21st century trade politics*, Oxford, Oxford University Press, p. 11.
3. Yelter Bollen, Ferdi De Ville and Jan Orbie, 2016, 'EU trade policy: persistent liberalisation, contentious protectionism', *Journal of European Integration*, vol. 38, n. 3, pp. 279-294.

(2018). Currently, the EU has nine FTA negotiations opened: with Malaysia, Thailand, Indonesia, Philippines, Myanmar (members of ASEAN –Association of South East Asian Nations) and India; in Latin America, the modernization of its agreements with Mexico and Chile, while the talks with MERCOSUL, which have been stagnating for more than 20 years, have been re-launched.[4] EU trade policy is characterised as 'liberal' since it broadly projects a preference for removing barriers to trade through a rules based system. Still, it has to be recognized that the EU also displays a 'mercantilist' approach that seeks to protect its sensitive sectors.[5]

Over the last years, however, EU Trade policy has become less insulated and is not exempt from rising tensions. Since the entry into force of the Treaty of Lisbon, the European Parliament (EP) plays a more important role, as it is necessary to keep it informed of on-going trade negotiations, a move that has given societal views increased relevance, beyond the traditional influence of interest groups. Some scholars have pointed out that although the Treaty of Lisbon does not grant the EP a role in drafting the negotiating mandate, it adopts a resolution before the start of negotiations that sets the terms of its eventual approval of a particular FTA.[6] Moreover, recent developments have highlighted the difficulties of pursuing the liberalization of trade in the context of increased contestation coming from societal groups and member states. A prime example of this was the suspension of negotiations for the Transatlantic Trade and Investment Partnership (TTIP) with the US in 2016 by Germany and France, whose governments saw strong societal opposition to the agreement, which was perceived to grant too much power to multinational companies in the dispute resolution mechanism proposed, as well as affecting sensitive sectors, from cultural products to agricultural standards. Another instance was the process of ratifying the CETA, which, in 2016, stumbled upon the regional parliament of a sub-national government: Wallonia in Belgium. After a brief re-negotiation with Canada, the agreement entered provisionally into force in September 2017, but will do so fully until all EU member states have ratified it.

---

4. European Commission, 2018, *Overview of FTA and other trade negotiations* (updated May2018). Available at: http://trade.ec.europa.eu/doclib/docs/2006/december/tradoc_118238.pdf (consulted 20/06/2018).
5. Aukje Van Loon, 2018, 'The political economy of EU trade policy: what do we (not) know?', *Z Politikwiss*, n.28. 28, p. 103.
6. Laura Richardson, 2012, *The Post-Lisbon role of the European Parliament in the EU's common commercial policy: Implications for bilateral trade negotiations*, College of Europe: EU Diplomacy Papers, n. 5, p. 9.

In 2018, the conclusion of negotiations with Singapore also saw rising contestation of the new provisions on investment contained in the Lisbon Treaty. The case made it to the European Court of Justice, which was asked its opinion on the division of competences between the EU and the member states. In its ruling, the Court favoured the centralization in the hands of the Commission, by stating that only the provisions relating to non-direct foreign investment and the regime governing dispute settlement between investors and states were of "shared competence". In a reaction to this, in May 2018, the Council adopted a 'New approach on negotiating and concluding EU agreements', which expressed its demand to become involved 'throughout all the stages of the negotiating process, and the importance of working to reach consensual decisions, to the greatest extent possible, in order to ensure that all member states' interests and concerns are adequately respected in trade agreements'. Additionally, the Council stressed the importance of 'keeping all interested stakeholders, including national parliaments and civil society informed'.[7] Thus, it is clear that concerns over the legitimacy of EU trade policy, which had hitherto lagged behind the push for greater efficiency and effectiveness,[8] have now come to the fore and are likely to complicate negotiations in the future.

Such tensions are the result of an expanded trade agenda that goes well beyond the reduction of tariffs and is more intrusive with national regulations, as well as the gradual breakdown of the liberal consensus that had pervaded in the EU since the mid-1980s. It is well known that nationalism and euro-scepticism are on the rise,[9] from the *Brexit* vote in Britain in 2016 to the ascent of governments in Central Europe that claim to subscribe to 'illiberal democracy'. The alarmingly high share of the vote obtained by so called 'populist', anti-EU, anti-immigrant parties in France, the Netherlands and Germany in 2017, and their victory in Italy in March 2018, to mention a few, represent real challenges to the very survival of the EU itself, let alone its trade policy.

---

7.   Council of the European Union, 2018, 'New Approach on negotiating and concluding EU trade agreements adopted by Council', *EU Press Release*, 22/5/2018.

8.   Alasdair R. Young, 2017, 'European trade policy in interesting times, *Journal of European Integration*, vol. 39, n. 7, p. 912.

9.   A majority of Europeans have a positive image of the EU (40%), above those who have a neutral image of the EU (37%), and those who have a negative image of the EU (21%). Although the image of the EU has improved since 2013 (30%), it has not recovered from its peak before the Great Depression: 52% in 2007. European Commission, 2018, *Eurobarometer 89: Public opinion in the European Union*, Spring 2018, Q9A, p. 15.

Perhaps the most important developments impinging on EU trade policy come today from the international arena. The arrival of Donald Trump to the presidency of the US is undermining the very foundations of the transatlantic community of values upon which the postwar order had been built. Despite the internal difficulties described above, EU member states have found themselves united by the decisions emanating from Washington, from the abandonment of the Paris Treaty on Climate Change to the denouncement of the nuclear agreement with Iran. With regard to trade, President Trump has been adopting a series of nationalist and protectionist measures, allegedly aimed at reducing the US trade deficits with its main partners and repatriating jobs. He first pulled out of the Trans-Pacific Partnership (TPP), then forced a surreal negotiation of the North America Free Trade Area (NAFTA) on Canada and Mexico, and has now announced the unilateral imposition of steep tariffs to steel and aluminium on Canada, Mexico and the EU and, a week later, on China, triggering a mirror response that threatens to escalate into a full-blown trade war. This new trade policy on behalf of the US has pushed the EU to seek new allies and to reinforce its ties with existing ones in the defence of open markets and the rules-based trade system on which its economy and place in the world depends so much. As European Council President Donald Tusk, stated at the end of January 2017, 'we should use the change in the trade strategy of the US to the EU's advantage by intensifying our talks with interested partners'.[10] What role is there for LAC in this context?

The changing context in Latin America

The international context in which the region is inserted is changing rapidly. Just as the EU, LAC is shaken by the shift in the US administration's approach to trade. Mexico has been in first line of fire, and is currently immersed in a tricky re-negotiation of the NAFTA, as well as facing the imposition of tariffs on steel and aluminium, to which it has already responded with retaliatory measures.[11] This attitude has cast uncertainty among other

---

10. 'United we stand, divided we fall', *Letter by President Donald Tusk to the 27 EU heads of state or government on the future of the EU before the Malta summit*, 31 January 2017. Available at: http:// www.consilium.europa.eu/en/press/press-releases/2017/01/31-tusk-letter-future-europe/ (consulted 20/06/2018).

11. Secretaría de Economía (Mexico), 2018, 'México impondrá medidas equivalentes a diversos productos ante las medidas proteccionistas de EE.UU. en acero y alumnio', *Comunicado de Prensa* 044/18, 31 May 2018. Available at: https://www.gob.mx/se/prensa/mexico-impondra-medidas-equivalentes-a-diversos-productos-ante-las-medidas-proteccionistas-de-ee-uu-en-acero-y-aluminio (consulted 20/06/2018).

countries of the region, which are waiting to see whether the USA will respect their FTAs (Central America (Dominican Republic-Central America Free Trade Agreement -DR-CAFTA), Colombia, Peru and Chile). However, the small size of their economies and the fact that they do not contribute significantly to the US's trade deficit seems to have shielded them so far.[12]

Another recent trend that is rapidly changing in Latin America's international economic landscape is China's rise as a key partner for many in the region: it accounted for 13% of the region's total trade (8.8% of exports, 17.8% of imports) in 2015.[13] China has now displaced the EU as second economic partner (12% of total trade), after the US, on which LAC still relies heavily (37%). For Venezuela, Brazil, Argentina and Chile, China is now the first buyer of exports. This varies considerably from one partner to the other (see Figure 1). China also allocates loans and other funds through the Asian Development Bank and China's Eximbank.[14]

Another feature of the region is that, despite economic liberalisation since the 1980s, LAC is still not fully integrated to the world economy: its external sector accounts for 20% of GDP, according to the World Bank. It is not very integrated regionally either: only 18% of trade takes place within the region (Figure 1). There is still great reliance on a few powerful external partners: the US, China, and the EU. In this context, the EU is has become, perhaps even more than ever, a necessary partner for most countries of the region, not just for economic reasons, but also as political counterweight to the US.

In terms of growth, Latin America has abruptly been coming down from the commodities boom of the early 2000s. According to the World Bank, GDP contacted by 1% in 2016 and was expected to grow 1.8% in 2017. Brazil has been facing the worst recession in its history with negative growth two years in a row (2015-6), and a forecast just above 0% for 2017. Mexico, the economy that is most integrated to international markets, has not been growing fast enough for the last two decades and its currency has experienced strong volatility since Trump's campaign started picking

---

12. Office of the United States Trade Representative, 2018, *Trade Policy Agenda and 2017 Annual Report of the President of the United States on the Trade Agreements Program*, pp. 7, 12, 3.
13. Data retreived from http://trademap.org (consulted 20/06/2018).
14. 'China cierra el grifo del crédito a Venezuela', *El País*, 2/06/2018, available at: https://elpais.com/internacional/2018/05/02/actualidad/1525228067_970906.html (consulted 20/06/2018).

Alfonso Serrano, 'China fills Trump's empty seat at Latin America Summit', *The New Yorker*, 13/14/2018.

Figure 1. Main Trade Partners of Selected LAC Countries, 2016

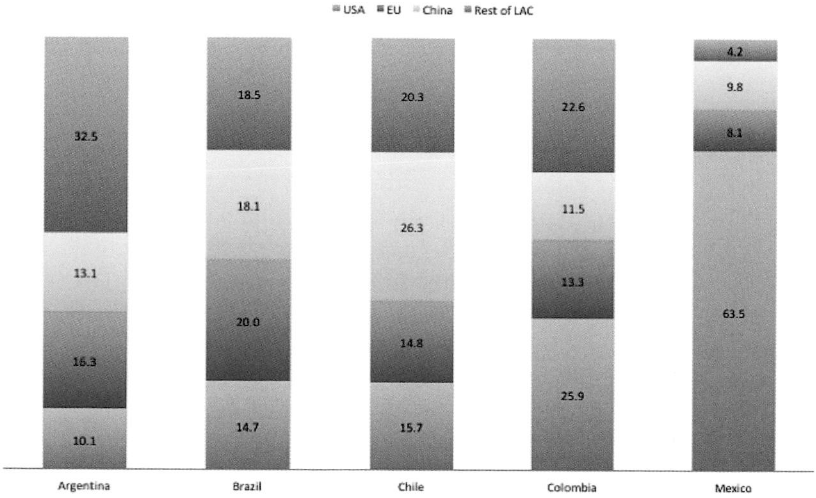

USA EU China Rest of LAC

	Argentina	Brazil	Chile	Colombia	Mexico
	32.5	18.5	20.3	22.6	4.2
					9.8
					8.1
	13.1	18.1	26.3	11.5	
				13.3	63.5
	16.3	20.0	14.8		
				25.9	
	10.1	14.7	15.7		

Source: Trademap.org

up in November 2016, due to its extreme dependence on the US market. Venezuela, on the other hand, is in complete disarray; since 2014 it has not even published data.

In the political arena, the so called 'Washington consensus' which in the 1990s coalesced LAC countries around liberal values, including a commitment to free trade, has been breaking apart since the middle of the 2000s with the onset of the Bolivarian revolution in Venezuela, and the arrival of other left wing governments in, Argentina, Brazil, Bolivia Ecuador, and Uruguay, which were not so interested in FTA negotiations. Consequently, the two South-American regional integration projects with which the EU had embarked on FTA negotiations, the Andean Community and MERCOSUL, stopped being viable partners in that endeavour (see section 3 below). Currently, the ebbing of "pink wave" after government changes in Brazil and Argentina brought back an interest in retaking the free trade agenda, so EU-MERCOSUL negotiations were accelerated between 2017 and 2018. Yet their domestic positions remain fragile.

Indeed, quite a few Latin American countries are facing social and political difficulties over the institutional consolidation of their democratic regimes. Several presidents have been removed in controversial and polarizing circumstances: Manuel Zelaya in Honduras (2009), Fernando Lugo in

Paraguay (2012) Dilma Roussef in Brazil (2016), Pedro Pablo Kucziynski in Peru (2018); a post-electoral conflict in Ecuador, a re-election dispute in Paraguay (2017) and riots followed by repression in Nicaragua (2018). Almost everywhere, democratic governance is also threatened by violence, organized crime and corruption scandals, especially in Mexico, Central America, the Caribbean, Brazil and Venezuela, with high rates of impunity and the consequent de-legitimisation of state authorities. The year 2018 has seen Argentina embark on talks with the International Monetary Fund (IMF) to tackle its economic situation, while several complex elections are due in Mexico and Brazil, which might complicate trade talks with the EU. This convulsed political panorama is quite distant from that of the 1990's when the EU launched its foreign policy strategy towards LAC anchored on trade policy. The following section provides an overview of current trade between the EU and LAC, to assess the challenges and opportunities it faces.

EU-LAC trade relations today: an overview

EU-LAC trade relations are highly asymmetrical, in a North/South fashion. In general, the EU imports raw materials and commodities from LAC, while it exports capital goods, intermediate products and finished goods of high value added.[15] The exceptions are Mexico, which exports mainly manufactures, and partially Brazil, which has an important industrial base, but more geared towards the internal market, shielded by a more protectionist trade policy. The relationship is also asymmetrical in terms of the significance of to each other: according to Trademap.org, while in 2016 the EU represented 12 percent of LAC's total external trade,[16] and features a second or third place as main trade partner of most countries, for the EU, LAC only represented 6.1 percent of exports and 5.3 percent of imports,[17] and is a very minor partner, way behind other players, notably from Asia.

EU trade with LAC is highly concentrated in five states: Brazil and Mexico, the two largest markets, followed by Argentina, Chile and Colombia (see Figure 2), which together account for more than 80 percent of total EU-LAC trade. According to data retrieved from *Eurostat*, in 2016,

---

15. For an indepth study of LAC trade in the current international context, see Luz María de la Mora Sánchez, *Hacia dónde se dirige el régimen de comercio internacional y sus implicaciones para América Latina*, Mexico, CEPAL, 2018.
16. Data retrieved from: Trademap.org
17. Data retrieved from: Eurostat.eu (consulted 20/06/2018).

Figure 2. EU Total Trade with LAC Main Partners, 2007–2016 (%)

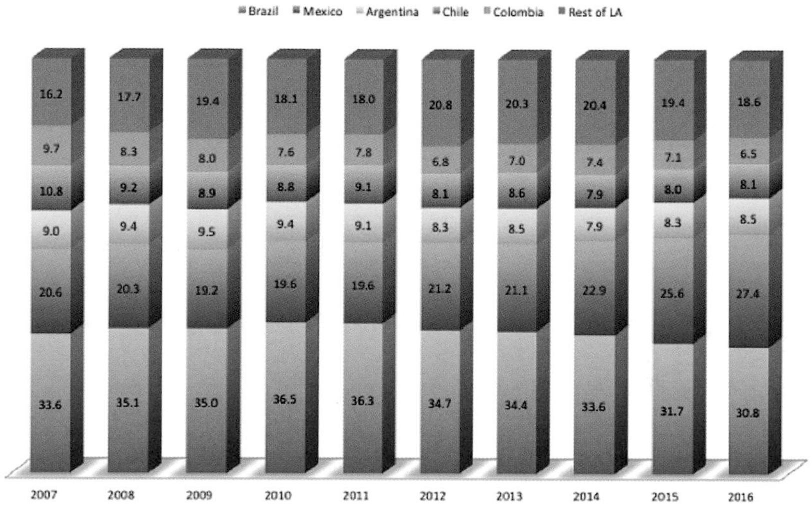

Legend: Brazil ■ Mexico ▪ Argentina ▪ Chile ▪ Colombia ■ Rest of LA

	2007	2008	2009	2010	2011	2012	2013	2014	2015	2016
	16.2	17.7	19.4	18.1	18.0	20.8	20.3	20.4	19.4	18.6
	9.7	8.3	8.0	7.6	7.8	6.8	7.0	7.4	7.1	6.5
	10.8	9.2	8.9	8.8	9.1	8.1	8.6	7.9	8.0	8.1
	9.0	9.4	9.5	9.4	9.1	8.3	8.5	7.9	8.3	8.5
	20.6	20.3	19.2	19.6	19.6	21.2	21.1	22.9	25.6	27.4
	33.6	35.1	35.0	36.5	36.3	34.7	34.4	33.6	31.7	30.8

Source: Eurostat.eu

Brazil alone accounted for 30.8 percent of the value of EU total trade with the region, although its share has been declining, from the 33.6 percent it represented in 2007. This is probably due to the deep recession that hit the country from 2014 onwards which contracted demand for EU imports, and to the fall of commodity prices since 2011, which are the main component of Brazilian exports to the EU. The latter factor is also behind the fall in the share of the value of total trade by other main partners: Argentina, from 9 percent in 2007 to 8.5 percent in 2016, Chile, from 10.8 percent to 8.1 percent and Colombia, from 9.7 percent to 6.5 percent respectively. Actually, the trade deficit that the EU ran with these countries (and with the region as a whole) turned into a surplus in 2012 (see Figure 3).

The exception to this trend is Mexico, the second most important trade partner of the EU in the region: its share of total EU-LAC trade has grown by nearly 7 percent over the last decade (Figure 2). The reason behind this is probably twofold. On the one hand, Mexico is the only country in LAC whose exports are not dominated by commodities, but by manufactures, especially in the automobile sector, closely intertwined with those of Canada and the United States through NAFTA. On the other hand, Mexico's imports from the EU have grown fast in the last five years, as it has required

Figure 3. EU Trade Balance with Main LAC Partners, 2017–2016

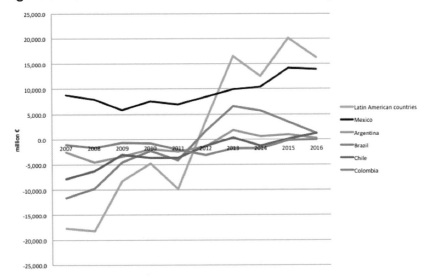

Source: Eurostat.eu

an increasing amount of intermediate and capital products for its export industry, heavily concentrated in the US, with which it runs a large surplus that has now become an issue the Trump administration wants to correct.

Beyond merchandise trade, it is worth noting that investment from Europe is as important as trade –if not more- for LAC economies, abundant in labour and natural resources, but not capital. Moreover, foreign direct investment has become an area of EU competence since the treaty of Lisbon, and a key element of the so called 'new trade agenda', which has moved from lowering barriers to trade to regulatory convergence, equal treatment for foreign companies in government procurement, and resolution disputes mechanisms for investor-state cases. These are key issues in the current trade talks the EU is engaged in with partners in Latin America, as discussed in section 5.

Figure 4 shows that, according to *Eurostat* data, EU investment has generally followed and upward trend since 2004, with Spain as the main individual investor, except for the years 2012-2013. Luxembourg is another important player, because due to its tax system, many European companies have their headquarters established there. It is interesting to note

Figure 4. European Direct Investment Flows to LAC, 2004–2016

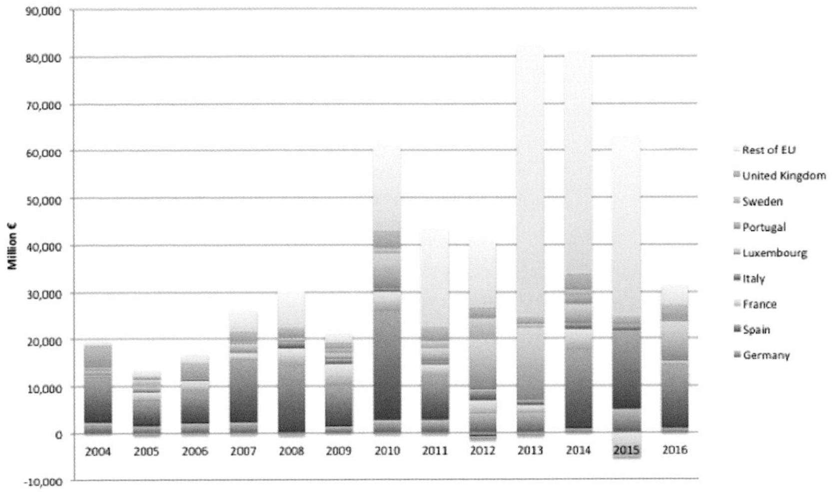

Source: Eurostat.eu

that investment from non-traditional partners ('rest of the EU' in Figure 4) has grown considerably, especially from the Netherlands, which has been investing heavily in Brazil and Mexico since 2013. On the receiving side, Brazil, Chile, Mexico and Peru stand out –apart from the Caribbean tax heavens of Bermuda, Barbados and the Caiman Islands.

An important feature of EU policy towards LAC since the 1990s has been its interest in fostering regional integration in the area, an objective it *pursued through trade policy*, by opening FTA negotiations with MERCOSUL (1995), the Andean Community (1996) and Central America (opened in 2002, concluded in 2014).[18] The plan to prioritize the negotiation of interregional FTAs has only worked partially, because after 20 years of pursuing this strategy, only the agreement with Central America has been concluded, while bilateralism seems to have worked better for deal-

---

18. With the Caribbean, the EU has a different relationship, based on the Cotonou agreement with the ACP Group, the small former colonies of European member states in Asia, the Caribbean and the Pacific. It has recently established a set of individual Economic Partnership Agreements (EPAs, 2008) with the members of the CARIFORUM that take into account the enormous asymmetries between the two sides.

ing with an increasingly diverse region.[19] The EU has FTAs with Mexico, Chile, Colombia, Peru and Ecuador, while regional integration agreements in LAC have been in flux, as discussed in the following section.

Regional integration in Latin America: a fluid panorama

Created in 1991, with the Treaty of Asuncion, MERCOSUL seemed to be very similar to the EU in that it involved the reconciliation of old foes and the establishment of a common market, including a customs union. The nature of MERCOSUL seemed to change after economic crises hit Argentina and Brazil in the early 2000s, and the common institutions were unable to maintain convergence as national responses started to drift. Later in the decade, the economic integration and liberalization agenda gave way to other concerns of a more political nature, as left-wing governments became less keen on free trade, and more interested in social affairs, energy and infrastructure. This fluidity in MERCOSUL's agenda was further compounded by Venezuela's application for membership in 2006 and accession in 2012, as well as the creation of UNASUR, which included the same issue areas that had recently been added to MERCOSUL. As a result of this shift, and other international factors, FTA negotiations between the EU and MERCOSUL, which had started in 2001, stalled by 2004 (see section 5). In the meantime, the EU established a Strategic Partnership with Brazil, which included discussion of some trade issues, in what seemed a consideration to pursue a bilateral path.[20]

The effects of Venezuela's Bolivarian revolution in the region were more disruptive to the Andean Community, which President Chavez left abruptly in 2006, followed by Bolivia, which has not completed its retreat, but remains a distant partner to the three remaining (Colombia and Peru, but less to Ecuador). This left the EU and its FTA negotiation in a dilemma, which it solved after a few years with a hybrid formula: it embarked on FTA negotiations with Colombia of a Multiparty Agreement in 2009 (concluded in 2013), which was followed by Peru (2013) and Ecuador (2014).

---

19. I have developed these ideas further in Lorena Ruano, 'Dealing with Diversity: The EU and Latin America today', *Chaillot Paper* n. 145, Paris, European Union Institute for Security Studies, April 2018.
20. Aukje van Loon, 2009, 'Diverging EU Trade Strategies in Latin America: External Challenges and Internal Debates', *Paper prepared for the 5th ECPR General Conference*, Potsdam, Germany, p. 20, footnote 33.

Figure 5. Regional Integration Schemes in LAC

- ▣ MERCOSUR
- ▢ MERCOSUR candidate
- ▢ UNASUR
- ▣ Pacific Alliance
- ▢ SICA
- ▢ CACM

The more liberal oriented governments of Colombia, Chile, Mexico and Peru launched the Pacific Alliance in 2011, a project born to construct a new form of regional integration and a common approach to their insertion in the world economy at large. Their method of integration is different from previous LAC schemes in that it tries to 'build from below', through small but practical steps, rather than building common institutions: the four countries have worked on the removal of as many technical trade barriers as possible among the members, the facilitation of mobility of business-men, students, scientists (removing visa requirements), and simplifying procedures as well as to attract investment. It has caught great international attention, featuring 49 observers (the EU and most of its member states among them), of which Costa Rica and Panama have become candidates to join.

The four countries have FTAs with the US and the EU, both of which constitute powerful signals of commitment to pursue an export led growth development strategy and open markets. In March 2018, Chile, Mexico and Peru signed the Comprehensive and Progressive Agreement for Trans-Pacific Partnership (CPTPP), which replaced the TTP after President Trump decided to pull out in January 2017, and the remaining members decided to pursue its negotiation under the leadership of Japan, in a gesture that signalled their continued commitment to trade liberalisation, and now, diversification away from the US. The Pacific Alliance is currently negotiating with Canada, Australia, New Zealand and Singapore to make them Associate Members.[21] It has also attracted the attention of MERCOSUL: in April 2017 at a gathering in Buenos Aires, ministers from both groups announced the intention to move towards the convergence of both groups.

The Pacific Alliance's relevance for the economies of its members remains marginal, especially for Mexico, the largest partner: its trade with the three other members combined amounts only to 1.2 percent of its total trade. For Chile, who trades most within the block, the other three partners represent 12 percent of its total trade.[22] Thus for the moment, its importance, is more political and symbolic, as a statement from its member states about their commitment to rules-based free trade, and their willingness to continue with their insertion into the international economy. For that reason, this is now the most interesting regional scheme with which to work for the EU, especially because it has the institutional infrastructure in place through FTAs with each member state.

Moreover, Figure 6 and Table 1 show that trade with the countries of the Pacific Alliance and Central America has been more dynamic than with the other regional integration schemes in LAC. The share of EU imports from Central America relative to imports from all of LAC has grown (from 5.2 percent in 2007 to 6 percent in 2016), as well as those from the Pacific Alliance (from 35.7 percent in 2007 to 45.1 percent), while those from MERCOSUL, the ALBA countries have declined.[23] In terms of EU exports to LAC, the Pacific Alliance's share has grown from 40.1 percent in 2007 to 47 percent, while that of MERCOSUL has grown marginally (from 37.1 percent to 37.9 percent) and the share of exports to other regional groupings has declined. Trade seems to become increasingly concentrated in the economies of the Pacific Alliance at the expense of other players in LAC.

---

21. 'Pacific Alliance, Associate Members Enter Fourth Negotiating Round, Look To Clinch Deal by July', Bridges, Vol. 22, n. 17, 17 May 2018. Available at: https://www.ictsd. org/bridges-news/bridges/news/pacific-alliance-associate-members-enter-fourth-ne-gotiating-round-look-to (consulted 20/06/2018).
22. Data retrieved from Trademap.org.
23. Since Venezuela is not fully integrated to MERCOSUL and was suspended in 2017, it is grouped with the ALBA countries, a bloc that it has led since the mid-2000s.

Figure 6. EU Trade with LAC Regional Integration Groups, 2007–2016 (million €)

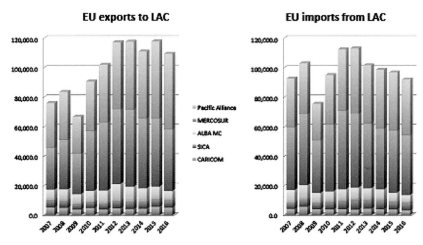

Source: Eurostat.eu

Table 1. Percentage of EU trade with regional integration groups relative to EU-LAC total, 2007-2016

EU imports from LAC

Partner/Time	2007	2008	2009	2010	2011	2012	2013	2014	2015	2016
Caricom	4.5	5.6	5.3	4.1	3.6	3.3	4.3	4.1	4.1	3.4
Sica	5.2	5.3	6.3	6.1	5.4	6.2	6.6	6.4	5.5	6.0
Alba Mc	8.7	8.9	8.5	6.9	6.6	7.2	7.2	7.3	6.2	5.4
Mercosul	46.0	46.9	47.0	47.8	47.3	44.3	43.2	41.8	43.4	44.1
Pacific Alliance	35.7	33.3	32.9	35.1	37.0	39.0	38.7	40.3	40.7	41.1

EU Exports To LAC

Partner/Time	2007	2008	2009	2010	2011	2012	2013	2014	2015	2016
Caricom	7.1	6.0	5.7	5.3	3.9	4.1	3.6	4.0	4.8	4.8
Sica	7.2	6.3	6.6	5.1	4.4	4.7	4.8	4.9	4.9	4.9
Alba Mc	8.6	8.6	9.0	7.9	8.1	9.4	8.1	7.6	6.7	5.4
Mercosul	37.1	40.0	40.8	44.5	45.0	43.0	44.3	42.7	39.2	37.9
Pacific Alliance	40.1	39.1	37.9	37.1	38.6	38.8	39.1	40.9	44.3	47.0

Source: Own calculations with Eurostat data

Current EU trade negotiations with Latin America

At the moment of writing, the EU has three trade negotiations opened with Latin America: the modernization of the EU-Mexico Global Agreement, the negotiation of the Interregional Association Agreement with MERCOSUL (IAA), and the modernization of the Association Agreement with Chile. This section addresses them in turn.

EU-Mexico

The intention to 'modernise' the EU-Mexico Global Agreement, in force since 2000, was first announced at the EU-CELAC (*Comunidad de Estados Latinoamericanos y Caribeños*) summit in Santiago in 2013, shortly after Mexico passed a set of reforms on the telecoms and energy sectors that Europeans had been awaiting. The 'update' is intended to adapt the existing 15 year-old agreement to the changes that had occurred in Mexico, the EU and the world economy in general, especially, to include the elements of the so called 'new trade agenda', present in the TPP, TTIP and CETA which were being negotiated at the time, and which went beyond the reduction of tariffs, already low after the Uruguay Round of GATT and the FTA between the EU and Mexico included in the Global Agreement. In particular, it was important to address non-tariff-barriers (NTBs), such as regulatory issues, and to facilitate investment.[24]

The negotiations took a while to start in earnest, as the EU gave priority to the negotiation it was carrying out with Canada (CETA) and the USA (TTIP). Moreover, although the Joint Statement of the VII EU-Mexico Summit reaffirmed the willingness to launch negotiations in 2015,[25] the internal EU process of defining a negotiating mandate, delayed the start of real talks until June 2016. And it was until 2017, with the arrival of Donald Trump to the US Presidency, that both parts found it urgent to accelerate negotiations.

In early 2017, Mexico launched a diversification strategy, with the EU as a priority, while it also aimed to improve the access of its exports to Latin America by strengthening the bonds with the Pacific Alliance and widen-

---

24. European Commission, *Commission Staff Working Document. Impact Assessment accompanying the document Recommendation fo a Council Decision authorising the European Commission and the High Representative of the Union for Foreign Affairs and Security Policy to open negotiations and to negotiate with Mexico a modernised Global Agreement*, SWD(2015) 289 final, Brussels, 16.12.2015.
25. *VII EU-Mexico-Summit Joint Statement*, Brussels, 12 June 2015, paragraph 3.

ing the economic complementation agreements with Brazil (ACE 53) and Argentina (ACE 6) in the framework of ALADI (*Asociación Latinoamericana de Integración*). in March 2017, when the USA withdrew from TPP, Mexico continued working with the 10 remaining members of the group to conclude a new agreement, the CPTPP, and in June of that year, the Pacific Alliance started negotiating an FTA with Australia, Canada, New Zealand and Singapore. On the side of the EU, Trade Commissioner Cecilia Malmström visited Mexico in January 2017 to announce the acceleration of the negotiations, followed by the visit by German Chancellor Angela Merkel in June, who criticised walls and defended free trade, sending out powerful signals of their intention to defend a rules-based approach to trade with Mexico as an ally. Thus, it was clear that the main factor pushing for the acceleration of negotiations was the changing international context, notably, the Trump factor.

On 21 April 2018, after nine rounds of intense trade negotiations, Mexico and the EU announced they had concluded the bulk of the new framework and reached an Agreement in Principle[26] on how to finalise the technical issues remaining. An important number of new areas have been added to the old FTA, such as updating the framework for financial services, intellectual property, digital trade, telecoms, energy, maritime transport, public procurement (including the sub-federal level), the mutual recognition of certain qualifications for professional services, and accumulated rules of origin for common partners. Simpler customs procedures will further benefit the EU's industry in sectors like pharmaceuticals, machinery and transport equipment. In the agricultural sector, the objective has been to liberalize 85% of what still remained protected, including the recognition by Mexico of 350 EU geographical indications, and the amplification of quotas for beef and milk products. The process for phytosanitary inspections was also simplified in order to speed up the time of approval from 4-5 years to 1 year. Few products compete directly in this sector between the two sides; the issue was more about how much Mexico would allow EU products to compete with those coming from the US.[27] Other important chapters that have been included in the new trade agreement relate to trade and sustainable development, gender, climate change, competition and cor-

---

26. 'New EU-Mexico Agreement: The Agreement in Principle', Brussels, 23 April 2018. Available at: http://trade.ec.europa.eu/doclib/docs/2018/april/tradoc_156791.pdf (consulted 20/06/2018).
27. Briefing by staff from the EU Delegation in Mexico at the *Formación de actualización sobre Unión Europea y temas estratégicos para la relación México-UE*, Mexico, ITAM, 30 May 2018.

ruption, reflecting the objectives as set out in the EU's new trade policy vision launched in 2015.[28]

Perhaps the most important innovation is the section on investment, which falls under EU competence since the Lisbon Treaty, and is actually more important for Mexico than trade in goods and services, as 27 percent of direct foreign investment came from the EU in 2017, while only 8 percent of its trade takes place with the EU.[29] Thus, the new agreement for the promotion and protection of investments will replace the 17 bilateral agreements Mexico has with some EU member states. Crucially, the 'modernised Global Agreement' establishes an investor-state dispute resolution mechanism similar to the one set up in CETA (as well as in the FTAs the EU recently concluded with Vietnam and Japan), which replaces *ad hoc* panels by a new Investor Court System, which is permanent, includes the right to appeal, and makes all decisions and documents public. Both parts also agreed to promote the establishment of this system at the multilateral level. Although Mexico was reluctant at the beginning to accept this new system, its acceptance by Canada in CETA and the pressure of the re-negotiation of NAFTA made it change its mind.[30]

The political statements of both parts that accompanied the announcement of the Agreement in Principle confirmed that they interpret the deal as a response to the disruptiveness of US trade policy, at an especially tricky moment in the renegotiation of NAFTA.[31] From the point of view of the EU, Commission President, Jean Claude Juncker stated that 'With this agreement, Mexico joins Canada, Japan and Singapore in the growing list of partners willing to work with the EU in defending open, fair and rules-based trade'.[32] Mexico's government stressed that 'Mexico and the European Union send a strong message to the world about the importance of maintaining open markets, [and] working together through the multilateral channels...'.[33]

---

28. European Commission, *Trade for All - Towards a more responsible trade and investment policy*, Brussels, 2015.
29. Stéphan Sbérro Picard, 2018, 'Europa, un gran aliado estratégico en la diversificación comercial de México', *Comercio Exterior*, vol. 14, April-June, p. 20.
30. Briefing by staff from the EU Delegation in Mexico.
31. Hans Von der Burchard and Christian Oliver, 'Mexico's EU trade deal land a punch on Trump: Accord with Brussels comes as Washington squeezes Latin American country in NAFTA talks', *Politico*, 22 May 2018.
32. 'EU and Mexico reach new trade agreement', *EU Press Release*, 21 April 2018.
33. Secretaría de Relaciones Exteriores (Mexico), 2018, 'Concluyen las negociaciones para un nuevo acuerdo integral México-Unión Europea', Comunicado de prensa conjunto SRE-SE, 21 April, 2018. Author's translation. Avalable at: https://www.gob.mx/sre/

In spite of the spectacular progress and the political will to conclude them, the fact is that the agreement is not finalised yet, and it is not clear that the next Mexican government, emanating from the July 2018 elections will be so keen on FTAs. If concluded, ratification will certainly be trickier than in the past on both sides, with EP elections coming up in 2019.

EU-MERCOSUL

In 1995, the EU and MERCOSUL signed an Interregional Framework for Cooperation Agreement (EMIFCA), which included the aim to launch trade negotiations for an Interregional Association Agreement (IAA) that would also include cooperation and political dialogue pillars. From the EU's point of view, geopolitical considerations were paramount. On the one hand, the US had embarked on the negotiation of a FTAA, which threatened to reduce the EU's share of trade in LAC. On the other hand, the EU was interested in exporting its model of regional integration, and MERCOSUL seemed to be the regional project closest to its experience.[34] In economic terms, access to the large and relatively protected MERCOS-UL market was promising for the EU's industrial products (especially in the automotive sector), services, telecoms, and the attractive opportunities for government procurement.

However, the internal negotiations within the EU to reach a mandate were long and tortuous, because MERCOSUL's main priority in exchange to opening its market was the liberalization of EU agriculture, as this is MERCOSUL's most competitive sector, which still faces substantial barriers of entry to the EU. This entailed a major reform of the EU's Common Agricultural Policy (CAP), a matter that has always been difficult and slow, dominated as it is by powerful interest groups, a strong path dependence, and the veto of those EU member states which benefit most from it, such as France, Ireland, Spain and Germany.[35] So it was not until June 2001, in the 5th round of negotiations, that the EU presented its first liberalisation

---

prensa/concluyen-las-negociaciones-para-un-nuevo-acuerdo-integral-entre-mexi-co-y-la-union-europea (consulted 20/06/2018).

34. Van Loon, 2009, p. 19-20.
35. I have analysed how the difficulties of CAP reform have complicated politically important negotiations with third parties in Lorena Ruano, 2005, 'The Consolidation of Democracy vs. the Price of Olive Oil: The Story of Why the CAP Delayed Spain's Entry to the EC', *Journal of European Integration History*, vol. 11, n° 2, pp. 97- 118; Lorena Ruano, 2005 , 'Institutions, Policy Communities and Enlargement: British, Spanish and Central European Accession Negotiations in the Agricultural Sector', in Frank Shimmelfennig and Ulrich Sedelmeier, eds., *The Politics of European Union Enlargement: Theoretical Approaches*, Abingdon and New York, Routledge, pp. 258-276.

offer to MERCOSUL, which excluded tariff cuts of its main exports, and the issue of exports subsidies which it wanted to discuss at the multilateral level in the Doha Round of WTO. At the next round, MERCOSUL responded with an offer that excluded the automobile industry. Ten rounds later, in September 2004, the last EU offer still excluded MERCOSUL's main exports (beef and sugar) from the tariff reduction basket of goods to be liberalized.[36] Negotiations were effectively blocked since then, and although there were EU-MERCOSUL summit meetings on the fringes of EU-LAC summits, and more trade negotiating rounds, only technical matters were advanced.

Besides the deadlock between both parties, which seemed intractable, other geopolitical considerations contributed to the stagnation of negotiations, notably the collapse of the FTAA negotiations in 2004, which reduced the urgency of the EU to reach a deal. Besides, as discussed in section 4, after economic crises hit Argentina and Brazil in 2000-2001, MERCOSUL's nature changed in economic and political terms, making it a less attractive partner for the EU.[37] In fact, the EU seemed to prioritise the bilateral channels with individual member states, notably with the establishment of the Strategic Partnership with Brazil in 2007, which included the discussion of trade related matters. With the other members, the EU also has bilateral cooperation framework agreements that encompass trade.

It was until 2016 that interest in concluding the trade negotiations returned with urgency, due to changes in the domestic and international contexts. At the domestic level, the arrival of centre-right governments in Brazil and Argentina renewed their interest in liberalizing trade, pursuing the economic integration within MERCOSUL, and even seeking a rapprochement with the Pacific Alliance. Their arrival has also created conflict with Venezuela, which was 'suspended' in December 2016 through the application of MERCOSUL's democratic clause. This left Venezuela as an observer to the trade negotiations, thus removing an important obstacle to meaningful talks with the EU, which, at the time of writing, has sanctions in place against that country. Meanwhile, in Europe, CAP reform returned to the agenda due to the future withdrawal of the United Kingdom from the EU, which will leave an important whole in the budget, and the need to reallocate resources to other priorities, as recognised by the new

---

36. Van Loon, 2009.
37. Mahrukh Doctor, 2007, 'Why Bother With Inter-Regionalism? Negotiations for a European-MERCOSUL Agreement', *Journal of Common Market Studies*, vol. 45, n. 2, pp. 281-2014.

French President, Emmanuel Macron, who advocated a discussion on farm subsidies 'without taboos'.[38] At the international level, both the EU and MERCOSUL saw the revival of negotiations as a response to Trump's protectionist and unilateralist trade policy.[39]

EU-MERCOSUL negotiations gathered pace, with six rounds of negotiations taking place between March 2017 and February 2018. There was significant progress in the 'new trade agenda' items, which were not present in the early 2000s, such as competition, sustainable development, intellectual property, services, investment and public procurement, but the contentious areas remained the same as in 2004: European agriculture (beef and ethanol) and MERCOSUL protectionism in the automobile sector. At the heart of the negotiation is whether the EU is ready to increase the original offer for beef quotas from 70 000 metric tons, while MERCOSUL has expressed it wants more than 200 000 in exchange for dropping its tariffs on cars and machinery exports from the EU. At the last round of negotiations, which concluded in March 2018, the EU signalled it was ready to open up further if MERCOSUL agreed to better access for EU cars and diary, the inclusion of maritime services, a flexibilisation of the rules of origin, and access to public procurement at the sub-federal level, as well as the recognition of several EU geographical denominations.[40]

At the time of writing, the window of opportunity is closing in fast without a firm conclusion to the trade negotiations, while the texts on the political and cooperation sections of the IAA were finalised in June 2018, to be sent to the member states for approval, as announced by Edita Hrdà, Executive Director for the Americas at the European External Action Service.[41] Domestic factors are reducing the room for manoeuvre, with the Brazilian election looming in October, and the Argentinian government busy with an 'adjustment' that has turned out more complex, costly and long than expected, having to call on the IMF for a $50 billion bailout in June 2018.

Completing this agreement would be very important economic terms, as the EU is the first trade partner of MERCOSUL (21 percent of its total

38. Emmet Livingstone, Maïa de la Baume and David M. Herszenhorn, 'Emmanuel Macron breaks French taboo on farm subsidies', *Politico*, 20 April 2018.
39. De La Mora, 2018, p. 65.
40. Hans von der Burchard and Ryan Heath, 'EU races against the clock to seal beef-for-cars trade deal', *Politico*, 26 January 2018; 'EU-MERCOSUL trade talks close with key gaps remaining', *Reuters*, 9 February, 2018; European Commission, *Report from the XXXIIth round of negotiations of the Trade Part of the Association Agreement between the European Union and MERCOSUL*, Asuncion, 21 February-2 March 2018.
41. https://twitter.com/EditaHrdaEU/status/1005410103347109888 (consulted 20/06/2018).

trade) and main investor.[42] Speaking at the EP, EU chief negotiator Sandra Gallina said that progress had been excellent at the technical level, but that she was now 'in need of big political help' to clear the remaining issues, otherwise leaders would have to explain 'why do don't want to finish this... geopolitically very important' agreement.[43]

EU-Chile

EU-Chile trade is governed by an Association Agreement, in place since 2003, the second that the EU established with a LAC country after the one with Mexico (2000). As the latter, it includes a political dialogue and cooperation pillar, although the trade part is more sophisticated than the one with Mexico. In 2015, the EU decided it was necessary to modernise the agreement with Chile (as it had started doing with Mexico) in order to 'broaden the scope of the Association Agreement and adjust it to the new political and economic global challenges [...] and to the level of ambition of recently concluded agreements and negotiations being conducted by the EU and Chile'.[44]

After a year of consultations and impact assessment, the negotiating mandate did not take too long to be approved by the Council, so negotiations started in November 2017. At the time of writing, three rounds have taken place, with good progress in all areas. The new areas to be included in the modernised agreement relate to the new investment protection framework (as with Mexico, Canada Japan and Vietnam), rules of origin, technical barriers to trade, services, intellectual property, geographical indications, public procurement, competition, sustainable development, and gender issues related to trade.[45]

As with Mexico and MERCOSUL, the Trump factor has been at play in accelerating the pace of negotiations. At the opening of negotiations, DG Trade Commissionner Cecilia Malmström hinted in her speah that this agreement is intended to strenghthen the position of both sides against protectionist temptations in world trade, when she stated that it was necessary to 'address the full range of political and global challenges', while

---

42. De La Mora, p. 64-65.
43. Quoted by von der Burchard and Heath, 'EU races against the clock to seal beef-for-cars trade deal', 2018.
44. Council of the European Union, *EU-Chile Modernised Association Agreement: Directives for the negotiation of a Modernised Association Agreement with Chile*, Brussels, 22 January 2018, 13553/17 ADD1 DCL1, p. 2.
45. Ibidem; De la Mora, p. 64.

the HRVP, Federica Mogherini said that both partners were 'to continue championing global peace and security, free and open markets, inclusive societies and the promotion of global common goods'.[46]

The new agreement is more important to Chile in economic terms, since the EU accounts for 15% of its foreign trade, it is its second export market after China, and more importantly is the source of nearly half of its FDI.[47] For the EU, the value of the agreement is more symbolic and political, as a sign to the USA that it is coalescing with other members of international society to defend open markets and rules based trade.

Conclusion

This chapter has argued that the current protectionist trend in US trade policy has triggered a reaction on the part of both the EU and some LAC countries (Mexico, Chile and the members of MERCOSUL) to accelerate, relaunch and start trade negotiations as way to coalesce around the defence of rules based free trade and open markets. However important they are in economic, symbolic and geopolitical terms, their successful conclusion is far from straightforward, as they depend on international, regional and domestic factors on both sides.

For the EU, trade is a most powerful instrument in its world standing and vital for its economic prosperity, so it has recently been pursuing an ambitious agenda of trade negotiations, both in contents and in geographical scope. The new agreements are based on the so called "new trade agenda" that includes regulatory convergence, a new court system for investment protection, public procurement, and the linkage of trade with issues like sustainable development, competition, corruption and gender equality; beyond LAC, the EU has also been negotiating agreements with several countries in Asia and Canada. Thus, it seems that the wave of nationalism and populism that is sweeping across its member states has not fully dented on the liberalism that still characterises EU trade policy. However, recent institutional changes, described in the first section, have made this insulation more difficult, as the Council and the Parliament seek to follow negotiations more closely while national ratification processes could become trickier in parliaments where nationalist parties gain ground.

---

46. 'EU and Chile to start negotiations for a modernised Association Agreement', EU Press Release, Brussels, 13 November 2017.
47. De la Mora, p. 65.

On the LAC side, this is an economically strained region, politically unstable and divided, and with a very fluid panorama in terms of integration schemes, among which the Pacific Alliance has become the most dynamic in its trade with the EU. For those countries which display a more liberal outlook in their economic and trade policies (Mexico, Chile, Colombia, Peru and recently Brazil and Argentina) their to vulnerability commodity prices, US policy swings and the rising role of China, have meant that, in their eternal search for diversification, the EU has gained importance. Therefore, they have displayed an impressive effort to strengthen their economic links with it, among themselves and with other extra-regional partners.

The modernization of the EU-Mexico Global Agreement advanced at full speed during 2017 and the first half of 2018, and is nearly completed, while that country is under enormous pressure from a complex revision of NAFTA. The conclusion of the agreement is now awaiting the electoral process in Mexico and much depends on the economic profile that the new government will display, while the process of signature and ratification could take several years. With MERCOSUL, the re-launch of long-time dormant IAA negotiations in early 2017 gathered pace, but their conclusion stumbled upon the same issue that blocked them 14 years ago: EU beef quotas and MERCOSUL's opening of its market in the automobile sector. The window of opportunity is quickly closing in as the most complex elections in Brazil's recent history loom, while Argentina deals with an IMF bailout. With Chile, fewer problems threaten the modernisation of its Association agreement, whose negotiations have just started. The 'Trump factor' has clearly provided the political will to advance with these three negotiations. Yet domestic variables both in LAC countries and EU member states remain volatile and could become significant obstacles to the consolidation of this new geo-political coalition to defend rules-based trade.

References

'China cierra el grifo del crédito a Venezuela', *El País*, 2/06/2018, available at: https://elpais.com/internacional/2018/05/02/actualidad/1525228067_970906. html (consulted 20/06/2018).

'EU and Mexico reach new trade agreement', *EU Press Release*, 21 April 2018.

'Pacific Alliance, Associate Members Enter Fourth Negotiating Round, Look To Clinch Deal by July', Bridges, Vol. 22, n. 17, 17 May 2018. Available at:

https://www.ictsd.org/bridges-news/bridges/news/pacific-alliance-associate-
-members-enter-fourth-negotiating-round-look-to (consulted 20/06/2018).

'United we stand, divided we fall', *Letter by President Donald Tusk to the 27 EU heads of state or government on the future of the EU before the Malta summit*, 31 January 2017. Available at: http:// www.consilium.europa.eu/en/press/press-releases/2017/01/31-tusk-letter-future-europe/ (consulted 20/06/2018).

Bollen, Yelter, Ferdi De Ville and Jan Orbie, 2016, 'EU trade policy: persistent liberalisation, contentious protectionism', *Journal of European Integration*, vol. 38, n. 3, pp. 279-294.

Briefing by staff from the EU Delegation in Mexico at the *Formación de actualización sobre Unión Europea y temas estratégicos para la relación México-UE*, Mexico, ITAM, 30 May 2018.

Council of the European Union, 2018, 'New Approach on negotiating and concluding EU trade agreements adopted by Council', *EU Press Release*, 22/5/2018.

Council of the European Union, 2018, *EU-Chile Modernised Association Agreement: Directives for the negotiation of a Modernised Association Agreement with Chile*, Brussels, 22 January 2018, 13553/17 ADD1 DCL1.

De la Mora Sánchez, Luz María, 2018, *Hacia dónde se dirige el régimen de comercio internacional y sus implicaciones para América Latina*, Mexico, CEPAL.

Doctor, Mahrukh, 2007, 'Why Bother With Inter-Regionalism? Negotiations for a European-MERCOSUL Agreement', *Journal of Common Market Studies*, vol. 45, n. 2, pp. 281-2014.

European Commission, 2015, *Commission Staff Working Document. Impact Assessment accompanying the document Recommendation fo a Council Decision authorising the European Commission and the High Representative of the Union for Foreign Affairs and Security Policy to open negotiations and to negotiate with Mexico a modernised Global Agreement*, SWD(2015) 289 final, Brussels, 16.12.2015.

European Commission, 2015, *Trade for All - Towards a more responsible trade and investment policy*, Brussels, 2015.

European Commission, 2018, *Eurobarometer 89: Public opinion in the European Union*, Spring 2018.

European Commission, 2018, *Overview of FTA and other trade negotiations* (updated May2018). Available at: http://trade.ec.europa.eu/doclib/docs/2006/december/tradoc_118238.pdf (consulted 20/06/2018).

European Commission, 2018, *Report from the XXXIIth round of negotiations of the Trade Part of the Association Agreement between the European Union and MERCOSUL*, Asuncion, 21 February-2 March 2018.

Livingstone, Emmet, Maïa de la Baume and David M. Herszenhorn, 2018, 'Emmanuel Macron breaks French taboo on farm subsidies', *Politico*, 20 April 2018.

Ruano, Lorena, 2005, 'Institutions, Policy Communities and Enlargement: British, Spanish and Central European Accession Negotiations in the Agricultural Sector', in Frank Shimmelfennig and Ulrich Sedelmeier, eds., *The Politics of European Union Enlargement: Theoretical Approaches*, Abingdon and New York, Routledge, pp. 258-276.

Ruano, Lorena, 2005, 'The Consolidation of Democracy vs. the Price of Olive Oil: The Story of Why the CAP Delayed Spain's Entry to the EC', *Journal of European Integration History*, vol. 11, n° 2, pp. 97- 118.

Ruano, Lorena, 2018, 'Dealing with Diversity: The EU and Latin America today', *Chaillot Paper* n. 145, Paris, European Union Institute for Security Studies.

Meunier, Sophie and Kalypso Nicolaïdis, 2006, 'The European Union as a conflicted trade power', *Journal of European Public Policy*, vol. 13, n. 6, pp. 906-925.

Office of the United States Trade Representative, 2018, *Trade Policy Agenda and 2017 Annual Report of the President of the United States on the Trade Agreements Program*, pp. 7, 12, 3.

Richardson, Laura, 2012, *The Post-Lisbon role of the European Parliament in the EU's common commercial policy: Implications for bilateral trade negotiations*, College of Europe: EU Diplomacy Papers, n. 5.

Sbérro Picard, Stéphan, 2018, 'Europa, un gran aliado estratégico en la diversificación comercial de México', *Comercio Exterior*, vol. 14, April-June, p. 18-22.

Secretaría de Economía (Mexico), 2018, 'México impondrá medidas equivalentes a diversos productos ante las medidas proteccionistas de EE.UU. en acero y alumnio', *Comunicado de Prensa* 044/18, 31 May 2018. Available at: https://www.gob.mx/se/prensa/mexico-impondra-medidas-equivalentes-a-diversos--productos-ante-las-medidas-proteccionistas-de-ee-uu-en-acero-y-aluminio (consulted 20/06/2018).

Secretaría de Relaciones Exteriores (Mexico), 'Concluyen las negociaciones para un nuevo acuerdo integral México-Unión Europea', Comunicado de prensa conjunto SRE-SE, 21 April, 2018. Author's translation. Avalable at: https://www.gob.mx/sre/prensa/concluyen-las-negociaciones-para-un-nuevo-acuerdo-integral-entre-mexico-y-la-union-europea (consulted 20/06/2018).

Serrano, Alfonso, 'China fills Trump's empty seat at Latin America Summit', *The New Yorker*, 13/14/2018.

Van Loon, Aukje, 2009, 'Diverging EU Trade Strategies in Latin America: External Challenges and Internal Debates', *Paper prepared for the 5th ECPR General Conference*, Potsdam, Germany.

Van Loon, Aukje, 2018, 'The political economy of EU trade policy: what do we (not) know?', *Z Politikwiss*, n. 28, pp. 97-110.

VII EU-Mexico-Summit Joint Statement, Brussels, 12 June 2015.

Von der Burchard, Hans and Christian Oliver, 2018, 'Mexico's EU trade deal land a punch on Trump: Accord with Brussels comes as Washington squeezes Latin American country in NAFTA talks', *Politico*, 22 May 2018.

Von der Burchard, Hans and Ryan Heath, 2018, 'EU races against the clock to seal beef-for-cars trade deal', *Politico*, 26 January 2018; 'EU-MERCOSUL trade talks close with key gaps remaining', *Reuters*, 9 February, 2018.

Young, Alasdair R. and John Peterson, 2014, *Global parochial Europe: 21st century trade politics*, Oxford, Oxford University Press.

Young, Alasdair R., 2017, 'European trade policy in interesting times, *Journal of European Integration*, vol. 39, n. 7, pp. 909-923.

Chapter Five

The Diffusion of Fundamental Rights in the Atlantic Basin through EU Trade Policy

Kimberly A. Nolan García

Although trade-based labor clauses have become a standard feature of US trade policy since 1994, and have been included in European Union (EU) accords since at least 2000, the inclusion of labor guarantees in trade has become increasingly common since 2008. Trade-related labor provisions, or labor clauses, refer to any standard introduced into a trade agreement to address labor standards, labor relations, or working conditions, then mechanisms for mechanisms for monitoring or promoting their compliance, or frameworks for cooperation on these labor matters.[1] In 2015, 76 trade accords included labor clauses, which means that given the growth of regional trade accords and spread of bilateral accords themselves in the same time frame, 80 percent of trade accords in force in the world now include some form of labor provision (ILO 2016, pp 23).

The EU remains a leader in this regard: policies since 2006 --to be addressed in this chapter—combined with unilateral provisions targeted to less-developed states, including the Generalized System of Preferences program (GSP), GSP+, and Everything but Arms arrangements currently extend labor rights obligations to 92 states through EU trade policy (ILO 2016, pp 24). The EU model is thus worth exploring just in terms of the spread of is reach through bilateral and LDC programs, and the potential then for the expansion of labor rights guarantees globally through EU trade policy.

Trade accords between the EU and Latin American countries are extensive, given that most LAS states continue to carry the bulk of their trade in North America, and in particular with the United States. The EU has full agreements with Caribbean states under the Cariforum Economic Partnership Agreement (since 2000) and Central American countries under the EU-CA Free Trade Association (2013). The EU also has bilateral agreements with four other Latin American states, Mexico, Chile, and Peru

---

1. This definition draws on that adopted by the International Labor Organisation (2016, pp 14).

and Colombia. Ecuador decided to join the Colombia and Peru agreement after dropping out of negotiations for an EU-Andean FTA, and negotiations for Ecuador's inclusion were completed in 2014 (EPRS, 2014). The EU accord with MERCOSUL (excluding Venezuela) now under consideration includes pillars on political cooperation and will feature a chapter on Trade and Sustainable Development. The extension of EU trade to the Latin American region in recent years, and the attachment of labor and human rights guarantees to those accords through EU policy represents the expansion of new forms of monitoring and enforcement of such guarantees into the region.

However, the EU model is interesting for additional reasons. First, while the US, Canada, Australia and Chile each created policies to include labor guarantees to trade accords, the EU conception of labor rights is the most expansive of all of the competing models (Lazo Grandi, 2009). The European Commission sets the international instruments of European and International *human rights* law as equal to international labor standards, which is an approach that contrasts to the limited focus on labor rights taken by the US in particular. As the EU continues to promote labor rights guarantees through trade, the result is more accurately the extension of human rights norms, promotion and protection. Second, as major trading states begin the process of reopening and revisiting older trade agreements in order to update them to meet the requirements of modern trade in services, e-commerce and so on, non-traditional areas of trade like social standards have been included as central areas of regulation and cooperation. Even as the EU model evolves as thinking on how to best link labor guarantees to trade changes, the European Commission has developed policies that seek to retrofit older accords with newer social standards. In the process of modernization of previously signed accords, labor rights and human rights guarantees are among the areas that must be included to the updated accords, often for the first time, to keep them consistent with EU policy on social guarantees in today's trade mandates.

This chapter considers the EU model for linking trade-based labor rights guarantees to trade policy in the context of the modernization of older EU trade accords, and the effort to retrofit older accords with new labor chapters. It describes first how social guarantees like human rights language was include in EU trade policy, how the emphasis on human rights protections gradually opened to include labor rights protections, and eventually led to dedicated chapters on Trade and Sustainable Development. It then compares the labor mechanisms and institutions of the "new generation" labor clauses to show how specific aspects of the labor chapters serve to promote and protect labor standards among EU trade partners, and therefore contribute to the enforcement of international labor standards in the Atlantic Basin. The last section discusses how the modernisation of older accords reinforces EU commitment to social guarantees through trade policy, with reference to the EU-Mexico agreement.

The importance of trade-based measures for the promotion of labor rights guarantees

The motivation to include labor rights guarantees into trade accords comes in part from the perception that trade competition leads to the erosion of domestic labor standards, especially in less-developed states. State leaders face incentives to relax regulations in order to attract international investors, which exacts downward pressure on labor standards and wage rates globally (Harrison and Scorse 2003; Pangalangan 2002), creating comparative advantages in labor costs among less-developed states (Rodrik 1996). While the record remains mixed, some quantitative studies have indeed shown that increases in trade are associated with increased labor rights violations, especially among developing countries. Some studies explore the effect of globalization writ large on labor rights indicators, and find that the opening of markets and extension of neoliberal economic principles, of which trade is a central factor, leads to the erosion of national labor protections (Blanton and Blanton, 2016; Blanton and Peksen, 2016.) There is also some evidence for weakened labor standards as a result of increased participation in trade (Mosley and Uno, 2007; Rodrik, 1997, and Cingranelli and Tsai, 2003), but evidence as well that increased trade leads instead to labor rights improvements (Greenhill, Mosley and Prakash, 2009; Davies and Vadlamannati 2013; Neumayer and de Soysa 2006). Country case studies suggest that labor standards are sometimes subject to selective regulation in the processing zones established to facilitate exports, leading to substandard working conditions (Frundt,1999; Frundt, 1998 and Gordon, 2000). Studies that focus on child labor in these areas show that the use of child labor tends to increase in highly labor-intensive exports sectors (Maskus, 1997), though child labor decreases with trade openness in other sectors of the economy (Neumayer and de Soysa, 2005).

Given the potential negative development consequences posed to less-developed states with trade liberalization, trade agreements are then increasingly seen as the best arena for promoting common standards to counteract the "race to the bottom" dynamic (Ross and Chan 2002). Including language and mechanisms intended to promote labor standards and decent working conditions into trade is one way to reestablish the minimum standards of employment for all workers party to trade agreements, because they establish regulations at the supranational level that can mitigate the incentives to limit rights at the national level.

Others argue that if labor costs, a function of weaker standards, are used as a comparative advantage in trade, labor standards should then be subject to dispute resolution just like tariff assessments, intellectual property rights, and investment rules (Ehrenberg, 1996; Moorman, 2001). Many trade-based clauses of the US models introduce fines and trade sanctions as consequences for labor rights violations in the trade accord structures. When labor conditionality is attached to trade agreements, labor rights compliance then becomes enforceable through dispute resolution as for other trade issues. States that relax labor standards to promote trade face strong incentives to improve labor rights performance and conform to promote labor rights in their countries to avoid negative and potentially costly consequences to their trading relationships (Rodrik 1996). Including social clauses meant to protect and promote labor obligations to trade agreements could mediate the potential negative effects of the intensification of trade on labor outcomes.

Though trade based social clauses are increasingly being incorporated into trade accords, there are still very few empirical studies available to understand the effect of including social accords on labor rights outcomes. One reason is the lack of comparative cross-national data, and the difficulties of creating comparable measures of labor rights compliance across states limits studies to qualitative assessments and country cases (Salem and Rozental, 2012). While Aissi, Peels and Samaan (2018) suggest an analytical framework going forward to establish metrics to critically and systematically assess social clause effectiveness, what we do know about the impact of trade based clauses on labor outcomes is skewed toward explaining US enforcement models, simply because EU, Canadian and other trade models have no petitions or cases from which to draw evidence.

Even so, quantitative assessments of the effects of trade-based labor clauses on promoting labor outcomes exist, though limited. The ILO 2016 study, which incorporates cross-national labor market outcomes from 2011 to 2014, finds support only for increases in labor force participation rates, including for increasing the employment of women (ILO, 2016, pp 81). While there are no negative effects, meaning attaching labor clauses to trade accords does not lead to the deterioration of labor standards, other tests were inconclusive, suggesting that additional work should be done on country-level effects.

Because clauses are new, impacts may take a number of years to take effect, and the impacts on workers maybe indirect: trade agreements often include regulations that require that trading partners adopt international standards like those expressed in the ILO *Fundamental Principles and Rights at Work* (1998), which in turn must become part of domestic law. It is domestic law and enforcement that then promotes international labor standards, and through this channel that changes labor market outcomes and respect for labor standards over time might be estimated. This channel of the improvement of labor rights within countries is suggested by the Postnikov and Bastiaens (2014) study, which tested EU accords and found that states were likely to adopt core labor standards into domestic labor regulations when facing the prospect of negotiating a trade deal, and that doing so created an *ex-post* improvement in labor protections (a finding also found by Kim (2012) in the case of US accords).

Hafner-Burton (2009) uses a data set that combines both EU and USA accords, and included human rights clauses and labor rights clauses in her study of the effects of binding enforcement measures for compliance as compared to non-binding mechanisms. She finds that one third of states improve their labor rights practices in preparation for signing an FTA with the within the two years of that FTA coming into force (2009, 161). In terms of effects while the FTA is in place, states that belong to EU FTAs with enforceable standards (meaning those with consultation mechanisms and access to sanctions) are more likely to improve their human rights practices over time than states that do not belong to accords with hard en-forcement mechanisms (2009, 162). Further, joining trade agreements with enforceable clauses has a greater demonstrated effect on influencing state behaviour than signing the UN personal integrity rights instruments.

Qualitative studies are skewed toward explaining outcomes for US based models, where access to trade sanctions, may alter the suitability of these studies to explain outcomes across other clauses that do not have bind-ing enforcement mechanisms, like those of the EU. Among the US pro-grammes, the US Generalized System of Preferences programme stands out as one which generally promoted overall improvements in labor rights protections in partner countries, particularly in Central America, and largely through the unilateral threat of suspending market access (Compa and Vogt, 2001; Frundt, 1998). In specific Central American cases, like the Dominican Republic, pressure from civil society through the GSP process helped to spur reform of the labor inspectorate (Shrank, 2009). In other Central America states, the GSP may have helped to resolve specific problems of union representation (Frundt, 1998), without making much progress on improving working conditions overall (Rodas-Martini 2006). Yet, when the same countries were graduated out of the GSP and subjected to a new set of institutional arrangements for labor under the CAFTA-DR labor clause, the few cases that were filed led to labor rights improvements only in very limited ways and only in a few states, and labor rights protections deteriorated in Honduras and Guatemala (Nolan García and O'Connor, *forthcoming*). The experience of Central America under CAFTA-DR, compared with the GSP gives evidence for Greven's claim that the effect of U.S. labor provisions on the promotion of labor rights depends in part on the presence of strong domestic social actors and social pressure (Greven, 2005).

Results have been more modest at the labor clause associated with the North American Free Trade Agreement. Scholars generally agree that NAFTA has been limited in its impact on the labor standards and practices of its partners, and in particular on Mexico, which faced larger challenges than the U.S. or Canada in implementation and enforcement of its labor regulations. Few cases filed under the NAALC have resulted in substantial improvement of labor rights protections in Mexico, or in the US (Dombois, 2002; Finbow, 2006; Garvey, 1995; Harvey, 1994), though there are exceptions as regards changes to labor policy and practices within Mexico (Aspinwall, 2009; Graubart, 2008; Kay, 2005; Singh and Adams, 2001), and again, largely due to outside pressure from civil society on Mexico to promote labor protections (Nolan García, 2014).

In sum, both quantitative and qualitative studies suggest that the adoption of trade-based labor clauses has helped in some cases to at least mitigate the erosion of labor protections, and in some cases have promoted labor standards in individual country cases. Even though clearly there is more work to be done on evaluating the trade and labor linkage cross-nationally, evidence so far points that there are important gains to be made from including labor clauses in trade agreements.

Social guarantees in EU trade agreements

The first EU agreements with social clauses, the Lomé Conventions of 1975 and their subsequent revisions, established trade cooperation between the EU and seventy-seven African and Caribbean States under preferential tariff regimes. These conventions included language around human rights protection in Article 5(2), and a monitoring mechanism. When Lomé was later replaced by the Cotonou Agreement in 2000, stronger language and enforcement mechanisms were introduced. The procedures for a formal review on human rights violations and the potential for trade sanctions in the event of grave violations are listed in Article 96. From 1996 through 2011, the clause was applied in 23 cases, including for reasons unrelated to human rights, as the consultation mechanism can be applied for coups, election fraud and breaches of the rule of law. Of these 23 cases, the application of human rights consultation mechanisms for human rights violations has occurred only in 2001 for Liberia and Zimbabwe, in 2004 for Togo, and in 2011 for Guinea-Bissau (Hachez 2015, p18-19). In practice, there has never been a full or partial trade embargo under Cotonou; rather, to avoid leveraging humanitarian costs on populations, sanctions come in the form of arms embargos, travel bans, revocations of visas, or freezing the assets of elites (Aaronson and Zimmerman 2008, 141).

Labor issues appear in EU accords in the early 2000s in the context of bilateral association agreements with Mediterranean states, including Tunisia, Morocco, Algeria, Egypt, Israel, Jordan and Lebanon. Though different in the design of institutions, these accords limited labor rights language to the non-discrimination of migrant workers in terms of social security, working conditions or wages.

It was the Association Agreements with South Africa (in force since 2000) and Chile (in force since 2003) that extended labor guarantees beyond migrant workers to the general working population of partner states, and beyond non-discrimination language. Both of these accords included space for cooperative activities related to international labor standards, though they did not reference the ILO instruments by name. Among areas for cooperation, the modernization of labor relations and promotion of social dialogue, better working conditions, and labor as key to development were emphasized. These areas would later become central to EU sustainable development chapters in later agreements, and to the eventual modernization of the Chile accord.

The European Commission's 2006 blueprint for bilateral trade, *Global Europe: Competing in the World* marked the emergence of a new emphasis on the protection and promotion of labor rights as a key component for sustainable development. These "new generation" agreements of the EU consider trade-related labor and environmental issues as part as a global approach to trade and sustainable development. After 2006, these goals were expressed in dedicated Social Development chapters attached to the accords, which include human rights, labor rights and environmental standards, cooperative activities, new instruments for social dialogue and steps for remediation. They are also the first EU accords to reference international instruments specifically such as the 1998 ILO Declaration, the United Nations (UN) Declaration on Full Employment and Decent Work, rather than strictly EU treaties and law.

The 2010 EU-South Korea agreement was the first to be ratified under the new focus, and accordingly, a new social clause incorporating both labor and environmental issues appears in Article 13. Treaties with Central America, Colombia and Peru, Georgia, Moldova, and Ukraine followed under the "new generation" model, with dedicated social rights guarantees in sustainable development chapters.

Later EU policy statements reinforced the use of trade instruments to promote and protect human rights. The ratification of the Lisbon Treaty in 2009 established human rights considerations as one of the principles guiding the Union's external activities. Then in 2012, the EU *Strategic Framework on Human Rights and Democracy*, established the priorities of the EU in promoting consistency around human rights and democracy in policies, and improving their effectiveness in EU external relations (Council of the EU, 2012). The *Framework*, together with the 2015 Action Plan for implementation, effectively mainstreams human rights and labor rights guarantees in EU foreign policy, including trade policy. Finally, *Trade for All* (2015) serves as the core policy pronouncement for the EU's new and comprehensive approach to streamlining human rights, labor rights and sustainability into trade policy specifically. For the first time, the EU shift in perspective is described as an opportunity to promote the diffusion of EU values around the world through trade structures and institutions (2015, p. 20).

New guidelines were developed by the EC and the Directorate General for Trade on how to operationalize EU commitment to European instruments of human rights protections and international law, and international fundamental labor rights conventions, into practical measures to then include in the trade negotiation process and design of new trade agreements. Among these measures was a new process that requires the Commission to include human rights criteria in all impact assessments for trade accords. The European Commission and DG TRADE devised specific guidelines that provide a methodology for executing human rights impact assessments (AIs), including the *Better Regulation Guidelines, the Better Regulation*

Toolbox. Guidelines on the Analysis of Human Rights Impacts in Impact Assessments for Trade-Related Policy Initiatives represents DG TRADE's in-house methodology for assessing the human rights impact of trade policy (European Commission, 2015). Together, these guidelines provide a concrete and systematized approach to assessing the potential human rights impacts of trade, and the estimation the magnitude of those effects.

The post-2012 guidelines are at the core of the current modernisation of EU accords to include sustainable development principles to older accords that do not include them, like the Association Agreement with Chile, and the Global Agreement with Mexico, and to new accords coming on line, like the EU-MERCOSUL Association Agreement and potential agreement with Indonesia. Beyond including the same human rights and labor rights guarantees in sustainable development chapters as the "new generation" agreements, they are also the first to undergo extensive pre- and post- negotiation impact assessments, including wide stakeholder consultations. Finally, as the 2012 Framework cites both international labor rights and human rights instruments, it also represents a return to the original emphasis on human rights guarantees from the early 1990 EU efforts, although with an extension of the types of international instruments and international law that is now included as part of EU policy.[2]

Institutions of EU chapters on trade and sustainable development

The "new generation" agreements are all similar in a number of aspects. Each agreement references the ILO 1998 *Declaration* in asserting that domestic law should remain consistent with the ILO core labor rights, meaning Freedom of Association, the effective recognition of the right to

---

2. The 2012 Framework cites a number of European and international human rights instruments as the sources and definitions for what the EU considers *fundamental rights*. These include Charter of Fundamental Rights of the European Union, The European Convention on Human Rights, The Universal Declaration of Human Rights, the conventions of the ILO 1988 Declaration of the Fundamental Principles and Rights at Work, and the core UN human rights treaties: *International Convention on the Elimination of All Forms of Racial Discrimination* (ICERD); *International Covenant on Economic, Social, and Cultural Rights* (ICESCR); *International Covenant on Civil and Political Rights* (ICCPR); *Convention on the Elimination of All Forms of Discrimination against Women* (CEDAW); *Convention against Torture and Other Cruel, Inhuman or Degrading Treatment or Punishment* (CAT); *Convention on the Rights of the Child* (CRC); The *International Convention on the Rights of Persons with Disabilities* (ICRPD); and *International Convention for the Protection of All Persons from Enforced Disappearance* (ICPED).

Collective Bargaining; elimination of all forms of forced or compulsory labor; the effective abolition of child labor; and elimination of discrimination in respect to employment and gender. They recognize the right of each Party to set its own levels of labor protection and establish priorities for its enforcement, while at the same time introducing no derogation principles which reaffirm that it is inappropriate to encourage trade or investment through lowering the levels of labor protection in domestic labor law and regulations. No EU agreement extends new burdens to Parties beyond implementing and enforcing existing domestic labor laws and international labor obligations.

From this common recognition of which labor rights are to be promoted in EU accords, the post 2006 agreements differ across the level of institutionalization in implementing the cooperative mechanisms by which partner states will meet their obligations.

Cooperative Activities

Cooperative activities play an important role in the diffusion of labor rights protection, including through information exchange and technical assistance, and therefore contribute to the spread of best practices through state to state dialogue. As such, fomenting cooperation is important to the trade and sustainable development emphasis of labor chapters. Even for agreements where the areas of cooperation are more limited in scope in comparison to other agreements, these still offer an extensive range of areas on which to cooperate and exchange information. These areas include the implementation of both international labor standards and domestic efforts at promoting decent work, and capacity building for administration of social security, human resources and job training. The EU-Singapore agreement presents the model of the most comprehensive set of cooperative activities. These entail information exchange, research activities, and the exchange of views around labor aspects of trade and sustainable development, including the linkages between international trade and domestic employment, laws and practices of industrial relations regimes, the collection of labor statistics, and other aspects of social protection.

However, state to state cooperation on labor issues is only possible to the extent that such cooperation is facilitated through bilateral institutions charged with managing cooperative activities. This points to a larger issue on how and when states determine where to begin to cooperate on labor issues, and it is where cases received for resolution and dialogue can have an agenda setting effect. The long list of the cooperative activities promoted in the early years of the labor side agreement of NAFTA through the National Administrative Offices established by the agreement for this purpose, which responded to recurrent labor rights issues across North America as expressed in the case files, gives credence to this claim. However, as will be noted below, the generation of even cooperative activities can only happen when states understand which areas of labor rights enforcement are problematic in partner states, that is, when cases draw attention to those issues. Without cases, as in the UE model, it is difficult to imagine a process by which partners would identify where to focus cooperative activities.

Monitoring mechanisms

In terms of dispute settlement procedures and case resolutions, EU agreements include some mechanism for the resolution of issues about the enforcement of labor standards that may arise during the course of the agreement. For all accords, dispute measures are unrelated to the dispute channels set for commercial issues in the general agreements. Also, dialogue and consultations, rather than sanction mechanisms, are central to EU agreements, though this has been the subject of controversy inside the Commission as well as across stakeholders. For example, Postnikov details how the European Trade Union Confederation (ETUC) lobbied to include enforceable trade sanctions in the EU Korea and EU Chile agreements, and the resistance by EU officials to do so (2013).

In the EU model, when issues arise, they are first discussed through offices established for this purpose ("points of contact") by each Party. If dialogue here does not solve the labor issue, all agreements allow for a series of additional stages of increasingly higher-level dialogue --across varying timelines-- to reach a solution, including meetings of the Sub-Committee (or Board) on Trade and Sustainable Development, in which Labor Ministries participate. If consultations fail, the next stage is recourse to a panel of experts, which creates non-binding preliminary and final reports, the end of which results in the creation of an Action Plan, the implementation of which is overseen by the Commission or Board. To date, no labor disputes have been brought to the board.

Each of the EU agreements provide a common basic outline of how a roster should be assembled from a list of potential experts on labor law, international trade, or trade disputes, and how such panels are to be formed. The EU-Singapore agreement stands out as including a particularly developed set of guidelines for both establishing a Roster of potential experts and for invoking the Panel of Experts, in Article 13.17.

Roles for stakeholders and civil society

The EU agreements reserve important for stakeholders, social partners and civil society in the implementation and monitoring of the labor chapters and any disputes resulting from them. The European Transparency Initiative (ETI) of 2008 established a framework for Civil Society Dialogues, including for trade, which aims to increase transparency on how trade policy is made, but also address concerns about the impact of trade on civil society. Following this framework, all new generation accords feature a formal venue for the participation of representatives from labor, business and environmental groups of all participating states.

The Domestic Advisory Groups (DAG) represents civil society interests in the Trade and Sustainable Chapter of agreements and serves to advise the Commissions and other bodies on its implementation. The members of the group are to meet annually, and the DAG is to also meet with Sub-Committee on Trade and Sustainable Development to discuss the implementation of the sustainable development chapter.

However, across agreements, the additional roles for stakeholders vary. While for all EU agreements, stakeholders are to be included through the DAG to discussions on the implementation of the agreement, often in parallel with government to government meetings, in almost all other areas, stakeholders play a very limited role. Stakeholders hold the most expansive role in the Singapore agreement. There is no DAG in this accord, instead stakeholders serve in multiple Advisory Groups to the Board in dialogues with the Parties, are invited to make comments on the initial drafts of reports by the panel of experts, and Parties must inform stakeholders of results of Action Plans resulting from expert panels.

While these formal channels serve the purpose of fulfilling the ETI mandate, there has been plenty of criticism of them, along the lines of how well they channel civil society representation versus merely fill an administrative function. Orbie et. al. (2014) raise the question of the selection of representatives to the Councils. Because these are not transparent, they ask whether there is a deliberate exclusion of representatives critical of trade itself (pp 528). Further it is not clear as to whether members from partner states are truly representative of their respective interest groups, or whether they are independent from their governments (pp 528). The major concern however is whether and how the work of these consultative channels is fed back in to EU policymaking in any concrete way, or whether there is follow up (pp 529). Some work suggests that the councils are lacking on all dimensions and therefore are ineffective in promoting the opinions of the public at large on trade policy. For example, Postnikov (2013) writes that the Commissions almost never meet.

In response, the EU has recently released a set of actions to address the shortcomings of the role of stakeholders in enforcing EU accords, in part as response to this ongoing criticism, and in part as a result of the feedback the Commission received during stakeholder consultations that were implemented for the first time as part of the impact assessments for the modernized EU-Chile and EU-Mexico accords and for the new EU-MERCOSUL accord (Commission Services, 2018). Core to this programme is strengthening the role of the DAGs and the joint civil society forums to facilitate their role in monitoring implementation of the Trade and Sustainable Development chapters, including new money to facilitate communication across the DAGs of each accord.

It is important to note that none of the EU agreements have received cases for discussion to date, in part because in contrast to the other models, there is no formal channel for stakeholders to bring cases to dialogue with the parties. While the new EU directive does project a more streamlined response system in terms of establishing timelines to respond to requests, it does not mention any new rules in place to support complaints from stakeholders in labor rights issues in EU trading partners (Commission Services, 2018). In order to promote labor clauses as a tool not just for the implementation of labor standards, but also to promote cooperation between states to improve labor related domestic practices, it is case filings that identify issues and priorities around to which to focus resources and effort. In the absence of cases, stakeholder inputs can reveal major labor rights enforcement issues that could be addressed through state to state dialogue, or provide the material for cooperative activities, which is the linchpin for spreading best practices.

Strengthening the EU model in the modernization process

The Commission has proposed the modernisation of the EU-Mexico and EU-Chile accords, which are earlier agreements, concluded respectively in 2000 and 2002. As the first accords of the Latin American agreements, they are less advanced than the more recently negotiated EU agreements with other LAS states, and very recent EU agreements like the EU agreement with Canada (CETA). While the EU- Mexico accord, for example, was already less advanced than NAFTA, the negotiations of the TTP, to which both Mexico and Chile are party, threatened to make EU agreements obsolete in relation to competing agreements with those countries' other trade partners like the US, in terms of comprehensive coverage. For example, The EU-Mexico and EU-Chile accords have limited WTO+ provisions on intellectual property rights, services, investment and regulatory provisions compared to later EU agreements. For example, more recent agreements include TRIPS + provisions while the Chile and Mexico accords do not, and while the EU-Mexico and EU-Chile agreement incorporate some GATS+ features, more recently negotiated agreements have further developed regulatory issues, including data protection.

Equally important is that neither the EU-Chile or EU-Mexico accords included sustainable development provisions, though some of the labor, human rights, and in the case of Mexico, quality of democracy issues were partly covered by political dialogues, both should be aligned with the *Trade for All* agenda.

The modernization of these accords, and the signing of additional ones based on the 2012 framework, provides an opportunity to improve upon the weaknesses of the "new generation" model presented in the preceding section. Important issues remain in the design of the sustainable development chapters, which in turn affects how well the clauses can be enforced, and ultimately their usefulness as tools to promote labor rights through EU trade.

Clearly the first step in modernising the older accords in this direction is in introducing sustainable development chapters that mirror the formal institutions of the post-2006 agreements, and that are in line with the 2012 Guidelines and *Trade for All* directives. The established pattern of EU "new generation" clauses each include a) the same emphasis on the right to establish national labor regulation and law, and determine national priorities for the application of labor law, b) a no derogation clause, c) reaffirm national commitments to the ILO fundamental labor standards of the 1998 Declaration by ensuring national labor regulations are consistent with the Declaration and d) refer to the ILO fundamental labor standards in establishing labor standards for the trade agreement itself. They also include e) major emphasis on state to state cooperation on labor issues f) some combination of institutional structures to manage cooperation, g) dispute resolution mechanisms between states which rely on dialogue, panels of experts and action plans to improve labor rights protections within states and h) formal if limited, roles for stakeholders. New Chile and Mexico accords, and forthcoming MERCOSUL and other agreements, should incorporate then all of these elements as the minimum acceptable framework for trade and build from there.

Modernization of the EU-Mexico Global Agreement

In April of 2018, the European Commission announced that it had reached a provisional framework agreement with Mexico on the modernization of the EU-Mexico Global Agreement, first signed in 1997, and in force since 2000. In addition to creating new rules for trade in services, adding deep reductions on tariffs of many goods, especially agriculture, and widening procurement and investment opportunities for both actors, the agreement will feature for the first time a dedicated chapter on Trade and Sustainable Development.

The Trade and Sustainable Development chapter has an enhanced role for the ILO in comparison to earlier accords. For example, while the ILO 1998 *Declaration* remains the base instrument for identifying which core or fundamental labor rights are included in the agreement, the chapter makes emphasized reference to the need for both parties to make progress on signing and ratifying the core Conventions of the Declaration (EU Commission 2018, p3). This is important because it offers a new tool for dialogue on securing Mexico's compliance with Convention 98 on the Right to Organize and Bargain Collectively, which Mexico signed but has tabled for ratification. Freedom of association and collective bargaining rights are at the core of Mexico's "protection contract" system, which limits union registration and the right to affiliation to unions of a worker's choice, the result of which has been the denial of worker's voices in workplace issues. The refusal to ratify Convention 98 and its consequences for workers has been the source of multiple filings in the ILO Committee of experts (CEACR) and the Freedom of Association panels. Creating an expanded role for the ILO here both places this agreement beyond earlier accords in terms of reach, and provides for additional channels for Mexico's compliance with the fundamental Conventions.

This agreement also creates new channels for engagement with civil society not found in other accords, and novel for EU-Mexico relations. The EU established new channels for engagement with Mexican civil society as part of the stakeholder engagement for impact assessments, and from there has built in as part of the agreement funding to continue that dialogue. As part of this initiative, NGOs and other social actors would be able to apply for EU funding to sustain programs to promote labor rights and social dialogue in Mexico, which is a virtually undeveloped area of EU-Mexico cooperation.

Finally, part of the enforcement process of the chapter includes sustained and periodic high level dialogue between Mexico and the EU on Mexico's human rights record. The accord then establishes for the first time a channel of Mexican accountability to the EU for these important issues, which could serve to pressure Mexico to improve its performance here.

Moving forward on cooperation on labor

Any new agreement from the EU will include channels for state-to-state cooperation around labor issues as part of the new emphasis on labor and human rights guarantees in trade as representing EU core values. Cooperative activities can play an important role in the diffusion of labor rights protection, including through information exchange and technical assistance, and therefore contribute to the spread of best practices through state to state dialogue. As such, fomenting cooperation is important to the trade and sustainable development emphasis of the labor chapters. Even the agreements where the areas of cooperation are more limited in scope, as compared to other agreements, the still of offer an extensive range of areas on which to cooperate and exchange information, across implementation of both international labor standards and domestic efforts at promoting decent work, capacity building for administration of social security, human resources and job training.

However, this analysis has argued that the mechanisms for cooperative mechanisms are best used when there are cases that draw attention to which types of labor issues should be addressed by consultations. The major failing of the EU model is that even given the expansive role for stakeholder consultations and participation in advisory groups, there is no channel for any civil society actor to bring cases or complaints against trade partners. One solution is to open the institutional and monitoring mechanisms to stakeholders, by giving Domestic Advisory Groups standing to request Government Consultations. In doing so, parties to the agreements and any commissions formed to implement the labor chapters could not just incentivize the role of civil society in the agreements, but harness the agenda setting aspect of receiving cases to determine where to prioritize cooperative activities, and thus give momentum to the cooperative aspects of the labor chapters. The "next generation" of EU trade and labor agreements could continue to emphasize the "cooperation through dialogue" that is at core of the European approach to labor standards and trade, but notably improve upon the effectiveness of both by opening the dispute mechanisms to stakeholder requests. Doing so may create the incentives for stakeholders to become more invested in the process, thus generating cases to discuss, and with this, reinforcing the cooperative aspects of the accord.

References

Aissi, Jonas, Rafael Peels, R. and Daniel Samaan. (2018), Evaluating the Effectiveness of Labor Provisions in Trade Agreements—An Analytical Framework. *International Labor Review*. First view, September 8, 2017. https://doi.org/10.1111/ilr.12066

Aspinwall, Mark. 2009. *Side Effects: Mexican Governance Under NAFTA's Labor and Environmental Agreements*. Stanford: Stanford University Press.

Blanton, Robert G., and Shannon Lindsey Blanton. 2016. "Globalization and Collective Labor Rights." *Sociological Forum* 31 (1): 181–202.

Blanton, Robert G., and Dursun Peksen. 2016. "Economic Liberalization, Market Institutions, and Labor Rights," *European Journal of Political Research* 55 (2):474-91.

Cingranelli, David L, and Chang-yen Tsai. 2003. "Democracy, Globalization and Worker's Rights: A Comparative Analysis." Unpublished MS, Binghamton, NY: Departmemt of Political Science.

EU Commission Services. 2018. *Feedback and way forward on improving the implementation and enforcement of Trade and Sustainable Development chapters in EU Free Trade Agreements*. Non paper of the Commission services (February 26). EC:Brussels. http://trade.ec.europa.eu/doclib/docs/2018/february/tradoc_156618.pdf, accessed May 10, 2018.

Council of the European Union. (2012). *EU Strategic Framework and Action Plan on Human Rights and Democracy*. https://www.consilium.europa.eu/uedocs/cms_data/docs/pressdata/EN/foraff/131181.pdf, accessed 12 December 2017.

Davies, Ron, and Krishna Chaitanya Vadlamannati. 2013. "A Race to the Bottom in Labor Standards? An Empirical Investigation". *Journal of Development Economics* 103, pp 1-14.

Dombois, Ranier. 2002. "Labor Regulation by the North American Agreement on Labor Cooperation: A Problem of Deficient Design?" *Paper Prepared for the 54th Annual Meeting of the International Industrial Relations Society*.

Ehrenberg, Daniel S. 1996. "From Intention to Action: An ILO/ WTO Enforcement Regime for International Labor Rights." In *Human Rights, Labor Rights and International Trade*, edited by Lance Compa and Stephen F Diamond, 163–80. Philadelphia: University of Pennsylvania Press.

European Commission. 2018. *EU-Mexico Free Trade Agreement, EU Textual Proposal, Chapter on Trade and Sustainable Development*. April.

European Commission. 2015a. *Trade for All: Towards a more Responsible Trade and Investment Policy*. http://trade.ec.europa.eu/doclib/docs/2015/october/tradoc_153846.pdf, accessed January 29, 2018.

European Commission. 2015b. *Guidelines on the Analysis of Human Rights Impacts in Impact Assessments for Trade-related Policy Initiatives*. http://trade.ec.europa.eu/doclib/docs/2015/july/tradoc_153591.pdf, accessed January 26, 2018.

European Parliamentary Research Service (EPRS). 2016. *EU–Latin America Trade Relations: Overview and Figures*. EPRS document PE 579.086. Brussels: EPRS.

Finbow, Robert. 2006. *The Limits of Regionalism: NAFTA's Labor Accord*. Burlington, VT: Ashgate.

Frundt, Henry J. 1998. *Trade Conditions and Labor Rights: US Initiatives, Dominican and Central American Responses*. Miami: University Press of Florida.

— — —. 1999. "Cross-Border Organizing in the Apparel Industry: Lessons from Central America and the Caribbean." *Labor Studies Journal*, vol 24 (1):89-106.

Garvey, Jack I. 1995. "Trade Law and Quality of Life: Dispute Resolution under the NAFTA Side Accords on Labor and the Environment." *The American Journal of International Law* 89 (2 (April)): 439–53.

Gordon, Michael. 2000. "Export Processing Zones." In *Transnational Cooperation among Labor Unions*, edited by Lowell Turner, 60–78. Ithaca: Cornell University Press.

Graubart, Jonathan. 2008. *Legalizing Transnational Activism: The Struggle to Gain Social Change from NAFTA's Citizen Petitions*. University Park: University of Pennsylvania Press.

Greenhill, Brian, Layna Mosley, and Aseem Prakash. 2009. "Trade-based Diffusion of   Labor Rights: A Panel Study, 1986–2002". *American Political Science Review* 103 (4, November) 669-690.

Greven, Thomas. 2005. *Social standards in bilateral and regional trade and investment agreements instruments*, Friedrich-Ebert-Stiftung Occasional Paper 16. Geneva: FES.

Hafner-Burton, Emilie M. 2009. *Forced to Be Good: Why Trade Agreements Boost Human Rights*. Ithaca: Cornell University Press.

Harrison, Ann E., and Jason Scorse. 2003. "Globalization's Impact on Compliance with Labor Standards." *Brookings Trade Forum* 2003 (1): 45–96.

Harvey, Pharis J. 1994. "Failure of the Labor Side Agreement." In *NAFTA's First Year: Lessons for the Hemisphere*, edited by Sarah Anderson and John Cavanaugh, 12–19. Washington, D.C.: Alliance for Responsible Trade.

International Labor Organisation. 2016. *Assessment of Labor Provisions in Trade and Investment Arrangements*, International Labor Organization: Geneva, 202 pp.   http://www.ilo.org/global/publications/books/WCMS_498944/lang--en/ index.htm, accessed 20 January, 2018.

Kay, Tamara. 2005. "Labor Transnationalism and Global Governance: The Impact of NAFTA on Transnational Labor Relationships in North America." *American Journal of Sociology* 111 (3): 715–56.

Kim, Moonhawk. 2012. "Ex Ante Due Diligence: Formation of PTAs and Protection of Labor Rights." *International Studies Quarterly* 56 (4), 1–16.

Lazo Grandi, Pablo. 2009. "Trade Agreements and Their Relation to Labor Standards: The Current Situation." *ICTSD Issue Paper*. Geneva.

Maskus, Keith E. 1997. "Should Core Labor Standards Be Imposed through International Trade Policy?" Policy Research Working Papers. Washington, D.C.: The World Bank.

Moorman, Yasmin. 2001. "Integration of ILO Core Rights Labor Standards into the WTO." *Columbia Journal of Transitional Law* 39.

Mosley, L., and S. Uno. 2007. Racing to the Bottom or Climbing to the Top? Economic Globalization and Collective Labor Rights. *Comparative Pol. Studies* 40 (8): 923–48.

Neumayer, Eric, and Indra De Soysa. 2006."Globalization and the Right to Free Association and Collective Bargaining: An Empirical Analysis." *World Development* 34(1): 31-49.

— — —. 2005. "Trade Openness, Foreign Direct Investment and Child Labor." *World Development* 33(1):43-63.

Nolan García, Kimberly A. 2014. "Internalización de las normas laborales internacionales bajo el marco del TLCAN: El caso mexicano," *Norteamérica* 9:1, pp 111-141.

Nolan García, Kimberly A. and Elizabeth O'Connor (*forthcoming*). *The Effectiveness of Trade Based Clauses in Improving Labor Rights Protections: The Case of the CAFTA-DR Labor Clause*. Geneva: International Labor Organization.

Orbie, Jan, Deborah Martens, Myriam Oehri and Lore Van den Putte. 2016. ""Promoting Sustainable Development or Legitimizing Free Trade?: Civil Society Mechanisms in EU Trade Agreements, *Third World Thematics* 1 (4): 526-546.

Pangalangan, Raul C. 2002. "Sweatshops and International Labor Standards: Globalizing Markets, Localizing Norms." In *Globalization and Human Rights*, edited by Raul C Pangalangan and Alison Brysk, 98–114. Berkeley: University of California Press.

Postnikov, Evgeny, and Ida Bastiaens. 2014. "Does Dialogue Work? The Effectiveness of Labor Standards in EU Preferential Trade Agreements." *Journal of European Public Policy* 21 (6): 923–40.

Rodas-Martini, Pablo. 2006. Labor Commitment in the Central America Free Trade Agreement (CAFTA): A Non-Negotiated Negotiation. *Integration and Trade*, 10 (25), 281-296.

Rodrik, Dani. 1996. "Labor Standards in International Trade: Do They Matter and What Do We Do About Them?" In *Emerging Agendas for Global Trade: High Stakes for Developing Countries*, 35–79.

———. 1997. *Has Globalization Gone Too Far?* Washington: Institute for International Economics.

Ross, Robert, and Anita Chan. 2002. "From North-South to South-South: The True Face of Global Competition." *Foreign Affairs,* September.

Salem, Samira, and Faina Rozental. 2012. Labor Standards and Trade: A Review of Recent Empirical Evidence. *J. of International Commerce and Economics*, August: 1–36.

Singh, P. and Roy J Adams. 2001. "Neither a Gem Nor a Scam: The Progress of the North American Agreement on Labor Cooperation." *Labor Studies Journal* 26 (1)

Chapter Six

Public Attitudes to Regional Integration in Atlantic Latin America

Mark Aspinwall

This chapter looks at the causes of individual attitudes to regional integration in Latin America. Many scholars have considered how individuals perceive European integration, and some others have examined the attitudes of Latin Americans and US citizens to free trade and regionalism. But few have applied the lessons from Europe to Latin American states to identify the structure of attitudes there. A better understanding of how citizens in Latin America perceive regional integration is important, and especially a clearer understanding of what structures their attitudes—whether it is material incentives; ideology and party identification, education levels, or something else.

The results of this study will help us better understand public attitudes in Latin America, and it will help close some of the gaps in understanding across the Atlantic region. While we know a great deal about the structure of public attitudes in Europe toward European integration, the same is not true of Latin America. In Europe, integration is perceived by citizens not simply as a means to create (or destroy) economic opportunities—a material rationale—but is also seen as a means by which the dominant cultural identity may be weakened by outsiders who gain access through free movement rules. It is also seen as a means to control domestic politicians, prevent backsliding on reforms and ideally to control corruption. Whether those same perceptions are present in Latin American attitudes to regional integration is the aim of this study. Do residents of Latin American countries see regional integration in the same way as their counterparts around the Atlantic Basin? Are there patterns in their support for regional agreements?

Attitudes to regional integration

EU studies mainly look at attitudes to European integration and the EU, whereas due to lack of data there is less work on Latin American attitudes to regional integration (but see Seligson 1999; Maldonado and Marin 2018;

Davis et al 1998; Merolla et al 2005; Deutschmann and Minkus 2018). These studies often do not seek to explain support for a particular regional agreement, but rather support for the more abstract notion of regional integration.

In Europe, anti-European Union attitudes are not necessarily explained by opposition to free trade, although some findings have highlighted the importance of material considerations (such as occupation). Other studies suggest that ideology or party support (political cues), and education are more important than material considerations.

In one of the earliest studies seeking to understand support for European integration, Matthew Gabel found strong support for utilitarian explanation of public attitudes to European integration (Gabel 1998). Public support in original member states was more likely to be influenced by political values and cognitive mobilization, while in newer member states attitudes were more shaped by elite actions and utilitarian concerns. There was also some evidence that support for the government predicts support for integration in a positive way.

In an important and widely cited study, Hooghe and Marks (2005) found that community identity was a stronger predictor of support for European integration than a utilitarian calculus. In other words, where citizens saw themselves as having an exclusively national identity, they tended to be more anti-EU. Also, where political elites were divided about European integration, citizens tended to be more negative toward it, especially among those individuals who see their identity as exclusively national.

Other work shows that educational levels have mixed effects on support for integration. Hakhverdian et al (2013) show that the impact of educational levels on support for European integration has become stronger, probably because of a deepening cleavage between the winners and losers of globalization. Human capital, convertible skills, networking, mobility, and related factors lead to utilitarian variation. These skills and attributes are affected by education. Educational attainment and Euroscepticism are negatively correlated, but educational attainment interacts with utilitarian considerations, political cues, and identity.

They delineate between an earlier research tradition that identified utilitarian explanations for anti-Europeanism, and later ones that see identity, cultural and national attachments, political parties, the media, and other domestic factors as important. Cuing by media and political parties plays a role in support for European integration, but cue influence declines as education increases. Identity is affected by perceptions of cultural and sovereignty threats. Nationalism and cultural intolerance predict Euro-scepticism, but Euro-scepticism is predicted by education levels as well. These relationships are established in the literature, but they find that the gaps have become more pronounced over time, particularly since the Maastricht Treaty in the early 1990s. This is because the salience and reach of the EU have increased.

Yet other work indicates that economic ideology interacts with local economic conditions. Garry and Tilley (2015) show that EU citizens are affected by both economic ideology and the context of their national political economy. Those who are leftist and live in member states with high income inequality and low state ownership are supportive of European integration, while those on the left who live in member states with low income inequality and high state ownership are more sceptical. This is because of anticipated economic effects of European integration in comparison with pre-existing national conditions.

A number of recent studies have shed some light on how citizens of Eastern and Central Europeans countries view European integration. This is pertinent because their lower income levels make them somewhat comparable with Latin American states themselves engaged with questions of regional integration. In some cases, public attitudes were closely connected to perceptions of material gain. Jackson et al (2011), for example, showed that positive attitudes toward the EU among Poles before and after entry in 2004 were related to the size of EU transfers and gains in personal income. Poles viewed the EU in instrumental terms. Herzog and Tucker (2010) show that economic winners in Eastern and Central Europe were consistently more likely to support EU membership than economic losers over the 1991-2003 period, and that this relationship strengthened as membership became more likely. This relationship was also found by Tucker et al (2002): economic winners in Eastern and Central Europe are more likely to support membership, as are those who support the free market. The rationale is that EU membership serves to prevent backsliding on economic reforms by these countries.

On the other hand, some research indicated that citizens in applicant member states had already (during the period before entry) assimilated the European issue into the Left-Right ideology dynamic and into the identity dynamic, much as had occurred in older member states. Cichowski (2000) found that attitudes about joining the EU in applicant countries was most strongly predicted by individuals' attitudes toward democracy and capitalism, and also by individuals' political partisanship. Thus, utilitarian explanations understood as sector-specific benefits are less predictive in these cases.

Elgün and Tillman (2007) found that public support for EU membership in Eastern and Central European applicant states depends on attitudes toward national politics and social identity (ie, respondents' beliefs about cultural threats). Also, the educational level of citizens affects their attitudes, depending on how much exposure citizens have to the impacts of integration. The more exposure they have, the more important the 'human capital' variable as a predictor of support. They argue that utilitarian attitudes depend on exposure to integration effects and educational experience. Finally, attitudes to the EU in Romania are affected by views of domestic political problems, such as corruption, and perceptions that the EU can improve local governance and reduce corruption by monitoring national politics.

Where does this brief review of findings leave us?

Essentially, it leaves us with a mixed picture in terms of predicting what might cause support for regionalism in the Atlantic states of Latin America. It could well be that non-economic and non-cultural factors drive and structure attitudes—including exposure to the outside world in general, and individuals' attitudes to immigrants and national pride. On the other hand, citizens may perceive regional integration in purely material terms—how much have they benefited from participation in the regional organization? In the next section I set out several hypotheses based on the brief review of literature above. In the section that follows I test these hypotheses using the LAYEM datasets. And in a final section I conclude.

Hypotheses

Drawing from this work to deduce plausible causal relationships, I hypothesize that attitudes toward regional agreements will be structured by several material, ideational, cognitive, or identity variables, including education, income levels, attitudes to globalization, national identity, ideology, and contact with the outside world (such as travel, remittances, living outside, and presence of foreigners in the country).

The dependent variable is attitudes toward regional integration of which their country is part, which means NAFTA in the case of Mexico, and MERCOSUL in the case of Brazil and Argentina. For Colombia, I test explanations of the US-Colombia preferential trade agreement (which came into effect in 2012), and separately, explanations of MERCOSUL, of which Colombia is an associate member.

I hypothesize that attitudes to these regional accords is explained by:

- *Income levels.* Higher income levels are likely to be associated with higher support for regional agreements because higher-income citizens are more likely to be engaged in international economic activity.

- *Exposure to international economic effects.* Receipt of remittances or time spent in other countries will be associated with higher support for regional trade agreements because of the positive economic connotations of international economic activity. Exposure to foreigners within the country will be associated with lower levels of support for regional agreements because of the competition effect felt by domestic workers.

- *Education.* Those with higher levels of education will be more supportive of regional agreements because their economic opportunities and/ or cultural awareness will be higher.

- *Ideology.* Those whose self-placement in ideological space is more to the Right will be more in favor of regional agreements because their ideological worldview accords more closely with liberal trade accords. Those whose self-placement in ideological space is more to the Center in Left-Right space will be more in favor of regional agreements because (following findings in Europe), they are less likely to oppose liberal trade accords for either nationalist reasons (Right) or economic outcomes reasons (Left).

- *Attitudes to economic globalization.* Those who favor economic globalization will also favor regional agreements because of the role the latter play in fostering economic openness.

- *Identity.* Those who hold attitudes of national pride will be less supportive of regional agreements because the agreements are likely to erode national economic protections or permit the entry of foreign influences, such as products, services, practices, customs or ideas.

Data and methodology

I use data from the 2014 wave of the biennial Las Americas y el Mundo (LAYEM) survey for Mexico, Colombia, Brazil, and Argentina. These surveys question citizens in numerous Latin American countries about their attitudes to the outside world. I employ simple linear regressions and two logistic models to determine causal probabilities between variables. I used the linear regressions to determine support for MERCOSUL and NAFTA (which are on a 0 to 100 scale) and the logistic models to assess the likelihood of answering that either Colombia or the US benefited most from the free trade agreement between the two countries. The questionnaire used in the LAYEM polls asked a variety of questions about individual attitudes. Some of the responses were on a 0 to 100 scale, while others were on 4-point Likert scales, or were categorical yes or no responses. This required adjustment of the datasets by converting all values of the variables to standard deviation units so the coefficients would be comparable.

Models were constructed in the following manner. First, I test several control variables (gender, household income, education) along with ideology against the dependent variable. Ideology is tested in two ways: first, I look at the effect of self-placement in Left-Right space, to see if more Right-leaning respondents are more positive about regional agreement; second, I look at the effect of distance from the ideological center (extremism), to see if those whose ideologies are more extreme are less likely to support regional agreements.

After these initial tests, I then add a variable to measure the impact of travel abroad on attitudes to regional agreements. The presumed relationship is that more travel abroad will lead to more positive attitudes to regional agreements. I also add a variable on remittances to determine whether this has an impact on attitudes to regional agreements. Here the relationship is also assumed to be positive, given the possibility of more opportunities for regional workers and the material benefits that flow.

Next, I add a variable to measure the impact of national pride on attitudes to regional agreements. Again, the hypothesized relationship is that higher levels of national pride will lead to lower levels of support for regionalism, given the likely foreign influences that flow from membership of regional organizations. Finally, I add a variable on attitudes to economic globalization to ascertain how these attitudes may affect views about regional agreements. Obviously, the more positively an individual views economic globalization, the more positively I expect her to view regional agreements.

I used the Akaike Information Criterion to evaluate model fit of different models using the same data sets. The AIC estimates the information lost in each model and therefore its outcomes most be interpreted as the lower the number, the better the model (Akaike 1987). For all cases analyzed here, the model with the best AIC score was the one including all variables except one where it scored the second best (Mexico 2014). This result allows us to rely on the interpretation of the models including all variables of the four categories (sociodemographic, exposure, nationalism and attitudes toward globalization).

Results

The results for Argentina indicate that in most respects, attitudes to regional integration are structured differently than in Europe. Neither household income, nor education, nor Left-Right ideological position have an impact on attitudes toward MERCOSUL. However, when the Left-Right spatial position is converted to distance from the Center, the relationship *is* significant at the 0.05 level (See Appendices for all results). As individuals' ideological views move farther Left *and* Right, they become more opposed to MERCOSUL. The effect is very strong—even just slight movements away from the Center have a large effect on attitudes to MERCOSUL. This is consistent with some findings in Europe (Aspinwall 2002) and is explained by reference to the economic nationalism of the Left (preserve state choice on economic matters) and the cultural nationalism of the Right (exclude the foreigner).

Travel abroad is a not significant explanatory variable. Interestingly, though national pride is statistically significant at the 0.05 level, it is in the opposite direction expected—that is, the more important a person feels that pride in Argentina is, the more supportive of MERCOSUL she is. This is the opposite of Europe, where national identity is associated with anti-regional integration views. At the same time, addition of these two variables strengthens the explanatory power of ideological extremism. In other words, controlling for gender, education, household income, travel abroad, and national pride—ideological extremism remains a statistically significant explanation of support for MERCOSUL.

A final independent variable, support for economic globalization, also fails to explain support for MERCOSUL. In this full model, ideological extremism washes out as an explanatory variable, but position toward the Right of the ideological spectrum does become a predictor of MERCOSUL support (significant at the 0.1 level), and with a large effect. Men were also more supportive of MERCOSUL in this model, but it is the only model in the entire study in which gender made a statistically-significant difference in terms of support for regional agreements.

In conclusion results from 2014 attitudes in Argentina suggest that support for regionalism is not structured in the same way as in Europe. Explanatory variables found in Europe largely fail to predict MERCOSUL attitudes, with the exception of ideological extremism (and in one model, Right ideology).

In Brazil the results are very different. In all but one model, ideology is not associated at all with MERCOSUL support. In the simplest sociodemographic model, household income and education are highly significant and have a large impact on attitudes to regionalism. The higher the household income and the more education, the more positive are people's views toward MERCOSUL.

In a second model, exposure to international influences also contributes explanatory power. In this case, 'exposure to international influences' is measured both by travel abroad and by receipt of remittances. The remittances variable has no impact at all, but oddly, travel abroad is negatively associated with MERCOSUL support—the more a person travels outside Brazil, the less they support MERCOSUL. Education and income remain significant explanations too. In addition, position to the Right on the Left-Right spectrum is associated with support for MERCOSUL. This contrasts with Argentina, where closeness to the ideological Center is what predicted support for MERCOSUL.

The third model considers the impact of attitudes to foreigners living in Brazil and national pride. Neither are significant explanatory variables. However, in the variant which measures Left-Right placement (as opposed to ideological extremism), four variables are significant predictors of support for MERCOSUL—higher income, more education, ideologically Right positioning, and less travel abroad. Finally, in a fourth model, I add in attitudes to foreign trade and economic globalization. Neither help predict regionalism support. In fact, in this model, all variables lose explanatory power.

In sum, explanations for MERCOSUL attitudes are very different in Brazil than in Argentina. Material and cognitive explanations work best, along with foreign travel (though the latter in the opposite direction predicted).

For Colombia, I review the results for attitudes to MERCOSUL first, then look at attitudes toward the US-Colombia Free Trade Agreement. Attitudes to MERCOSUL are similar to what was found in Argentina. Gender, income and education do not predict MERCOSUL positions, nor does Left-Right ideology. However, in the initial model, extremism does predict support for MERCOSUL, in the direction anticipated—that is, less centrist respondents are more opposed to the regional agreement.

Adding travel abroad and receipt of remittances in the second model does not improve predictability. Neither are statistically significant predictors. However, national pride is associated with more pro-MERCOSUL opinion, as with Argentina. Attitudes to foreigners in Colombia is also statistically insignificant as a predictor, though in this third model, extremism and national pride are significant and have powerful effects.

In the fourth model, I add attitudes to economic globalization and to free trade as variables. Both economic globalization and free trade are significant and strong predictors of MERCOSUL opinion, and the relationships are positive. Ideological extremism in this model remains a significant and strong predictor of MERCOSUL opinion in a negative direction.

In conclusion, like Argentina, closeness to the ideological center helps us understand why Colombians support MERCOSUL. Moreover, national pride is positively associated with MERCOSUL support in some models, and so is attitude to economic globalization and free trade. The latter, unsurprisingly, are positively associated with support for the regional agreement.

Interestingly, attitudes toward the US-Colombia Free Trade Agreement are structured differently. Those with higher levels of education are most likely to believe that the *US benefitted* more than Colombia from the Agreement, and the relationship is highly significant in all models. On the other hand, ideological position is not associated with preferences on the Agreement. In fact, the only other variables that explain attitudes to the Agreement are national pride (negatively associated and significant at the 0.01 level in the full model) and opinion on economic globalization (negatively associated and significant at the 0.001 level). What this means is that those who feel national pride and those who support economic globalization do not believe that the United States benefitted most from the trade accord with the United States.

Turning this analysis around, I next examined the probability of answering that *Colombia benefitted* more from the Agreement. In this analysis, education is also highly significant, and is negatively associated with beliefs that Colombia benefitted more. Ideological extremism is also negatively associated with this dependent variable. Ideological extremists (Left and Right) do not believe that Colombia benefitted most from the Agreement, as per my earlier hypothesis. Finally, national pride, positive opinion on economic globalization, and positive opinion on free trade are all statistically significant predictors of beliefs that Colombia benefitted more from the Agreement.

The case of Mexico presents very interesting findings, some consistent with the other countries in this study, and others at odds with them. For Mexico, the dependent variable is attitudes toward NAFTA.

In the initial model, household income and position in Left-Right space are both highly significant and strong influences on personal attitudes about NAFTA. Like with Brazil, higher income in Mexico translates to more support for regionalism. And like with Argentina and Colombia, ideology is strongly associated with support for NAFTA, though in the Mexican case, it is not distance from the ideological Center that matters. Instead, support for NAFTA increases as ideology moves to the Right. Education is significant, but interestingly the relationship is *negative*. The more education one has, the less supportive of NAFTA.

In model 2, adding variables related to foreign exposure (travel abroad and receipt of remittances) does nothing to improve predictability. In fact, controlling for foreign exposure, both income and Right ideology remain highly significant and positively associated with NAFTA support. Education is also significant (though less so), and negatively correlated.

Model 3 looks at the effect of attitudes to immigrants in Mexico and at the effect of national pride. Positive attitudes to immigrants increase support for NAFTA, and education, income, and right ideology also still matter. In fact, ideological positioning to the right is the most powerful predictor in this model. In another version of this model, attitudes to foreigners in Mexico also positively predicts NAFTA support, as does national pride.

Finally, in a fourth model I add two variables measuring attitudes to economic openness. They are economic globalization and free trade. Free trade is insignificant, but views on economic globalization are strong predictors of attitudes to NAFTA. Not surprisingly, the more favourable someone is to economic globalization, the more they support NAFTA.

The Mexican case coincides with findings in some of the other countries. Favourable attitudes to the outside world and to national pride are positively associated with NAFTA attitudes. Material considerations matter—the more income someone has, they more favourably inclined toward NAFTA. On the other hand, Mexico presents a curious picture with regard to education, in that it is the less educated who are more favourable toward NAFTA, possibly because NAFTA benefitted relatively low-skill manufacturing in Mexico. Likewise, Mexico is an outlier on the relationship between ideology and integration. While Argentina and Colombia data suggest that ideological centrism predicts regionalism support, for Mexico it is Right ideology.

Discussion and conclusion

Returning to our hypotheses, those which predicted a material influence on support for regional integration had mixed results. In Brazil and Mexico, income matters, in the expected direction—those with more of it are more supportive of regional integration. In Argentina and Colombia, income did not matter. However, attitudes to economic globalization did matter (in Colombia and Mexico, but not Argentina or Brazil). So material incentives are only partly explanatory.

The analysis of ideological effects reveals some similarities to Europe in that non-Centrist respondents are less supportive of regionalism in Argentina and Colombia (but not in Brazil or Mexico). In Mexico, those to the Right were more supportive of NAFTA, confirming that hypothesis, but in Brazil there was no real ideological effect.

National pride—my proxy for identity—is positively associated with support for regionalism in all countries except Brazil, disconfirming hypothesis 6 and contrary to findings in Europe. Latin Americans apparently see no conflict between positive attitudes to their own country, and support for regionalism. This suggests a positive sum perspective on the national and regional questions.

Cognitive variation does provide an explanation for regionalism support in Brazil, Colombia, and Mexico, but in different ways. More education leads to higher support for MERCOSUL in Brazil, but lower support for NAFTA in Mexico, possibly because of the kinds of opportunities that NAFTA provides for Mexicans. In Colombia, those with higher levels of education believe that the US benefitted more from the FTA with Colombia, while those with less education believe that Colombia benefitted more. This is consistent with a Leftist=anti-imperialist attitude, though Leftist ideology provides no explanatory purchase here.

In terms of exposure to other cultural influences, there is little to report (and what there is to report is counter-intuitive). Brazilians who travel abroad are *less* likely to support MERCOSUL. Mexicans with positive attitudes to immigrants and foreigners in Mexico are more likely to support NAFTA. Both findings contradict the hypothetical relationship in hypothesis 2.

In conclusion, what is particularly striking about attitudes in Latin America is not simply that the structure of support for regionalism differs between Latin America and Europe, but that there is no common structure of opinion across Latin America itself. Two of the region's most closely associated partnerships—Argentina and Brazil, show quite radically different results.

More broadly, material variation does matter, though not across all four of the countries studied. As in Europe, regionalism is politicized, but again, not in all four countries studied. Cognitive variation also matters in some cases but not in others. And identity also matters across three of the four countries, but opposite to the expected impact. Those who have pride in their nation also tend to support regionalism.

References

Akaike, Hirotugu (1987) 'Factor analysis and AIC' *Psychometrika* vol. 52, no. 3, pp 317-32.

Azpuru, Dinorah and Dexter Boniface (2015) 'Individual-level Determinants of Anti-Americanism in Contemporary Latin America' *Latin American Research Review*, Volume 50, Number 3, 2015, pp. 111-134.

Baker, Andy, and David Cupery (2013) 'Anti-Americanism in Latin America: Economic Exchange, Foreign Policy Legacies and Mass Attitudes toward the Colossus of the North' *Latin American Research Review* vol. 48, no. 2: pp 106–130.

Cichowski, Rachel (2000) 'Western Dreams, Eastern Realities: Support for the European Union in Central and Eastern Europe' *Comparative Political Studies*, vol. 33, no. 10, pp 1243-1278.

Davis, Charles L., Matthew J. Gabel and Kenneth M. Coleman (1998) 'Citizen response to regional integration in the Americas: The cases of Costa Rica and El

Salvador' *Studies in Comparative International Development*, Summer, Vol. 33 Issue 2, pp 88-110.

Deutschmann, Emanuel, and Lara Minkus (2018) 'Swinging Leftward: Public Opinion on Economic and Political Integration in Latin America, 1997–2010' *Latin American Research Review* vol. 53, no. 1, pp. 38–56.

Elgün, Özlem and Erik R. Tillman (2007) 'Exposure to European Union Policies and Support for Membership in the Candidate Countries' *Political Research Quarterly*, vol 60, no. 3, pp 391-400.

Gabel, Matthew (1998) 'Public Support for European Integration: An Empirical Test of Five Theories' *Journal of Politics*, vol. 60, no. 2, pp 333-54.

Garry, John and James Tilley (2015) 'Inequality, state ownership and the European Union: How economic context and economic ideology shape support for the European Union' *European Union Politics* vol. 16, no. 1, pp 139-154.

Hakhverdian, Armen, Erika van Elsas, Wouter van der Brug, and Theresa Kuhn (2013) 'Euroscepticism and education: A longitudinal study of 12 EU member states, 1973–2010' *European Union Politics*, vol. 14, no. 4, pp 522–541.

Herzog, Alexander and Joshua A. Tucker (2010) 'The dynamics of support: the winners–losers gap in attitudes toward EU membership in post-communist countries' *European Political Science Review*, vol. 2, pp 235-267.

Hooghe, Liesbet and Gary Marks (2005) 'Calculation, Community and Cues: Public Opinion on European Integration' *European Union Politics*, vol. 6, no. 4 pp 419-43.

Jackson, John E., Bogdan W. Mach, and Jennifer L. Miller-Gonzalez (2011) 'Buying support and regime change: the evolution of Polish attitudes towards the EU and voting between accssion and 2008' *European Union Politics* vol. 12, no. 2, pp 147-67.

Maldonado, Gerardo and Karen Marin (2018) Apoyo a la Integración Regional en América Latina. Unpublished paper. CIDE, Mexico City.

Merolla, Jennifer, Laura Stephenson, Carole Wilson and Elizabeth Zechmeister (2005), Globalization, Globalización, Globalisation: Public Opinion and NAFTA Law and Business Review of the Americas, vol. 11, Issue 3&4, pp. 573-596.

Seligson, Mitchell A. (1999) 'Popular Support for Regional Economic Integration in Latin America' *Journal of Latin American Studies*, Vol. 31, No. 1 (Feb.), pp. 129-150

Tanasoiu, Cosmina and Constantin Colonescu (2008) 'Determinants of Support for European Integration: The Case of Bulgaria' *European Union Politics*, vol. 9, no. 3 pp 363–377.

Tucker, Joshua A., Alexander C. Pacek and Adam J. Berinsky (2002) 'Transitional Winners and Losers: Attitudes toward EU Membership in Post-Communist Countries' *American Journal of Political Science* vol. 46, no. 3 pp 557-571.

Standardized effects on MERCOSUL approval Argentina 2014

	(1)	(2)	(3)	(4)	(5)
Variables	Sociodem	+Exposure	+Nationalism	+AttGlob	All
Gender	0.137	0.157	0.0806	-3.401*	-3.223
	-0.893	-1.046	-1.026	-2.034	-2.11
Household income	1.204	1.148	1.168	-2.118	-1.92
	-0.265	-1.109	-1.083	-2.343	-2.406
Level of education	0.545	0.488	0.674	0.338	-0.456
	-0.621	-1.162	-1.112	-2.218	-2.438
Left-right scale	1.363	1.331	1.101	3.292*	3.550*
	-0.162	-0.99	-0.99	-1.869	-1.947
Extremism	-2.212*	-2.188**	-2.386**	-1.31	-1.192
	-0.0241	-0.994	-0.988	-1.866	-1.919
Times abroad		0.257			1.016
		-1.27			-3.022
Feeling proud of being Argentinian			1.861*		-0.847
			-1.003		-1.774
Positive opinion on economic globalization				-2.878	-3.016
				-2.052	-2.136
Constant	65.91***	65.88***	65.82***	66.65***	66.88***
	0	-1.041	-1.018	-2.032	-2.138
Observations	517	503	512	128	124
R-squared	0.017	0.017	0.024	0.066	0.068

pval in parentheses

*** $p < 0.001$, ** $p < 0.01$, * $p < 0.05$

Standardized effects on MERCOSUL approval Brazil 2014

Variables	(1) Sociodem	(2) +Exposure	(3) +Nationalism	(4) +AttGlob	(5) All
Gender	-1.347	-2.656	-1.466*	-0.454	2.349
	-0.107	-1.735	-0.836	-1.725	-3.872
Household income	2.635**	3.049*	2.670***	3.347*	3.464
	-0.00291	-1.778	-0.882	-1.768	-4.109
Level of education	3.803***	4.776**	3.878***	3.840*	8.196
	-0.000103	-2.162	-0.977	-2.078	-5.57
Left-right scale	0.75	3.471*	0.778	0.582	1.741
	-0.425	-1.899	-0.939	-1.785	-4.152
Extremism	1.318	0.614	1.326	0.348	-1.08
	-0.151	-1.821	-0.917	-1.833	-4.061
Times abroad		-6.645**			-6.947
		-2.651			-10.31
Receives remittances		0.509			0.394
		-1.753			-4.112
Positive opinion on foreigners in Brazil			-		-
Feeling proud of being Brazilian			0.615		0.132
			-0.834		-4.419
Positive opinion on economic globalization				4.050**	3.88
				-1.693	-3.89
FT is good for Brazil				-0.0535	0.855
				-1.715	-3.597
Constant	52.16***	52.44***	52.12***	52.71***	47.56***
	0	-1.987	-0.856	-1.814	-4.968
Observations	1,161	282	1,158	284	68
R-squared	0.037	0.071	0.039	0.06	0.099

pval in parentheses

*** $p < 0.001$, ** $p < 0.01$, * $p < 0.05$

Standardized effects on NAFTA approval Mexico 2014

Variables	(1) Sociodem	(2) +Expo	(3) +Natio1	(4) +Natio2	(5) +AttGlob	(6) All(1)	(7) All(2)
Gender	-0.862	-0.906	-0.577	-0.0358	-0.346	-0.564	-1.127
	-0.244	-0.745	-1.056	-0.0454	-1.467	-1.514	-3.028
Household income	2.923***	2.995***	2.597**	0.109**	2.012	1.718	0.712
	-0.00027	-0.805	-1.178	-0.0504	-1.733	-1.832	-0.759
Level of education	-1.675	-1.712**	-2.386*	-0.043	-0.744	-0.478	-0.111
	-0.0512	-0.87	-1.27	-0.0506	-1.78	-1.842	-0.429
Left-right scale	3.851***	3.750***	4.368***	0.138***	4.463**	3.251*	1.212*
	-2.40E-07	-0.75	-1.099	-0.0449	-1.748	-1.868	-0.696
Extremism	0.368	0.208	0.849	0.00274	0.755	0.132	0.0734
	-0.625	-0.759	-1.069	-0.0463	-1.62	-1.74	-0.971
Times abroad		-0.496				5.152	0.328
		-1.007				-4.937	-0.314
Receives remittances		0.636				-2.021	-6.243
		-0.701				-1.645	-5.083
Positive opinion on immigrants in Mexico			1.975*			0.353	0.398
			-1.032			-1.604	-1.809
Proud of being Mexican			0.685	0.0879**		-1.711	-2.681
			-1.08	-0.0419		-1.567	-2.456
Positive opinion on foreigners in Mexico				0.114**			
				-0.0456			
Positive opinion on economic globalization					4.196***	4.627***	5.524***
					-1.515	-1.64	-1.957
FT good for Mexico					0.854	0.328	0.494
					-1.519	-1.599	-2.406
Constant	61.68***	61.65***	61.87***	0.012	62.43***	63.16***	48.69***
	0	-0.781	-1.13	-0.0473	-1.56	-1.666	-16.37
Observations	994	985	479	507	192	183	183
R-squared	0.046	0.047	0.064	0.059	0.11	0.117	0.117

pval in parentheses *** $p < 0.001$, ** $p < 0.01$, * $p < 0.05$

Standardized effects on MERCOSUL approval Colombia 2014

Variables	(1) Sociodem	(2) +Exposure	(3) +Natio1	(4) +Natio2	(5) +AttGlob	(6) All(1)	(7) All(2)
Gender	0.462	0.574	0.879	0.769	0.609	1.270	1.126
	(0.595)	(0.871)	(0.901)	(0.885)	(0.927)	(0.975)	(0.954)
Household income	0.687	0.592	0.749	0.422	0.125	0.0812	-0.264
	(0.425)	(0.866)	(0.886)	(0.864)	(0.935)	(0.974)	(0.945)
Level of education	0.518	0.550	0.564	0.398	0.307	0.467	0.263
	(0.610)	(1.021)	(1.045)	(1.028)	(1.082)	(1.127)	(1.100)
Left right scale	-0.520	-0.673	-1.033	-0.950	-0.734	-1.618	-1.286
	(0.576)	(0.935)	(0.973)	(0.937)	(0.974)	(1.040)	(0.994)
Extremism	-2.020*	-1.999**	-2.005**	-1.815**	-2.098**	-2.182**	-1.889**
	(0.0242)	(0.897)	(0.932)	(0.899)	(0.947)	(0.998)	(0.960)
Times abroad		2.013				0.411	0.977
		(2.679)				(2.821)	(2.799)
Receives remittances		-1.426				-1.762*	-1.612
		(0.917)				(0.983)	(0.979)
Opinion on immigrants in Colombia			0.592			-0.636	
			(0.893)			(1.000)	
Proud of being Colombian			1.856	1.834*		1.236	1.305
			(1.163)	(1.091)		(1.325)	(1.221)
Opinion on foreigners in Colombia				0.567			0.204
				(0.920)			(1.001)
Opinion on economic globalization					2.762***	2.542**	1.980**
					(0.949)	(1.016)	(0.984)
FT good for Colombia					0.921	2.031**	1.689*
					(0.974)	(1.034)	(1.001)
Constant	54.30***	54.52***	54.83***	54.58***	54.81***	55.92***	55.43***
	(0)	(0.969)	(0.985)	(0.958)	(1.004)	(1.095)	(1.062)
Observations	685	682	639	653	603	557	573
R-squared	0.010	0.014	0.016	0.014	0.026	0.038	0.030

pval in parentheses   *** p<0.001, ** p<0.01, * p<0.05

Standardized Pr of answering USA benefits the most in USA-Col FT

Variables	(1) Sociodem	(2) +Exposure	(3) +Nationalism(1)	(4) +Nationalism(2)	(5) +AttGlob	(6) All(1)	(7) All(2)
Gender	-0.0702	-0.059	-0.0611	-0.0409	-0.115	-0.0789	-0.0681
	-0.304	-0.0686	-0.0717	-0.0719	-0.0775	-0.0815	-0.0817
Household income	-0.104	-0.106	-0.107	-0.0741	-0.0286	-0.0282	-0.00314
	-0.167	-0.0764	-0.0777	-0.0791	-0.0863	-0.09	-0.0912
Level of education	0.533***	0.524***	0.507***	0.574***	0.518***	0.502***	0.581***
	0	-0.0792	-0.0813	-0.0821	-0.0867	-0.0913	-0.0922
Left-right scale	-0.0859	-0.108	-0.101	-0.0648	-0.0711	-0.0932	-0.0894
	-0.206	-0.0691	-0.0727	-0.0715	-0.078	-0.0846	-0.0835
Extremism	0.0398	0.0563	0.00538	0.02	-0.0173	-0.0158	-0.0445
	-0.56	-0.0689	-0.0721	-0.0712	-0.0771	-0.0824	-0.0814
Times abroad		0.499*				0.444	0.438
		-0.283				-0.273	-0.279
Receives remittances		-0.0299				-0.0125	-0.0329
		-0.0716				-0.0831	-0.0826
Opinion on immigrants			-0.0589			0.0297	
			-0.074			-0.0827	
Feeling proud of being Colombian			-0.165*	-0.204**		-0.157	-0.204**
			-0.0898	-0.0899		-0.102	-0.103
Opinion on foreigners				-0.128*			-0.102
				-0.0758			-0.0853
Opinion on economic globalization					-0.251***	-0.263***	-0.226***
					-0.0808	-0.0864	-0.0861
FT is good for Colombia					-0.0587	-0.0452	-0.0129
					-0.0822	-0.0879	-0.0878
Constant	1.006***	1.047***	0.996***	1.039***	1.089***	1.098***	1.151***
	0	-0.0769	-0.073	-0.0734	-0.0782	-0.0881	-0.0891
Observations	1,147	1,138	1,038	1,063	947	856	878

pval in parentheses *** $p < 0.001$, ** $p < 0.01$, * $p < 0.05$

Standardized Pr of answering Col benefits the most in USA-Col FT

Variables	(1) Sociodem	(2) +Exposure	(3) +Nationalism(1)	(4) +Nationalism(2)	(5) +AttGlob	(6) All(1)	(7) All(2)
Gender	0.0238	0.012	0.0165	-0.00799	0.0714	0.0407	0.00576
	-0.773	-0.083	-0.0863	-0.0866	-0.0915	-0.096	-0.0961
Household income	0.108	0.105	0.0851	0.062	0.146	0.125	0.087
	-0.236	-0.0917	-0.0938	-0.0957	-0.0987	-0.103	-0.106
Level of education	-0.449***	-0.447***	-0.414***	-0.467***	-0.501***	-0.487***	-0.551***
	-1.61E-06	-0.0948	-0.0967	-0.0974	-0.101	-0.106	-0.107
Left-right scale	0.167*	0.192**	0.164**	0.124	0.0706	0.0673	0.0754
	-0.0304	-0.0784	-0.082	-0.0805	-0.0864	-0.093	-0.0921
Extremism	-0.253**	-0.267***	-0.234***	-0.240***	-0.209**	-0.247**	-0.206**
	-0.00214	-0.0833	-0.0863	-0.0854	-0.0907	-0.0962	-0.095
Times abroad		-0.299				-0.343	-0.334
		-0.235				-0.255	-0.261
Receives remittances		0.0919				0.0625	0.0706
		-0.0841				-0.0964	-0.0969
Opinion on immigrants			0.0566			-0.0779	
			-0.089			-0.0959	
Feeling proud of being Colombian			0.248**	0.280**		0.325**	0.369**
			-0.124	-0.124		-0.151	-0.153
Opinion on foreigners				0.101			0.0239
				-0.0913			-0.0988
Opinion on economic globalization					0.208**	0.260**	0.204**
					-0.0961	-0.103	-0.102
FT is good for Colombia					0.272***	0.264**	0.198*
					-0.0991	-0.106	-0.105
Constant	-1.744***	-1.768***	-1.728***	-1.776***	-1.747***	-1.760***	-1.811***
	0	-0.0906	-0.0916	-0.0925	-0.0969	-0.108	-0.109
Observations	1,147	1,138	1,038	1,063	947	856	878

pval in parentheses *** $p < 0.001$, ** $p < 0.01$, * $p < 0.05$

Chapter Seven

EU Values in EU External Relations:
An Introduction to Current Legal Instruments

Kirstyn Inglis

Values have always lain at the heart of EU integration among the EU Member States, and international norms have informed these values while the EU has also been a driver of values at international level. Political momentum has been gathering at EU level, driven by the EU and the Member States' concerns to reject protectionism in order to harness globalisation, while at the same time to preserve the successes of their integration over the last 60 years, spanning their own values at home as well as in their actions abroad. Mirroring the trust, engagement and integration that it has achieved through pursuing values over its lifetime, the EU is projecting values out into the world as integral to its global interests. This reveals the lesions in multilateral provision for institutions, procedures, rules and standards. This necessarily affects relations between Brazil and the EU, whether in the context of bilateral Brazil-EU relations or in the context of EU-MERCOSUL relations, or in international fora. The EU's values-based agenda in its external relations highlights the highlight the challenges of protecting democracies and national sovereignty, and public policy-making in a globalising world.

The EU's Treaty of Lisbon in 2009 clarified definitions of values in the EU's external actions. It also increased the capacity of the EU Member States for common international actions at EU level, in terms of the legal basis and financing for external EU actions and the institutional arrangements the implement them, notably with the creation of the European Union's External Action Service (EEAS). Currently, the values agenda of the EU in relations with third countries are progressively being worked out from bilateral—including at local levels—to multilateral level, including rules and institutions, including trade and investment treaties.

The evolution of the instruments agreed at EU level to support this new external relations agenda has been gathering momentum recently, notably since the European Union's 2016 Global Strategy on Foreign and Security Policy (EUGS), and its revision in 2017, which has its purpose to enhance the consistency of the EU's External Action. The 2017 EU GS includes building resilience at home and in third countries, and it marks a shift away from crisis containment towards "a more structural, long-term non-linear approach to vulnerabilities, with an emphasis on anticipation, prevention and preparedness".[1] It is rooted in the ten priorities fixed by European Commission President Jean Claude Juncker for his term in office (2014-2018), which included the priority to make the European Union a stronger global actor.[2] Juncker's programme was more than a stock-taking of the economic and political crisis from which the EU was surfacing. It addressed the fact that the EU was ill-prepared for the global challenges ahead. It was already aiming to restore public confidence among EU citizens in the democratic legitimacy of the EU, including in the global arena. The upgrading of the role of the High Representative,[3] In terms of the context of the EU GS was published hot on the heels of the "Brexit" vote of the United Kingdom's population and came at the time of rising populism and euroscepticism within the European Union, including societal resistance to international trade and investment agreements under negotiation at that time on ground of the threats they posed to democratic values, national sovereignty and the public policy space, among other things.

The "undivided and indivisible" political commitment of the EU Member States to the external agenda in the form of the *Rome Declaration 2017*[4]—which marked the 60th anniversary of the European Union at a time when the *White Paper on the Future of Europe* laid bare the indecision on their own internal agenda—is noteworthy. The political demand by the Heads of State and Government at European Council level in October 2017,[5] instructing follow up action on the Global Strategy to be taken by the relevant EU institutions, further underlines that commitment as does the review of a range of internal policy areas in order to reviewing

---

1. See European Commission Joint Communication *A Strategic Approach to Resilience in the EU's External Action*, JOIN (2017) 21 final of 7 June 2017
2. For Juncker's 2014 Political Guidelines of 15 July 2018, go to https://ec.europa.eu/commission/publications/president-junckers-political-guidelines_en, last visited on 28 March 2018.
3. See Juncker's political, 14 July priorities 2014, *Ibid.*, at Priority 9.
4. See, *Declaration of the leaders of 27 Member States and of the European Council, the European Parliament and the European Commission*, Rome, 25 March 2017, to be found at http://www.consilium.europa.eu/en/press/press-releases/2017/03/25/rome-declaration/, last visited on 27 February 2018.
5. See "concrete policy initiatives and action, focused on the five priorities for the EU's external action identified in the strategy: strengthening security and defence; investing in the resilience of states and societies to our East and South; developing an integrated approach to conflicts and crises; promoting and supporting cooperative regional orders; and reinforcing a global governance based on international law, including the principles of the UN Charter, and the Helsinki Final Act".

pre-existing strategies on climate diplomacy, energy diplomacy, economic diplomacy and cultural diplomacy to bring them into line with the EU GS. The December 2017 Joint Declaration of EP, Commission and Council of Ministers promises faster decision-making on priority actions in the external agenda.[6]

Today the Union's current values-based external agenda is taking on increasingly coherent and concrete form, pulling together the Union's international commitments as well as the respect of EU level labour, environment and human rights standards. Significantly, the EU Commission's commitment to transparency in its conducting of EU international negotiations on trade and investment has taken on a whole new dimension. This throws into stark contrast the lesions in governance at multilateral level even where global consensus on values are clear in what is an increasingly complex and contested global order. The policy landscape has been speeding up in the last 3 years in measures to be agreed by the Member States at EU level, and in all EU external relations with third countries including in trade and investment, and the EU Global Strategy for Foreign and Security Policy of 2016, revised in 2017,[7] and the Juncker Package 2017.[8] The Union's concern to engage with its own citizens

This contribution begins by listing the primary law EU Treaty provisions providing the legal basis for values in EU external actions, and then lists the policy instruments that provide the foundations for how the EU and its Member States are working out these values in the international arena today. Here, a subsection is dedicated to transparency in international negotiations, which has taken on new meaning recently and which will inevitably impact on future EU-Brazil relations. This contribution then briefly explores the structure and content of the relations between Brazil and the EU recent evolutions in the current EU values-based approach in the context of the Trade and Sustainability Chapter in the pending (not yet concluded) Association Agreement between the EU and MERCOSUL.

---

6. See *Official Journal* 2017 C446/1.
7. See European Commission *Report on the Implementation of the Trade Policy Strategy Trade for [of 2015] Delivering a Progressive Trade Policy to Harness Globalisation*, COM(2017) 491 of 13 September 2017.
8. To consult the Package, of 14 September 2017, and ongoing implementation of its deliverables, go to http://trade.ec.europa.eu/doclib/press/index.cfm?id=1711, last visited on 18 May 2018.

Primary law and institutional foundations

The EU's need to upgrade its external powers and actions was obvious already at the turn of the Century, and the European Convention (2002) gives useful understanding of the evolution, rationale and current directions of the EU values agenda today, including substantive content as well as institutional arrangements[9]. The need for reforms were clear as much because of the complexity in the interplay between the Member States and the European Institutions as in their interactions with third countries adhering to different values systems—this in addition to the limitations and inadequacies of international institutions, rules and procedures supporting international values creation, implementation and enforcement.

Already the Mandate for Working Group VII of the Praesidium on "External Action" recognised the globalisation challenges facing the EU and expressed that "only a strong and united Union can protect its political and economic interests and defend the values, which are at the heart of the Union itself",[10] setting broad parameters to the scope of options for the revision of the primary Treaties on how to define and formulate the Union's common actions, the decision-making processes and coherence between instruments of external actions, and how to improve the effectiveness of the EU on the international stage including the financing of such actions. It was also expressly mandated to explore reforms of the Union's external representation at international level and improving the synergy between diplomatic activity of the Union across the full breadth of concerned fields of policy activity as well as with the Member States. The obvious influence of the work of the Convention can be seen in the drafting of the eventual Treaty of Lisbon, both in the working out of the EU's external values agenda and in the introduction of the European External Action Service (EEAS) for the purposes of coherence and rationalisation of the EU external representation, building up the clarity and continuity in EU representation in third countries in particular, all in the aim of enhancing the Union's impact abroad.

---

9. Source documentation relating to the Convention on the Future of the European Union can be found at http://european-convention.europa.eu/EN/doc_register/doc_register9713.html?lang=EN&Content=WGVII, last visited on 16 May 2018.
10. The mandate for the working group on External Action which was drafted by the Praesidium, can be found at http://european-convention.europa.eu/pdf/reg/en/02/cv00/cv00252.en02.pdf last visited on 16 May 2018.

The reasoning of the Final Report[11] of Working Group VII is reflected in the final drafting of the Treaty of Lisbon in the clarifying and consolidation of the principles and objectives of all EU external actions as well as the strategies to pursue them in international relations, and how to implement them in practice.

In terms of clarity and consolidation of the principles and objectives, certain core primary law Treaty provisions emanating from the ToL must be mentioned. Article 2 of the Treaty on European Union (TEU) declares that:

> The Union is founded on the values of respect for human dignity, freedom, democracy, equality, the rule of law and respect for human rights, including the rights of persons belonging to minorities. These values are common to the Member States in a society in which pluralism, non-discrimination, tolerance, justice, solidarity and equality between women and men prevail.

Article 3 TEU expressly provides for the objectives of all EU external actions to promote peace, ensure the security of its citizens, and to promote its values and protect its interests in the world. Further, Article 21 TEU adds guidance on the principles and strategies for external actions:

> 1. The Union's action on the international scene shall be guided by the principles which have inspired its own creation, development and enlargement, and which it seeks to advance in the wider world: democracy, the rule of law, the universality and indivisibility of human rights and fundamental freedoms, respect for human dignity, the principles of equality and solidarity, and respect for the principles of the United Nations Charter and international law.
>
> The Union shall seek to develop relations and build partnerships with third countries, and international, regional or global organisations which share the principles referred to in the first subparagraph. It shall promote multilateral solutions to common problems, in particular in the framework of the United Nations.
>
> 2. The Union shall define and pursue common policies and actions, and shall work for a high degree of cooperation in all fields of international relations, in order to:

---

11. See CONV 459/02 of 16 December 2002, To be found at http://european-convention. europa.eu/pdf/reg/en/02/cv00/cv00459.en02.pdf, last visited on 16 May 2018,

(a) safeguard its values, fundamental interests, security, independence and integrity;

(b) consolidate and support democracy, the rule of law, human rights and the principles of international law;

(c) preserve peace, prevent conflicts and strengthen international security, in accordance with the purposes and principles of the United Nations Charter, with the principles of the Helsinki Final Act and with the aims of the Charter of Paris, including those relating to external borders;

(d) foster the sustainable economic, social and environmental development of developing countries, with the primary aim of eradicating poverty;

(e) encourage the integration of all countries into the world economy, including through the progressive abolition of restrictions on international trade;

(f) help develop international measures to preserve and improve the quality of the environment and the sustainable management of global natural resources, in order to ensure sustainable development;

(g) assist populations, countries and regions confronting natural or man-made disasters; and (h) promote an international system based on stronger multilateral cooperation and good global governance.

3. The Union shall respect the principles and pursue the objectives set out in paragraphs 1 and 2 in the development and implementation of the different areas of the Union's external action covered by this Title and by Part Five of the Treaty on the Functioning of the European Union, and of the external aspects of its other policies."

The Union shall ensure consistency between the different areas of its external action and between these and its other policies. The Council and the Commission, assisted by the High Representative of the Union for Foreign Affairs and Security Policy, shall ensure that consistency and shall cooperate to that effect."

In terms of reforms introduced by the ToL to the legal bases for external actions—which establish whether the competence for EU action is shared or exclusive, or limited to co-operation, and relevant decision-making procedures—the Treaty on the Functioning of the European Union is the reference point[12]. Various of the EU level actions will also have external dimensions[13] and will require co-ordination with the relevant EU services and instruments in the context of specific external actions. The extraterritorial effect of EU rules and regulations will also be relevant.

The EEAS, the European Union Global Strategy and values instruments

Taking up the thread of the Final Report of Working Group VII (December 2002) above concerning the implementation of the new legal and institutional constellation, the creation of the EEAS is relevant. Led by Frederica Mogherini,[14] it aims at improving coherence and efficiency in the Union's external relations.[15] By holding the double-hat of High Representative for Foreign Affairs and Security Policy at the same time as being Vice-President of the European Commission, Mogherini and her services in Brussels and partner countries, institutionalise this process towards ever more practical means of effecting coherence and efficiency in the Union's external actions. Mogherini's appointment was accompanied by the "new way of working" heralded in 2014 by the then new Jean Claude Juncker European Commission, all in the aim of increasing the collaboration between different portfolios of different Commissioners on the EU's external relations.[16]

---

12. For the decision-making procedures dedicated to external actions: Implementing measures of the common commercial policy are based on Article 207 paragraph 2, TFEU; Implementation of development cooperation policy are based on Article 209, paragraph 1, TFEU; Economic, financial and technical cooperation with third countries other than developing countries are based on Article 212, paragraph 2, TFEU, and; the general framework for humanitarian operations are based on Article 214, paragraph 3, TFEU.

13. For a full list of the legal bases in the TFEU, see the consolidated list provided by the European Commission on the Europa website of 17 December 2009, go to http://ec.europa.eu/codecision/docs/legal_bases_en.pdf, last visited on 16 May 2018.

14. Appointed in November 2014.

15. For fuller information on the responsibilities involved, go to https://ec.europa.eu/commission/commissioners/2014-2019/mogherini_en, last visited on 16 May 2018.

16. For the Mission Letter of the President of the European Commission to High Representative of the Union for Foreign Policy and Security Policy/Vice-President of the European Commission of 1 November, go to https://ec.europa.eu/commission/commissioners/sites/cwt/files/commissioner_mission_letters/mogherini_en.pdf, last visited on 16 May 2018. At p. 3, it provides that "You will work closely with the other Vice-Presidents and, in your area of responsibility, guide the work of the Commissioners for European Neighbourhood Policy and Enlargement Negotiations; Trade; International Cooperation and Development; and Humanitarian Aid and Crisis Management. You will also be able to draw on the Commission's policy instruments and expertise in many areas where our international partners are keen to work with us. These include policies under the responsibilities of the Commissioners for Climate Action and Energy, Transport as

The policy landscape for EU external relations has been speeding up and filling out, including in terms of the form and content of the European Union's values in its international relations. From early days on in the discussions contemplating the European Convention, the need for treaty reform and innovative ways of engaging with a globalising world was laboured, particularly the pros and cons of protectionism on the trade and investment front. A new stage has been set, with new forms of implementation in place and based on the new ToL clarity on the Union's aim and objectives together with reformed legal bases for EU actions in the global arena. The 10 Juncker Priorities in 2014-2019 have made use of this new toolkit.

The 2016 *European Union Global Strategy* (EU GS) should also be read against this backdrop, and is an expression of the intention to ensure better coherence between foreign policy decisions on the one hand, and deployment of instruments in the field of external relations on the other hand:

> Guided by the values on which it is founded, the EU is committed to a rules-based multilateral international order. The Union regards the respect for and promotion of international law - including the principles of the UN Charter—to be crucial for preserving peace, human rights, sustainable development and lasting access to the global commons. Multilateral organisations—in particular the United Nations—sit at the heart of this framework of international norms. They are providers of global governance as well as fora for the peaceful resolution of disputes and jointly tackling global challenges. To strengthen rather than just preserve the rules-based multilateral system, the European Union is committed to reform, transform, and further expand the existing system. The European Union leads by example with the implementation of new and reinvigoration of existing multilateral projects like the Paris Agreement, the Sustainable Development Goals, as well as the global effort on nuclear non-proliferation and disarmament. We will

---

well as Migration and Home Affairs, which have a strong external dimension". See also Juncker's ten political priorities, 14 July 2014, at Priority 9 providing for upgrading the institutional role and support for the High Representative and her mission: the HR "will have to a be strong and experienced player to combine national and European tools, and all the tools available in the Commission, in a more effective way than in the past. He or she must act in concert with our European Commissioners for Trade, Development and Humanitarian Aid as well as for Neighbourhood Policy. This will require the High Representative to more fully play his/her role within the College of Commissioners. To make this possible, I intend to entrust other external relations Commissioners with the task of deputising for the High Representative both within the work of the College and on the international stage".

seek to widen the reach of international norms and institutions. Not only is the EU committed to living up to its obligations under such regimes, rather it will strongly support expanding their membership, universalisation, full implementation, and enforcement[17].

Regarding the trade and investment agreements subsequently negotiated by the EU, in the face of globalisation, objections from social actors and national parliaments have threaten to disable negotiations that were intended, ultimately, to secure the benefits of international trade[18]. Their objections centre on the increasing scope of these agreements and the encroachment into the policy space that this involves, including the threat to democratic decision making in all fields of society. The Juncker Priorities and measures implementing it are clearly motivated by the need to restore the public's support for the democratic legitimacy of the Union and furtherance of the Union's external agenda.

The firm commitment to resisting protectionism and harnessing globalisation under the Juncker Package of September 2017, can be seen in the consensual political support of the Member States and the European Parliament.[19] Contributing to this apparent shift has been the impact of the societal resistance and political struggles among national parliaments during the course of 2013 over the initiatives for a Transatlantic Trade and Investment Partnership (TTIP) and the Comprehensive Economic and Trade Agreement (CETA), were very much values-based, and the lack of transparency of parties to international negotiations has been a core reason throughout. This resistance was threatening the future of the Union's trade and investment relations agenda. The accumulating internal crises at EU level have also been an undeniable and obvious contributing factor in a more strategic approach to anchoring values into EU external actions.

Already the formulation of the new agenda for trade and investment in the Commission Communication *Trade for All* (adopted in October 2015) was to hold out transparency, efficiency and values at its heart. In Com-

---

17. See European Commission Communication *Shared Vision, Common Action: A Global Strategy for the European Union's Foreign and Security Policy*, of June 2016, to be found at file:///C:/Users/kirst/Downloads/eugs_review_web.pdf, last visited on 10 March 2018. See also European Commission Joint Communication *A Strategic Approach to Resilience in the EU's External Action*, JOIN (2017) 21 final of 7 June 2017.

18. See European Commission *Report on the Implementation of the Trade Policy Strategy Trade for [of 2015] Delivering a Progressive Trade Policy to Harness Globalisation*, OP. Cit. n. 10, and European Commission Reflection Paper for Harnessing Globalisation COM(2017) 240 of 10 May 2017.

19. *Op. Cit.* n. 9.

mission President Juncker's September 2017 State of the Union address,[20] values were brought to the top of the list in his speech. The resounding political support of the Member States for the external values agenda in the Rome Declaration of March 2017 was followed by increased financial support for the external ambitions. Also, recent reporting for 2018 on the implementation of Juncker's 10 priorities in the first three years, highlights that the number of initiatives issued under the global actor priority are the second highest on the list. Being a priority area for action, the 2016 interinstitutional agreement between the European Commission, European Parliament and European Council is clearly facilitating the streamlining of decision-making at EU level in order to push ahead with this priority[21].

In recent years, the EU has been manifesting the objectives of Article 3 TEU in line with the principles and guiding strategies set out in Article 21 TEU, in increasingly concrete forms in its external relations, including by taking measures to give them effect at EU level. To this list of values must be added working conditions, food safety, public health, environmental protection and animal welfare[22]. In terms of labour standards, the EU is supporting collective bargaining systems under the International Labour Organisation (ILO) umbrella. Corporate social responsibility (CSR) and Responsible Business Conduct (RBC) is also expressly promoted, and the EU Member States are all active in the UN Global Compact on corporate social responsibility.[23] Multilateral Environment Agreements are central

---

20. See European Commission President Jean-Claude Juncker's State of the Union Address 2017 of 13 September 2017, Brussels to be found at http://europa.eu/rapid/press-release_SPEECH-17-3165_en.htm, last visited on 28 March 2018.
21. *Op. Cit.* n. 9.
22. In its 2017 Communication, *Report on the Implementation of the Trade Policy Strategy Trade for All: Delivering a Progressive Trade Policy to Harness Globalisation*, the declared aim is to bring about a "trade policy that is effective, transparent and based on values is needed more than ever before. The fundamentals of the Trade for All strategy thus continue to guide the EU's approach: openness combined with a level playing field, high standards of labour, environmental, consumer and social protection combined with the right policies at home remains the most fitting way to make globalisation work for all Europeans. The EU is committed to a rules-based multilateral trading system that underpins our prosperity, and that is essential to making trade a positive force around the globe in line with the Sustainable Development Goals. The EU's policy response seeks out partners such as Canada, Japan, Mexico, MERCOSUL, Australia or New Zealand who want to team up in building open and progressive rules for the realities of 21st century trade", See Commission Communication COM(2017) 491 final, to be found at https://ec.europa.eu/transparency/regdoc/rep/1/2017/EN/COM-2017-491-F1-EN-MAIN-PART-1.PDF, last visited on 10 March 2018.
23. See European Parliament *Resolution on EU-CELAC relations*, *Op. Cit.* n. 7. For the UN Global Compact on CSR for the Region of Europe, go to https://www.unglobalcompact.org/engage-locally/europe, last visited on 24 February 2018.

also, and in the broader sustainable development agenda, future EU efforts must "benefit prosperity, the planet and people around the world, especially in developing countries"[24] and expressly embrace those values underpinning the EU's UN commitments on climate change and development, specifically the 2030 Agenda for Sustainable Development,[25] the 2008 Declaration on Social Justice for Fair Globalisation, the EU Consensus on Development of 8 June 2017,[26] as well as the Paris Climate Agreement,[27] and the 2016 UN New York Declaration for Refugees and Migrants.[28] Concerning the latter, the New York Declaration has set the signatories the task of "[achieving] a more equitable sharing of the burden and responsibility for hosting and supporting the world's refugees by adopting a global compact on refugees in 2018".

Transparency becomes a value in its own right

Transparency is a key characteristic of decision-making at EU level, especially since the time of the 1990s BSE crisis and the consequent crisis of trust in EU governance. The culture of transparency and access to information regarding EU policy and law making enables the trust building among the peoples of the 28 Member States and in their institutions. The reforms

---

24. See *Op. Cit.* n. 4.
25. See European Commission *Next Steps for Sustainable European Future* COM(2016) 739 of 22 November 2016, to be found at https://ec.europa.eu/europeaid/sites/devco/files/communication-next-steps-sustainable-europe-20161122_en.pdf, last visited on 24 February 2018, at the section 2.3 *The European Union as a committed global partner to promote the 2030 Agenda*. For the European Parliament's position on the future rolling out of this strategy, European Parliament resolution of 6 July 2017 on EU action for sustainability, go to http://www.europarl.europa.eu/sides/getDoc.do?pubRef=-//EP//NONSGML+TA+P8-TA-2017-0315+0+DOC+PDF+V0//EN, last visited on 24 February 2018. See also EU Regulation (EU) 2017/1601 creating the EFSD Guarantee and the EFSD Guarantee Fund , *OJ* 2017 L 249/1–16.
26. See European Commission, *New European Consensus on Development, 'Our world, our dignity, o*ur future', to be found at https://ec.europa.eu/europeaid/new-european-consensus-development-our-world-our-dignity-our-future_en, last visited on 24 February 2018. For the political support for the policy development of actions under this process, see European Parliament Resolution of 1 June 2017 *the new European Consensus on Development–Our World, Our Dignity, Our Future*, to be found at http://www.europarl.europa.eu/sides/getDoc.do?type=TA&language=EN&reference=P8-TA-2017-0241, last visited on 24 February 2018.
27. In force since 1 November 2016, see the EU's implementation through the European Commission's Directorate General for Climate Action, https://www.unglobalcompact.org/engage-locally/europe, last visited on 24 February 2018.
28. See at p. 12, to be found at https://refugeesmigrants.un.org/declaration, last visited on 29 March 2018.

that followed have been crucial to re-establishing consumer trust in the EU's agriculture and food sectors, and the governance tools developed for the entire food chain are shaping the EU's approach to its international negotiations. Progressive Treaty reforms to decision-making processes over the lifetime of the European Union have held the aim of democratic legitimacy at their core, including by giving the European Parliament increased influence. The role of the directly elected European Parliament in the scrutiny over EU decision-making processes has been pivotal in the subsequent reform of the EU institutions and their democratic accountability as well as in the shaping of future EU external relations. Moreover, the inclusion of a broad range of stakeholders in the formulation of EU policy from earliest stages, welcoming the lobbyists representing NGOs and civil society as well as industry, is intended to make laws that are fit for purpose and capable of achieving the goals sought.

The TTIP, CETA and Ukraine Agreements all attracted society and political resistance globally, despite the considerable benefits anticipated. Issues of national sovereignty and democratic values—especially how to guarantee a country's capacity over its own public policy making—lie at the heart of the EU's values agenda. See further for comments on the EU-MERCOSUL draft Association Agreements, comprising trade provisions alongside sustainable development provisions and providing for structures to broaden transparency and the participation of civil society in implementation of the agreement.

Today, transparency has become a value in its own right, a gateway for the scrutiny and democratic accountability that enables such broad stakeholder engagement in all good faith. Time will tell whether the unprecedented promotion of transparency indeed goes far enough, and the ultimate gauge will be ratification of concluded agreements by national legislatures not to mention the growth, or not, of petitions by social networks that are capable of mobilising mass societal resistance on a global scale.[29] In particular, the European Commission requests that the negotiating mandates for the Council representing the Member States in international negotiations, be published. Also, to include civil society and national parliaments fully throughout international negotiations obviously implies delays where

---

29. See for example, the recent criticisms by the powerful civil society platform that represent of 170 NGOs worldwide, the Seattle to Brussels Network (S2B), general declaration of 1 February 2018. See also *Joint civil society statement on the EU-Japan free trade agreement* of March 21, 2017, Brussels/Tokyo to be found at http://s2bnetwork.org/statement-eu-japan/, last visited on 10 March 2018

such participation goes beyond information and seeks active collaboration in the negotiated outcomes.

Ongoing legal questions before the Court of Justice of the European Union[30] concerning the compatibility of the CETA with EU law will inevitably be significant. These development frame unavoidable legal and political challenges to negotiations for future trade and investment treaties in particular. Today therefore, in the context of its international negotiations, the EU is engaging in unprecedented transparency, beginning with the 2015 *Trade for All* Communication, which must be seen in the context of the unprecedented social resistance to the first progressive trade agreements to be negotiated on the basis of the Treaty of Lisbon provisions. While such agreements can take years to negotiate through the EU services, the final ratification remains to be secured before national parliaments. The very real threat of rejection of the final agreement[31] according to national constitutional arrangements has demanded new engagement mechanisms by the EU services. Misinformation and poor reporting and engagement on complex issues are made all the more sensitive by the lack of trust in experts or failure to give them enough time to explain. The Europa Portal reference library for ongoing and previous civil society dialogues relating to trade matters over the last fifteen years or more continues.[32]

The last dialogue in Brussels on the EU-MERCOSUL Agreement was on 20 March 2018. Additionally, as part of the initiatives under the Juncker Package, the new Advisory Group on EU Trade Agreements has been created, comprising:

> 30 organisations representing business, trade unions, consumers, the environment and other areas participated in the first meeting. The number of participants is intended to foster in-depth dialogue. The Com-

---

30. See Belgian Ministry for Foreign Affairs, Foreign Trade and Development Co-operation, *Minister Reynders Submits Request for an Opinion on CETA*, of 6 September 2017, to be found at https://diplomatie.belgium.be/en/newsroom/news/2017/minister_reynders_submits_request_opinion_ceta, last visited on 19 December 2017. For the form and content of the request, see *CETA : Belgian Request for an Opinion from the European Court of Justice*, to be found at https://diplomatie.belgium.be/sites/default/files/downloads/ceta_summary.pdf, undated, last visited on 19 December 2017.
31. Moreover, the apparently negative precedent the *Achmea* ruling sets in respect of the CETA ISDS provisions, implies that national parliaments of the EU Member States are effectively obliged to halt their ratification processes, see CJEU Case C-284/16.
32. See http://trade.ec.europa.eu/civilsoc/, last visited on 28 March 2018. Regular Civil Society Dialogue meetings with Commissioner Malmström and Director-General for Trade Jean-Luc Demarty, http://trade.ec.europa.eu/civilsoc/index.cfm , last visited on 24 February 2018.

mission's idea is to consult the group on new issues for trade negotiations and areas where it feels it needs a broader perspective. The Commission hopes the group's input will help it in its ongoing efforts to ensure that EU trade policy is state-of-the-art and progressive.[33]

The context of EU-Brazil and EU-MERCOSUL relations

For the EU Brazil relationship, Brazil was the first Latin American state to recognise EEC in 1960 and set up a permanent representation in Brussels. The EU-Brazil Framework Co-operation Agreement of 1992 was followed by the 1995 EU-MERCOSUL Framework Co-operation Agreement, and then Agreement for Scientific & Technological Co-operation was signed in 2004. As concerns trade relations, the negotiations for the inter-regional agreement between the EU and MERCOSUL regional integrations has spanned 20 years and European Commission reporting has been anticipating their conclusion since December 2017. How the EU's values are addressed in the EU-MERCOSUL Association Agreement as it stands in draft form today, is addressed further on.

With the Lisbon Summit of 2007, the EU-Brazil Strategic Partnership was established. The Strategic Partnership, rather than specifying rights and obligations of the Parties that characterise international treaty relations, it provides for the forward planning of the joint activities according to declared mutual interests, including political and economic. Brazil's Strategic Partnership will continue after signature of the EU-MERCOSUL Association Agreement. The EU-Brazil Joint Action Plan of 2008 began the programming for joint actions under the Strategic Partnership. The 1992 Co-operation Treaty between the EU and Brazil remains valid, as do subsequent Treaties on scientific and technological co-operation, and the sharing of staff resources, as well as on fusion energy research[34]. The influence on the rationale of these initiatives directly reflects the wording of reflecting the EU Global Strategy and efforts on sustainable develop-

---

33. See DG Trade website of 1 February 2018, to be found at http://trade.ec.europa.eu/doclib/press/index.cfm?id=1791, last visited on 3 February 2018.
34. See the 2004 Agreement for Scientific and Technological Co-operation and the 2017 Atlantic Research and Innovation Co-operation between the EU, Brazil and South Africa, involving the Strategic Partnership on Marine Research, and the Sharing of staff and resources and infrastructure since 24 January 2013, and also, the fusion Energy Research, 2009, in force since January 2013. See also the Research and Innovation Report on Brazil of 20 December 2016, - Report on the implementation of the strategy for international cooperation in research and innovation, COM(2014) 567 final, 11.

ment in particular. On the broader Latin American context, advances in the values-agenda for the EU-Community of Latin American and Caribbean States (CELAC) are tracked in the September 2017 Resolution of the European Parliament, giving insight into its preferences for future policy directions.[35] The EU-CELAC channels for political dialogue illustrate the common region-to-region values-approaches to the policy development, and pressing issues to be tackled in making progress.

To institutionalise the Strategic Partnership, a framework for governmental summits and ministerial meetings as well as collaboration between senior officials, is provided for according to a Joint Action Plans of 3 years duration. Both partners contribute financing based on flexible approaches and based on reciprocity, complementarity and mutual interests. The 2012 Multi-annual Joint Action Plan remains to be renewed, although activities reflecting the broader values of the relationship continue: examples include the renewal in March 2017[36] of the "sector dialogues" for constructive practical political and technical co-operation between EU and Brazilian institutions on a range of topics relating to environmental protection and sustainable development, human rights, energy efficiency, etc.[37] The EU budget contribution is EUR 5.7 million over 3 years for the current fourth phase of the sector dialogues. Recent project and open calls include human rights as well as cultural and economic diplomacy.[38] Reflecting Brazil's emergence from developing country status and the reorientation of the financing instruments by the EU, this new round of funding contribution from the European Union is sourced in the Partnership Instrument. The provision of financing to additional projects on the ground in Brazil as part of the economic and cultural diplomacy efforts of the European Union, as well as projects to further the Union's interests in facilitating trade and the

---

35. See European Parliament *Resolution on EU political relations with Latin America* (2017/2027(INI)), of 13 September 2017, to be found at http://www.europarl.europa. eu/sides/getDoc.do?pubRef=-//EP//NONSGML+TA+P8-TA-2017-0345+0+DOC+PD-F+V0//EN, last visited on 24 February 2018.
36. See http://sectordialogues.org/en/noticia/brazil-and-european-union-launched-new-phase -international-cooperation, last visited on 3 February 2018.
37. In the first 3 phases of the sector dialogues, 30 sector dialogues involved 228 projects involving 41 Brazilian and 27 EU institutions on topics including deforestation and biodiversity, marine research, sustainable production and consumption, climate change and energy efficiency, national disasters, genetic resources, preventing chemical accidents, etc. See the Balanço geral dos oito anos de execução do Projeto 2008 - 2016, to be found at http://sectordialogues.org/pt-br/resultado/publicacao-resultados-do-proje-to-apoio-aos-dialogos-setoriais-uniao-europeia-brasil, last visited on 28 March 2018.
38. For open calls, go to http://sectordialogues.org/encontre-projetos.php?ida=5, last visited on 28 March 2018.

EU-MERCOSUL agreement, are an important contribution to bottom-up approaches that ensure the ultimate success of the Union's international negotiations in their broadest sense.

Turning our focus to trade and investment provision, the EU-MERCOS-UL Association Agreement will contain such a chapter, and while no draft has been made public yet, public consultations on draft clauses have been broad. This is more than a trade agreement, notably for its political dialogue dimension. Anticipated human rights provisions are well-advancing the EU-MERCOSUL inter-regional Framework Cooperation Agreement of 1999. This current draft EU-MERCOSUL "Association Agreement", as it stands so far, includes provision for a Free Trade Area alongside various institutional and economic and political provisions, is the most advanced form since the beginning of the negotiations some 20 years ago, so far reaching 1,300 pages in length. Without official projections on the eventual conclusion between the Parties to the agreement, the window of opportunity for reaching agreement will necessarily be affected by the political backdrop on both sides of the Atlantic. For the EU, political availability and resources at EU level will surely be affected in 2019 by the change of European Commission and by the European Parliamentary elections, in addition to other pressing challenges, notably the secession of the United Kingdom from the EU—Brexit—at the end of March 2019. However, the December 2017 Joint Declaration of European Parliament, the European Commission and the Council of Ministers has already proved effective in progressing with today's priorities for the current term of the European Commission.[39]

The broader legal and political trends in the trade and investment treaties signed by the EU since the Treaty of Lisbon, is pertinent the future of the EU-MERCOSUL relationship. The European Commission's 2017 blueprint for trade and Investment actions is set in the context of the values-based approach that motivates EU financing and co-operation in the EU's broader external relations. The European Union remains open to trade and investment, intentionally rejecting protectionism while building its values into all forms of its international relationships, starting with small constellations of willing partners where needs be. The innovation of the "Trade and Sustainable Development Chapter" in EU Free Trade

---

39. For the Decisions, see *Official Journal* 2017 C446/1, reported on in the 2018 report on the 10 Priorities of the Juncker Commission, 2014-2019. (http://www.europarl.europa.eu/RegData/etudes/IDAN/2018/614679/EPRS_IDA(2018)614679_EN.pdf, last visited on 28 May 2018)

Agreements dates back only to 2011, with the entry into force of the EU-South Korea Free Trade Agreement (FTA).

Further shaping and reorientation of the institutional arrangements and provision for values in these chapters are now under reformulation at EU level. Implementation and enforcement of values through trade and investment treaties are increasingly becoming subject to improvements in the implementation of the social and environmental values, as well as in fleshing out provision for transparency and civil society inclusion in international negotiations and the implementation of trade and investment agreements. Only last year, in May 2017, five Member States' foreign affairs, trade and development Ministers—Belgium, Finland, Luxembourg, the Netherlands and Sweden—wrote[40] to the European Commissioner for Trade, Cecilia Malmstrom, providing suggestions on how to further improve the Trade and Sustainable Development Chapters of trade and investment agreements. Broadly speaking, they are urging for: regular reporting and implementation strategies; more co-operation with multilateral organisations for labour and environmental agreement secretariats; supporting local actors in their contributions to the processes, and increasing their work with EU delegations and embassies in third countries, and; further improving interlinkages between the trade and investment agenda with the 2030 sustainable development agenda and the 17 sustainable development goals. Clearly the political weight of these positions will be relevant to the international negotiators and the ultimate ratification of the agreement after it has been concluded.

Already in the Namur Declaration of December 2016[41] which was the idea of the Belgian politician Paul Magnette, Minister-President representing the Walloon State of Belgium and brought together some 40 or more lead academics from the EU, the US and Canada last December 2017 supported and further articulated growing public concerns as to the values involved and the way in which the EU negotiates international economic and trade agreements. In the Namur Declaration, they call for the EU to "seek in good faith ways to ensure the success of already advanced, let alone already signed agreements, in the spirit of this Declaration", before articulating and further advocating as legitimate, civil society demands for: respect

---

40. See Letter of five EU Member States to Commissioner Malmström of 11 May 2017 http://ec.europa.eu/transparency/regexpert/index.cfm?do=groupDetail.groupDetail-Doc&id=33338&no=22, last visited on 29 May 2018.
41. See the *Declaration of Namur* of 5 December 2016, to be found at http://declarationde-namur.eu/en/index.php/namur-declaration/, last visited on 18 December 2018.

for democratic procedures; compliance with socio-economic, sanitary and environmental legislation, and; guarantee public interests in the dispute resolution mechanism. While the European Commission's commitment to transparency and inclusion of stakeholders in its mandates and conduct of international trade and investment negotiations is indeed unprecedented compared to previous practice, not all demands of the civil society platforms, including the Namur Declaration, are addressed. In particular, to fully include national parliaments and regional assemblies in debates on the initial negotiating mandates would prove burdensome and increase the time frames for international negotiations. The challenge is to balance the legal safeguards for inclusiveness, accountability and scrutiny over international negotiations while at the same time achieve the eventual success of the negotiations and to come up with a functioning and effective trade relationship.

Both the letter from the five Member States to Commissioner Malstrom and the Namur Declaration contribute concrete suggestions of how to improve the implementation and enforcement of labour and environmental values. Very early exploration by European Commission services[42] is already underway into potential means for improving the implementation and enforcement of the trade and sustainable development chapters of future agreements. Avenues under exploration include a more assertive use of the TSD dispute settlement mechanism, build up the capacity of civil society stakeholders and enhancing coordination and joint action with Member States, the European Parliament, international organisations and trade partners.[43] A model based on sanctions is also explored, based on extending the practice under the TTIP and CETA agreements, based on state to state dispute settlement in situations of the lowering of labour or environmental standards. In both scenarios, these discussions are in their infancy and can-

---

42. See the "Non-paper" of the European Commission services entitled *Trade and Sustainable Development (TSD) chapters in EU Free Trade Agreements (FTAs)* of 11 September 2017, to be found at http://trade.ec.europa.eu/doclib/docs/2017/july/tradoc_155686. pdf last visited on 28 March 2018.
43. Non-paper of the Commission services of 11.07.2017. See also the European Parliament Resolution of 5 July 2016 on the implementation of the 2010 recommendations on social and environmental standards, human rights and corporate responsibility (2015/2038(INI)), to be found at   http://www.europarl.europa.eu/sides/getDoc. do?pubRef=-%2f%2fEP%2f%2fTEXT%2bTA%2bP8TA-2016-0298%2b0%2b-DOC%2bXML%2bV0%2f%2fEN&language=EN, last visited 28 March 2018. See also the European Economic and Social Committee (EESC) Opinion on the Commission communication 'Trade for all: Towards a more responsible trade and investment policy', http://www.eesc.europa.eu/?i=portal.en.rex-opinions.39089, last visited on 28 March 2018.

not yet be described as policy proposals as such. Views of the Council and Member States as well as the European Parliament will play an important role in the future relevance of these early opinions.

The values basis is the EU-MERCOSUL Association Agreement currently under negotiation is apparent in the Chapter on the Global Agreement Trade Related Provisions as well as in the Chapter on Trade and Sustainable Development (referring to the draft as it stood last December 2017).

Before introducing the Trade and Sustainable Development Chapter, it is relevant to comment on values relating to human rights, which are notable by their absence in both of the Chapters. The ongoing Sustainability Impact Assessment (SIA) in support of the EU-MERCOSUL Association Agreement will be concluded in the course of 2018, and is being conducted by the consulting arm of the London School of Economics. The SIA EU-MERCOSUL involves broad stakeholder consultation in the four MERCOSUL countries[44] and the last consultation to be held in Sao Paulo, Brazil, was in mid-March 2018. The 2009 SIA for EU-MERCOSUL negotiations at that time on the economic, social, environmental and sectoral analyses. Focused on human rights dimension has expanded considerably since then and this is reflected in today's SIA EU-MERCOSUL. The fact of such broad reference to advances in international relations on human rights deserves comment, see page 80 *et seq* of the SIA EU-MERCOSUL. Whereas labour, food and environmental standards for instance, involve a competitive advantage for which ever partner that does not bear the costs involved in implementing these standards, there is no comparable commercial justification for incorporating human rights. The Terms of Reference for the SIA note the emerging human rights institutional and legal framework in the EU and MERCOSUL countries and "certain human rights issues stand out across national boundaries". It promises to identify potential impacts of trade measures on the various human rights obligations of the EU and MERCOSUL partner countries within the trade provisions,[45] and is specifically screening the rights of indigenous peoples, gender discrimination, the right to highest attainable standard of physical and mental health, and the right to an adequate standard of living.

Returning to the Trade and Sustainable Development Chapter of the EU-MERCOSUL Association Agreement, lessons can certainly be drawn

---

44. See http://www.euMERCOSULsia.com/ last visited on 8 March 2018.
45. See Table 24 of the SIA, *Op. Cit.* n. 48.

from the wave of trade agreements that have ensued[46] since the expansion of the legal basis for such agreements in the Treaty of Lisbon (Art. 2017, TFEU). Working from a draft of the agreement[47] sourced from civil society platforms, relating to the negotiations between 21 February and 2 March 2018, values feature in heavily in both in the Chapter for the Global Agreement on Trade Related Provisions and, as is to be expected in the Chapter on Trade and Sustainable Development. Other specific chapters are dedicated to transparency, dispute settlement, private arbitration, trade in services, intellectual property rights, as well as a chapter on increasing dialogue on food safety, animal welfare, market access issues arising in agricultural biotechnology, anti-microbial resistance and sanitary and phytosanitary measures.

The Global Agreement contains the expression of the Parties values already throughout its preamble to the creation of the Free Trade Area. The very first stated objective is:

> a modern and mutually advantageous trade agreement which creates a predictable framework to boost trade and economic activity, while promoting and protecting our shared values and perspectives on the role of government in society and retaining the right of the Parties to regulate at all levels of government t achieve public policy objectives.

The second objective provides for sustainable development in its economic, social and environmental dimensions, consistent with, and supportive of, their respective international obligations. The following stated objectives include standard provisions of a free trade agreement and its relationship with the WTO agreements, such as reducing tariff and non-tariff barriers to trade in goods and agreement is foreseen on technical standards and conformity assessment including SPS measures. Noteworthy is that the agreement includes provision for integration in global value chains, the liberalisation of trade in services, intellectual property rights' enforcement and protection, and for dispute settlement.

---

46. Korea, Central America, Columbia, Peru, Georgia, Moldova Ukraine. Japan since 2017 and Mexico in 2018. Further agreements are being negotiated with Australia and New Zealand. The Mexico agreement, 36 Chapters long, is available in its draft form, and subject to ratification, go to http://trade.ec.europa.eu/doclib/press/index.cfm?id=1833&title=New-EU-Mexico-agreement-The-Agreement-in-Principle-and-its-texts, last visited on 28 March 2018.
47. Textual proposals can be sourced on the European Commission's website at http://trade.ec.europa.eu/doclib/press/index.cfm?id=1395, last visited on 28 May 2018.

Novel is the provision for creating a framework for the participation of civil society in the implementation of the agreement, as well as for providing a transparent and predictable regulatory environment and efficient procedures for economic operators and all the while respecting the public policy space for "public health, social services, public education, safety, the environment, public morals, social or consumer protection, privacy and data protection and the promotion and protection of cultural diversity". Moreover, the following Article is dedicated to the Parties' relations with civil society through an "association council or committee", which will comprise ministerial level representatives of the Parties and tasked with implementing the trade provisions.

Turning then to the Chapter on Trade and Sustainable Development, the rationale is to ensure that a level playing field in the environmental and social standards, to prevent backsliding in the standards set, guarding against any lowering any social, labour and environmental standards in the interests of improving trade or attract investment. The rationale is also to ensure effective implementation of the international and national standards set. Express provision—"the Parties recognise the importance of working together to achieve the objectives of this chapter"—is made for the two regional integrations to work together through multi-lateral fora to meet the objectives of this chapter, in the WTO and ILO, but also in the UN bodies, such as the UNEP and UNCTAD.

Reading the overall objective of the chapter on trade and sustainable development in the draft EU-MERCOSUL Association Agreement, it is to:

> *enhance* the integration of sustainable development in the Parties' trade and investment relationship, notably by establishing principles and actions concerning labor and environmental aspects of sustainable development of specific relevance in a trade and investment context [emphasis added].

Specific clauses in this chapter of the EU-MERCOSUL Agreement address ILO provisions and MEAs, together with the sustainable management of natural resources in areas of low carbon development, forestry, fisheries, biodiversity, including fighting illegal harvesting practices and promoting corporate social responsibility and fair and ethical trade initiatives.

As concerns the fundamental ILO conventions and other ratified up-to-date international labour conventions and working conditions, together with multilateral environmental agreements (MEAs), The approach is "a co-operative approach based on common values and interests", and while there is provision for dispute resolution (and keeping in mind that this clause is not final), the dispute resolution is based on "dialogue, consultation, exchange of information and co-operation to address any disagreement on the interpretation or application of this chapter"—in the current drafting, the standard dispute settlement chapter is excluded for dispute arising under the trade and sustainable development chapter. Meanwhile the transparency provision as it stands so far, rests on domestic rules and procedures, implying that where they are lacking, the transparency rights of civil society will be difficult to access. The transparency provision foresees that the Parties are open—ensuring awareness and encouraging public participation—about any trade and investment initiatives that might effect environmental protection or labour conditions, and *vice versa*.

Chapter Eight

Current Experience With Nutritional Information in the EU and Chile: How Brazil Could Benefit

Daniele Bianchi

Food does not escape from the intervention of lawmakers around the world. Today even eating habits fall under the protective hands of the law.

The fight against obesity and the search for simple ways to communicate nutritional messages to consumers is a priority in Brazil and in many other countries in Latin America. Governments on both sides of the Atlantic are working on legal solutions to protect consumers for public health reasons, with different approaches that are undoubtedly influenced by the political, economic and legal systems in which they are developed.

At the same time, practical testing is ongoing in Europe and Latin America on alternative nutritional labels for consumer information.

In some ways, two lines can be identified: on the one hand, a soft voluntary approach addressing an apparently educated and informed consumer; and on the other hand, a more direct approach stigmatising products for an unaware consumer. At first sight, these two lines appear so distant from each other and, in many aspects, diametrically opposed, that it might seem unfruitful even to dare a comparison. Yet it is possible to draw some lessons from the concrete implementation of the two approaches in order to develop a halfway approach that could be useful for countries still in the process of thinking or rethinking their nutritional information. This would be the case of Brazil.

In the end, there is common ground where both these approaches find a point of contact. The EU and Brazil are two important traders in the Atlantic. Following the freezing of negotiations on the Transatlantic Trade and Investments Partnership (TTIP) between the EU and the US after the last presidential election in the United States, the current negotiation of a trade agreement with MERCOSUL—where Brazil is the main actor—is again on top of the EU's political agenda.

The scope of this chapter is not, however, to examine the difficult negotiations for this future agreement, which have been ongoing for ages.

The fact that two important actors in the Atlantic ring are searching for solutions to protect their respective consumers will certainly have repercussions when and if the two actors conclude a common trade agreement, even if this agreement does not cover those areas directly.[1]

This chapter focuses on the evolution of nutritional information for consumers in the EU and Brazil, taking account of similar and parallel experience that is ongoing in other parts of Latin America. In the jungle of pure marketing, and in the marshes of the indications, labels and logos that invade the space on the packaging of foodstuffs, it is not always easy for the consumer to separate the wheat from the chaff.[2] In several European and non-European countries, testing is being carried out on nutritional information. Does this answer consumers' expectations? And which consumers?

Eating healthily today cannot be restricted to one social class but should be the normal choice for any consumer who is educated, informed and aware of their role. By reading the packaging of food products, consumers should be able to choose to buy products that are aimed at feeding their body, rather than products that are artificially highly processed—as are most processed products or soft drinks on the market, which only fill your body.

We shall discuss the advantages and disadvantages of the British, French and Chilean experience, before seeing how Brazil could benefit from this experience[3] and before putting forward an alternative proposal.

The role of the EU in consumer protection

The EU was not built in a day. It is the fruit of years of negotiations, compromises, legal evolutions and jurisprudential interpretations.

---

1. See the attempt of Trump administration to limit the ability of NAFTA's members (including the US) to warn consumers about the dangers of junk food in the current ongoing trade talks, as reported by *New York Times*, 20 March 2018.
2. See D. Bianchi, *Comment lire l'étiquette d'un aliment…et reconnaître faux produits naturels et vrais produits chimiques!*, Les points sur les i, Paris, Dec. 2017, p.170. Currently being translated into Italian, Portuguese and English.
3. Other experiences are ongoing in Sweden, Denmark, Norway and Iceland, in Europe, as well as in Australia and New Zealand. In South America, Ecuador is experiencing a variation of the UK traffic lights system and Uruguay is doing public consultations on a model based on the Chilean experience. This latter could have an impact as Uruguay is part of the MERCOSUL where the nutritional labelling is among the harmonised rules inside the group.

Today, it is inconceivable that consumers of the single European market should be subject to different rules across national borders, and even less so that the protection of public health should be affected by administrative or political barriers. Unfortunately, in their nationalistic deliriums, Europhobic parties (because referring to euro-scepticism is an understatement) put half a century of European construction at stake when asking their countries to consume only domestic products and to close their borders to imported products.

The need to complete the single market has been essential to harmonise large parts of national legislations that traditionally produced only for their own national market. Today, nobody (except disqualified politicians for internal reasons) doubts the enormous contribution made to European construction by food law and the case-law of the Court of Justice since the so-called 'Cassis de Dijon'[4] judgment.

Progress has also been determined by "difficult times,"[5] which have led to enhancing the construction of the single market not only for EU industry and trade but, much more, for European citizens, who have become increasingly reconciled around a set of common rules, values and principles.

Information is a key element in consumer protection, as established by Union law.[6]

Consumers have the same rights across the European Union regardless of their nationality: the same right to healthy products which comply with hygiene rules, the same right to have the same information on products to enable them to make an informed choice at the time of purchase, and the same right to be able to eat food safely in compliance with health, economic, ecological, social and ethical standards. They also have the same right to protection if a problem arises following the purchase or consumption of a food product in any EU country.

---

4. ECJ, 20 février 1979, case 120/78, Rec. 1979.
5. See C.Blumann, V. Adam, "La politique agricole commune dans la tourmente : la crise de la 'vache folle'," *RTDE*, Paris, n° 2, avril-juin 1997, pp. 239-293) ; N. DE Grove-Valdeyron, La protection de la santé et de la sécurité des consommateurs à l'épreuve de l'affaire de la dioxine, *RMCUE*, n°433, 1999, p. 700 et s.
6. Cf. article 12 TFEU, article 169 TFEU and article 38 Charte des droits fondamentaux de l'Union européenne.

Sellers of sensations

"Advertising is the soul of trade". Fortunately, the European legislator[7] intervened to impose certain rules on wandering souls that would have otherwise tried to mislead the consumer. The emotional effects provoked by advertising or images representing ingredients or by the denomination of a product must not be misleading to the consumer. Regulation (EU) No 1169/2011[8] (along with Regulation (EC) No 178/2002 laying down the general principles and requirements of food law) constitutes one of the foundations of European Food Law.[9]

Food information, used by multinationals as bait, is the identity card of a product and as such it should not be misleading.[10] The presentation of foods, in particular their shape, appearance or packaging, the packaging materials used, the way in which they are arranged and the setting in which they are displayed is subject to this basic rule,[11] as the European Court of Justice recently recalled to some sellers, not of food but of sensations or emotions.

The Court of Justice was confronted with an herbal tea in which raspberries and vanilla, attractively evoked in the name and on the images of the package, disappeared in the list of ingredients.[12] The Court has placed limitations on the protection of consumer expectations, in defining the concept of "average consumer, reasonably well informed and reasonably observant and circumspect."[13] It is a pity that the Court overestimated the knowledge and attention of a consumer, who often has neither the time nor the reflex

7. Directive 2006/114/EC of the European Parliament and of the Council of 12 December 2006 concerning misleading and comparative advertising (OJ L 376, 27.12.2006, p. 21) and Directive 2005/29/EC of the European Parliament and of the Council of 11 May 2005 concerning unfair business-to-consumer commercial practices in the internal market (OJ L 149, 11.6.2005, p. 22).
8. Regulation (EU) No 1169/2011 of the European Parliament and of the Council of 25 October 2011 on the provision of food information to consumers (also known as "FIC Regulation") (OJ L 304, 22.11.2011 p.18).
9. See D. Bianchi, "Politique agricole commune, régime juridique des produits agroalimentaires," *Juriclasseur*, fasc. 1326, août 2017 and the bibliography quoted.
10. Article 7 of Reg.(UE) n. 1169/2011.
11. See A. Di Lauro, "Le mensonge dans les règles de la communication : instruments pour une gestion soutenable et "adéquate" de l'information du consommateur," in *Production et consommation durables : de la gouvernance au consommateur-citoyen*, Québec , Les éditions Yvon Blais Inc., 2008, p. 517-541.
12. Judgement 4 June 2015, case C-195/14, Teekanne.
13. In particular judgements of 2 Feb. 1994, case C-315/92, Clinique, Rec., 1994, I-317; 18 May 1993, Yves Rocher, case C-126/91, Rec., p. 2361; 6 July 1995, case C-470/93, Mars, Rec., p. 1923.

to read the labelling, particularly when other elements of marketing disturb their already reduced attention to read the label of the product.

In the Darbo case,[14] the Court held that the consumer was not misled by the use of the words 'naturally pure' referring to a German jam containing pesticide residues, cadmium and a gelling agent which were indicated in the list of ingredients. While fully respecting consumer protection, the Court held that the presence of pectin was authorised by Community directives on the composition of jam, and that the presence of residues, within the tolerance limits, was the inevitable consequence of pollution.[15]

In its judgment in the above-mentioned herbal tea (Teekanne) case, the Court made a clearer path towards the protection of consumers by providing a shield against increasingly widespread abuse in the wild world of marketing. It stated that 'the list of ingredients may in some situations, even though correct and comprehensive, not be capable of correcting sufficiently the consumer's erroneous or misled impression concerning the characteristics of a foodstuff that stems from the other items comprising its labelling." The Court referred expressly to the images on the packaging, which misled the purchaser as to the true characteristics of the product.[16]

To enhance this protection, there should be more courage on the part of the competent national authorities in pursuing such abuses, instead of the complaint often being left exclusively to the goodwill of consumer associations or to "word of mouth" via social networks.

The role of states

It is probably in its regulation of aspects that may seem trivial (as there is little attention to them in our daily habits) that we see how helpful the European Union is. However, the European Union fails to be noticed and is often forgotten. The nutritional information system is nevertheless far from being perfect. The information on packaging is often complex and confusing, and it is certainly often not easy to read. This leaves room for the marketing of the food industry.

The EU legislator has left a margin of discretion to the national legislators as regards not only the controls but also the provision of supplemen-

---

14. Judgement of 4 April 2000, case C-465/98, Darbo, Rec. 2000, I, p. 2297.
15. Pt 27 of judgement Darbo.
16. Pt 40 and 41 of judgement Teekanne.

tary information on the labelling. First of all, European legislation requires producers to provide consumers with a mandatory nutritional declaration that includes the following: energy value; the amounts of fat, saturates, carbohydrate, sugars, protein and salt. If space permits, this information is to be presented in tabular format with the numbers aligned. The table is normally presented on the back of the package—but not only for a question of space. No manufacturer would indicate any potential "unpleasant" content in the principal field of vision.

The only concession that the legislature made to the need for clarity of consumer information was to authorise the presence of additional forms of expression and the presentation of such information on the front of the packaging.[17] This information is, however, subject to a double limitation: it is optional, and it must be based on sound and scientifically valid consumer research. Both conditions limit its scope and use.

Member States may recommend to food business operators the use of one or more additional forms of expression or presentation. This should not mislead the consumer, as it is intended to facilitate the understanding of the contribution or importance of the food to the energy and nutrient content of a diet. This is why the additional information must be supported by scientifically valid evidence of understanding of such forms of expression or presentation by the average consumer. The Commission should assess that such systems are objective and non-discriminatory, and that their application does not create obstacles to the free movement of goods.

In some countries, European and non-European, testing is ongoing to help consumers in the difficult task of eating in a healthy way.[18] We will examine three approaches: the precursor, the latest test and, outside Europe, the most courageous one.

The British model

In 2013, the United Kingdom introduced an additional nutritional information system.[19] The labelling system, known as the 'traffic light system',

---

17. See article 35 of Reg. n° 1169/2011.
18. See Daniele Bianchi, "Feu rouge pour les informations nutritionnelles complémentaires en étiquette," *Revue de Droit Rural*, April 2018.
19. See Technical Guidance On Nutritional Labelling and Front of Pack Nutritional Labelling Guidance, available at http://www.nutritionalinformationservices.co.uk/tag/food-labelling/

indicates the number of calories and four nutrients (fat, saturated fat, sugar and salt).

The British agency responsible for food safety (the Food Standards Agency, FSA) developed minimum thresholds for each of the four nutrients in order to rank them according to three colours: red (high), orange (medium) and green (low). The classification of each nutrient into one of these three colours is based on its content in food.

The basic criterion is the thresholds for nutrition claims on foodstuffs that define the terms 'low in fat' and 'reduced sugar'. The FSA sets the thresholds that entitle a product to move from 'orange' to 'red' on the basis of exceeding the basic threshold of 25 percent of the recommended daily intake of the nutrient in question.

In the original model, the FSA used the recommendations of the World Health Organization (WHO) and the British Committee on the Medical Aspects of Food and Nutrition Policy, which laid down a maximum daily intake of 50 grammes. The entry into force of the FIC Regulation increased the threshold (to 90 gr[20]) and therefore modified the criteria for the attribution of 'orange' or 'red'. This allowed certain big multinationals to change their initial reluctant opinion on the British model and to adopt it accordingly.

But other criticism can be made against this British traffic light system.

If the aim, according to the FIC Regulation, is to facilitate consumers' understanding of the contribution of the food to the energy and nutrient content of a diet or importance of the food, the result is partial or misleading.

The colour code system does not take into account all the nutrients, vitamins and minerals whose consumption must be encouraged.[21] Furthermore, nutritional food intake is unknown and it is suggested to consumers that, based on the content of the four nutrients only, a food is bad (red), good (green) or 'maybe good maybe not' (orange). Colour codes are defined per 100 g or 100 ml of the food and not per packet (except for the portion exceeding 100 g or 150 ml), which, for the consumer, does not make sense. No consumer will consume 100 g of butter, for instance, or not eat a half or a third of a pseudo-chocolate bar keeping the remaining portion in the fridge for the following day.

---

20. See annex XIII, part B of FIC Reg.
21. See annex XIII, part A of FIC Reg.

Finally, the combination of three colours simultaneously is ambiguous, since the average consumer can easily find himself confronted with similar products but with alternative colours depending on the content of the four nutrients, thus preventing any comparison.

The protests of several Member States, which found their production affected by this traffic lights system, led the Commission to initiate an infringement procedure[22] for alleged incompatibility with EU law in 2014. This procedure is still at the preliminary stage and pending.[23]

The French model

France introduced its additional nutritional information system at the end 2017[24] after having briefly tested four models. Among these four models, which were subject to testing in many supermarkets in various French regions, there was also the British model. The test served to prove that, at least for the French, the British 'traffic light system' was not useful as it was discarded.

The additional information system is optional, as laid down by European Law. In an annex, the Decree provides for technical specifications, addressed to the "volunteers", which establish the rules for determining the rating score per food based on nutritional aspects, on a scale of five colours. The score allows foods to be classified on a colour scale ranging from green to red, passing through yellow, orange and purple, coupled with letters (A/B/C/D/E) with a view to achieving greater visibility.

For each product, the overall score also takes into account a 'negative' and a 'positive' component. The first includes the amount of energy, saturated fat, sugars and salt. The second is calculated on the basis of the content of fruit and vegetables, nuts, fibres and proteins in food products. A special regime applies to milk, cheese and oils in order to reflect the 'specific character' of French food.

---

22. See Salas, G. Simoes, "Food: The European Commission Initiates Infringement Proceedings against the UK over its 'Traffic Light' Nutrition Labelling Scheme," *EJRR - European Journal of Risk Regulation*, 2014, pp. 531-534.
23. See Commission answer to European Parliament written question, 17 July 2017, n° E-003663/2017.
24. Cf. "Arrêté du 31 octobre 2017 fixant la forme de présentation complémentaire à la déclaration nutritionnelle recommandée par l'État en application des articles L. 3232-8 et R. 3232-7 du code de la santé publique," JORF n° 257, 3 novembre 2017. See. P. Borghi, "Rosso, giallo o verde? L'ennesima etichetta alimentare a semaforo," *Rivista di diritto alimentare*, Aprile-Giugno 2017, p. 79.

Known as the 'NutriScore', the French system is very similar to the UK model in its use of colours, even if it has a higher level of complexity. Complexity does not mean depth or accuracy of information, however, as we will see. Indeed, the only positive aspect highlighted by commentators,[25] when referring to the contribution of avoiding creating room for private initiatives, has been undermined by the initiative taken by some large food multinationals of adopting their own system[26] at European level, ironically called the 'evolved nutrition label'.

For the rest, the system raises the same reservations as the British model.

Moreover, the fact that the French system is built on certain nutrients, and not on the whole nutritional value of a product, makes its impact limited with regard to providing real information to ensure a balanced diet. In addition, the 'positive points' in the calculation actually alter the system, rather than improve it, because the simple addition of certain vegetables (often dehydrated) in the formulation of a prepared meal adds no value to the quality of food. Derogations for vegetable oils, milk or cheese only allow them to obtain the same colour code as industrial products.

This French NutriScore is a simplified system which, as some studies have shown[27], may have an impact on categories such as elderly people, low income, low level of education or low level of knowledge of nutrition. This concerns groups other than the average consumer identified by the case law of the Court of Justice.

The Chilean model

For once, Europe is not alone in exploring appropriate solutions for consumers. This reflects the fact, as is already the case for the environment, that public health and its corollary—consumer information—are problems without borders. South American tests show that innovative, and in some way more courageous, ideas can come from the other side of the ocean and not always from the northern hemisphere.

---

25. See Borghi, ibidem, *supra*.
26. Pepsi, Coca-Cola, Mars, Mondelez International, Unilever and Nestlé.
27. See Avis du Haut conseil de la santé publique (HCSP) du 24 août 2015; études de l'Institut national de la santé et de la recherche médicale (Inserm) in *Nutrients*, Aug. 2015, and *American Journal of Preventive Medicine* (AJPM), Dec. 2015.

Chilean legislation on the nutritional components of food and food publicity[28] merits a special mention. The lengthy legislative process and the four-year period needed to adopt implementing provisions are evidence of the difficulties (and pressures) with which the Chilean lawmaker had to cope.[29] The Chilean law, which concerns only the nutrient profiles, may be considered pioneering in several respects.

It provides for specific prohibitions for the sale and advertising of high-calorie food or food rich in nutrients (sugar, salt and saturated fat) in schools of lower level. These prohibitions also apply to advertising (including the use of gadgets, stickers or cartoon characters[30] to attract children) and to the free distribution of these foods for children under the age of fourteen.

This legislation is accompanied by an obligation for schools to organise courses for nutrition education and physical education designed to raise the awareness of young people about healthier eating habits.

Regarding the information on the label, the Chilean law imposes an obligation to display an octagon on the front of the package. Inside the octagon is the indication, in white letters on a black background, high in calories, high in saturated fat, high in sugars or high in salt. The use of the 'stop' signal in the Chilean Highway Code, and the use of an octagon and these colours, results in a certain stigmatisation of the products bearing it. This legislation is midway between complementary nutritional information and radical measures against so-called "junk food."[31]

Unlike the European models, this Chilean food label marking enables the consumer to immediately identify a product whose content is very rich in fat, sugar or salt.

---

28. Known as "ley de etiquetado de alimentos" of 6 June 2012, into force since 27 June 2016 : Ley No. 20.606 Sobre Composición Nutricional de los Alimentos y su Publicidad, available at: http://www.leychile.cl/Navegar?idNorma=1041570&idVersion=2012-07-06.
29. See décreto N° 13, Ministerio de Salud, of 16 Apr.2015. See Pilar Rodriguez, "La guerra entre Salud y el área económica del gabinete por el etiquetado de los alimentos", 20 November 2014, available at: http://ciperchile.cl/2014/11/20/la-guerra-entre-salud-y-el--area-economica-del-gabinete-por-el-etiquetado-de-los-alimentos/.
30. See Carreño, I. and Dolle, T. (2017). "The Relationship between Public Health and IP Rights: Chile Prosecutes Kellogg's, Nestlé and Masterfoods for Using Cartoons Aimed at Attracting Children," *European Journal of Risk Regulation*, 8(1), 170-177.
31. See Alberto Alemanno, "Health warnings on junk food", 25 March 2013, available at http://albertoalemanno.eu/articles/health-warnings-on-junk-food; Smith, E., Scarborough, P., Rayner, M., & Briggs, A. (2018). "Should we tax unhealthy food and drink?" *Proceedings of the Nutrition Society*, 1-7. doi:10.1017/S0029665117004165.

The Chilean socio-economic and legislative context explains the rationale for these measures, which do not have the disadvantage of being voluntary and complicated.

The Chilean food labelling law was preceded by a wide-ranging debate after the publication of very alarming data on obesity among young people and among the general population of Chile.[32] At the time the law was adopted, no soda (with the exception of 'zero' or 'light') and no breakfast cereal (except unprocessed) could meet the criteria for not displaying the black octagon.[33]

An apparent simplicity for an "unaware" consumer

These models have one thing in common: the Nudge theory.[34] Conceived by US researchers, this theory is based on the assumption that a 'nudge' allows individuals to make a 'choice' without obligation or sanctions in case of a wrong choice.

It is true that models based on prohibitions or sanctions often provoke counterproductive behaviours, but it is also true that these models of paternalistic liberalism are reaching their limits in the complexity of the problem they are trying to reduce to its simplest denominator. A balanced and healthy diet cannot be reduced to the choice of food identified in relation to three or four nutritional components, although these are the four most important.

The British, French and Chilean models have another thing in common. They refer to a kind of 'unaware' (or 'idiot') consumer, far from the notion of the "average consumer, reasonably well informed and reasonably observant and circumspect", stemming from the case law of the European

---

32. See Corvalan, C. et al., "Structural responses to the obesity and non-communicable diseases epidemic: the Chilean Law of Food Labelling and Advertising," *Obes Rev*, 2013, 14: 79–87; Mediano Stoltze F, Barker JO, Kanter R, Corvalán C, Reyes M, Taillie LS, Dillman Carpentier FR. "Prevalence of child-directed and general audience marketing strategies on the front of beverage packaging: the case of Chile." *Public Health Nutr.* 2018; 21(3):454-464.
33. See Vega, "Coca Cola cambió 59 fórmulas por nueva ley de etiquetado", 4 September 2016, available at: http://www.latercera.com/noticia/coca-cola-cambio-59-formulas--por-nueva-ley-de-etiquetado/.
34. See Thaler and Sunstein, *Nudge: Improving Decisions about Health, Wealth, and Happiness*, Yale University Press, 2008; Hansen, "The Definition of Nudge and Libertarian Paternalism: Does the Hand Fit the Glove?" *European Journal of Risk Regulation*, March 2016, pp. 155-174.

Court of Justice. The three models are based on the assumption that the consumer is not able to read the information on calories, protein, saturated fats and added sugars as indicated in the list of ingredients, in descending order, often accompanied by the content expressed in percentage. They are also based on the fact that the consumer may rely blindly on the 'subliminal' or less subliminal messages that the manufacturer printed on the label: 'artisanal product', 'grandmother's recipe', 'home-made', 'with added'...

The legislator then provides consumers with a tool of choice: a colour code (green or black), so that, like Pavlov's dog, they can make the right choice. Unfortunately, this additional information has not satisfied the need of consumers for simple and direct information. Indeed, the additional information could be seen more as marketing than information. And in some cases, it induces misinformation.

The optional nature of the French and British models weakens the idea of providing a system of comparison between thousands of products that do not bear the codes. Furthermore, if, as it seems, some manufacturers indicate the colour per portion, you can be assured that they will choose the size that enables them to obtain the green colour (or the yellow), regardless of the full content of the package. Another shortcoming is the fact that the colour is not a measure of the quality of a product (which, of course, does not depend on the presence of salt, sugar or fat) or of its being 'artisanal' or 'industrial' (which depends on the presence or absence of GMOs, additives, flavourings or highly technical processes). In fact, this is the best way to promote industrial products in which, unlike products made of a single or a few ingredients, the numerous components of the formulation may be differently determined or replaced by chemical substitutes.

A transparent and effective educational system should rather allow the recognition of food which does not use chemical ingredients (additives and flavours in the first place) and which has not been subject to highly industrial processes.

The colour marking is likely to result in a 'boomerang' effect for consumers by providing partial and potentially misleading information. These systems, no matter what their promoters say, do not enable the identification of 'good' or 'bad' food. The most obvious example is that of milk, which will not be marked in green, due to the presence of fats, whilst beverages with sweetener will display the green colour because they have a reduced caloric content. The same thing will happen to ham or meat products (orange/red colour) compared to pre-cooked meals: the latter may even obtain the green colour because the industry will be able to manipulate the formulation by subtracting calories, fats and sugars and adding flavourings and preservatives and subjecting the product to treatments for recreating the food finally represented on the package.

Extra virgin olive oil, the cornerstone of the Mediterranean diet because of its health benefits, will not obtain the green colour either, although 'light' products from the food industry would display this colour.

Moreover, these systems do not consider the recommended doses and daily intakes. There is therefore a risk that an industrial preparation with low fat can be labelled 'green' (and thus be considered beneficial) despite that it does not contain any component necessary for a balanced diet.

As highlighted by the doctrine, these three models all raise criticism from the point of view of compliance with EU law.[35] Indeed, there is a risk that they may be considered as protectionist measures hampering and distorting intra-EU trade and WTO rules on international trade.

In the light of experience, the European Commission was due to submit a report, by 13 December 2017, to the European Parliament and to the Council on the use of such additional forms of expression and presentation, their effect on the internal market, and the advisability of further harmonisation of these forms of expression and presentation.[36] As of this writing, the report is still due.

An alternative solution for an "aware" consumer

The European Union is not an abstract entity that imposes rules from the mythical city of Brussels. Without the contribution of the 'citizens/consumers', none of these rules would be meaningful. The consumer has a genuine power of life or death over the product, with economic consequences for the manufacturer - whether or not multinationals - whose survival depends on the sale of the product.

Consumers should not just be satisfied by food the health of which is based merely on the absence of contaminants or harmful residues (such as pesticides and antibiotics). This should go without saying! They should rather require that every food has the taste and nutrients that it must obviously have. Most processed products are only a reproduction of the natural

35. See Borghi, op cit, *supra*.
36. See article 35 paragraph 5 of FIC regulation.

food[37] through the addition of flavourings and additives, and through the use of techniques and processes for manipulating the ingredients.

While all these wonderful chemical mixtures may comply with the nutritional profiles of a so-called food in accordance with the rules, they nevertheless perfectly imitate the appearance, flavour and aroma of the most typical dishes without containing any of their most typical ingredients!

Ultra-processed food is characterised by a long list of ingredients that includes products one cannot normally find easily unless you are a chemist or an industrial manufacturer.[38] These are products that have also been subject to highly technological processes that not easily re-performed in a kitchen but rather in a laboratory.[39] This ultra-processed food is relatively cheap and, most importantly, ready for use or to pop into the microwave, thus creating the illusion that the time saved contributes to one's well-being. It is presented in attractive packaging covered with beautiful images, health claims and probably a colour mark. It usually also belongs to the ten multinationals controlling global food production.

Instead of referring to nutritional profiles that can be manipulated or artificially created by industrial processes and that have no connection to the quality of a product, it would be much simpler to distinguish food on the label, according to three categories and colours:[40]

- traditional or natural, in green (no preservatives or additives or vitamins added, no GMOs, nor any added sugars or treatment — like the substitution of components of an ingredient, water injection or irradiation... — apart from the simple mixing of ingredients, cooking or deep-freezing),

- processed, in yellow (food incorporating additives or flavourings, or that has undergone any industrial process)

- ultra-processed, in red (food incorporating more than five additives or preservatives, including an industrial process).

---

37. See D. Bianchi, *Comment lire l'étiquette...*, op.cit; p. 24.
38. E.g. hydrogenated oils, hydrolysed proteins, maltodextrine, inverted sugars, starch and syrup from different sources...
39. E.g. irradiation, recombination, addition or subtraction of components ...
40. This is a simplified version of the NOVA model which suggests four food groups based on their degree of processing: fresh foods, food ingredients, processed foods and ultra--processed food. See Monteiro et al., "NOVA. The star shines bright", *World Nutrition*, January-March 2016, 7, 28-38. See also Cediel G, Reyes M, da Costa Louzada ML, Martinez Steele E, Monteiro CA, Corvalán C, Uauy R., "Ultra-processed foods and added sugars in the Chilean diet (2010)", *Public Health Nutr.* 2018; 21(1):125-133.

This proposal has the advantage of offering consumers a simple way to use basic products and thus to rediscover the principles of good cooking and healthy eating. In its frenetic use for profit, the food industry has lost these principles. Good cooking has been confined to culinary TV shows, and healthy eating to laboratory handling and allusive labelling ('light', 'zero' and the 'green' colour of a traffic light).

The current general legal framework for food law in Brazil: lights and shadows

In Brazil, the labelling of packaged food is mandatory and is regulated by legislation[41] through bodies such as the Ministry of Health, the National Health Surveillance Agency (ANVISA),[42] the Ministry of Agriculture and the National Institute of Metrology, Quality and Technology. The Código de Defesa do Consumidor (Consumer Protection Code) supplements the legal framework and can be used for issues not clarified by other regulations.

Labelling rules apply to all food offered to consumers for domestic or international trade, whatever its origin. When exporting or importing food that is ready to be offered to a natural or legal person that acquires or uses food, the labelling rules of the country of consumption must therefore be observed. This shows the importance of labelling legislation in the framework of international trade.

What is important is the awareness of the consumer and their power. Achieving this is tantamount to a good nutritional education, and the efforts made by the Brazilian government deserve praise worldwide.

In Brazil, the promotion of healthy food as a strategy to prevent certain diseases, as well as to control nutritional diseases and malnutrition, is carried out by the Ministry of Health through the National Policy on Food and Nutrition (Política Nacional de Alimentação e Nutrição—PNAN).

One of the main achievements of this policy was the drafting of a strategic document: *"Guia Alimentar para a População Brasileira"* ("Food Guide for the Brazilian Population").[43] Published in 2014 by the Ministry

---

41. See in particular Resolução RDC N° 259, 20 Sept. 2002.
42. The legislation is available on the website of the Agency: http://portal.anvisa.gov.br/
43. http://www.paho.org/bra/index.php?option=com_docman&view=document&category_slug=seguranca-alimentar-e-nutricao-997&alias=1509-guia-alimentar-para-a-populacao-brasileira-9&Itemid=965

of Health, this document presents information and advice on food consumption, and aims at promoting a healthy lifestyle for individuals, families and communities in the Brazilian heterogeneous society. The document has the courage to put at the top of the list of recommendations the principle[44] that food is more than nutrient intake, and to draw consumers' attention to a socially and environmentally sustainable food consumption of fresh food or minimally processed food. This golden rule should be raised as a general principle of any food policy and as a guideline to the consumer in the jungle of labelling information.[45]

The guide identifies the dietary guidelines of the Brazilian population in order to promote health through educating the population on food and nutrition and through subsidising national food and nutrition policies and programmes. In addition, rather than formulating prohibitions,[46] it also promotes the recovery of a healthy diet based on typical Brazilian food, and the identification of foods whose consumption should be stimulated.

The priority actions of the governmental agencies[47] are the reduction of the levels of sodium, sugar, and fats, especially saturated and 'trans' fats in processed foods; the nutritional labelling of foods; and, more recently, allergens labelling.

In 2015, Brazil adopted a National Pact for Healthy Eating ("Pacto Nacional para Alimentação Saudável"),[48] to expand the supply, availability, and consumption of healthy foods and to combat overweight, obesity, and disease caused by a poor diet.

---

44. *"Prefira sempre alimentos in natura ou minimamente processados e preparações culinárias a alimentos ultraprocessados"*.
45. On the role of ultra-processed food, see Monteiro, Carlos Augusto; Levy, R. B. (Org.), *Velhos e novos males da saúde no Brasil : de Geisel a Dilma*, 1. ed. São Paulo, Hucitec/NUPENS-USP, 2015. v. 1; v. Monteiro et al., "Dietary guidelines to nourish humanity and the planet in the twenty-first century. A blueprint from Brazil", 2015, *Public Health Nutr.* 18, 2311-2322.
46. See National Plan for Coping with Non transmissible chronic diseases (2011–2022) Brazil. Ministry of Health Secretariat of Health Surveillance. Secretariat of Strategic and Participatory Management. Vigitel Brazil 2010: Surveillance of risk factors and protection for chronic diseases by telephone survey. http://bvsms.saude.gov.br/bvs/publicacoes/vigitel_2010.pdf.
47. See Jane Mara Block, Adriana Pavesi Arisseto-Bragotto, Maria Manuela Camino Feltes, "Current policies in Brazil for ensuring nutritional quality", *Food Quality and Safety*, Volume 1, Issue 4, 21 December 2017, pp. 275–288, https://doi.org/10.1093/fqsafe/fyx026.
48. Decreto No. 8.553, de 3 de Novembro de 2015, art. 1, Planalto.

Although less complex and sophisticated than European legislation, the Brazilian legislation has many characteristics comparable to its European equivalent. It would be difficult to make an exhaustive list of these elements in a few pages. However, it is possible to identify some lights and shadows in this legislation, in particular in relation to nutritional labelling.

The regulation of nutritional labelling has been mandatory in Brazil since 2003[49] and harmonised in the scope of Mercosul. The nutritional labelling of food forms part of the PNAN strategies as this labelling is considered an instrument that may facilitate the choice of healthy food by the population. The nutriment to be indicated in the nutritional table includes information such as caloric value; carbohydrates; proteins; total and saturated fat, 'trans' fats; cholesterol; fibre; calcium; iron and sodium, and the percent of the daily value of each nutrient per serving of fat. Brazilian consumers are confronted with the same difficulties as their European counterparts: the table is complicated to read. The Brazilian legislator should have made a particular effort in simplifying the appearance of the nutritional messages and should have taken into consideration the level of education of the population. The compulsory nutritional labelling not only targets the consumers of Alto de Pinhciros in São Paulo or Ipanema in Rio but also some 12 million illiterate inhabitants out of a total of 210 million inhabitants.

Other nutritional information also appears on the label and is subject to rules. EU rules on nutrition and health claims have been established by Regulation (EC) No 1924/2006. Since 2012 this other additional information is mentioned in Brazil as supplementary nutritional facts or nutritional claims[50], which suggest that a food possesses particular nutritional properties, especially but not only in relation to its energy content and/or its content of proteins, fats, carbohydrates and fibre, as well as its vitamin and mineral content.[51] Compared to European legislation,[52] where flavourings are divided into two categories (artificial, created by chemical synthesis in

---

49. See Resolução RDC N° 359, 23 Dec. 2003, Resolução RDC N° 360, 23 Dec. 2003 completed by Resolução RDC n° 163,17 Aug. 2006. Technical Regulation of Portions of Packed Foods for Nutritional Labeling Purposes. http://portal.anvisa.gov.br/documents/33880/2568070/res0359_23_12_2003.pdf/76676765-a107-40d9-bb34-5f05ae897bf3.
50. See Informação Nutricional Complementar (INC), Technical Regulation on Complementary Nutrition Information. Technical Report n° 54, November, 12, 2012. http://bvs-ms.saude.gov.br/bvs/saudelegis/anvisa/2012/rdc0054_12_11_2012.html.
51. I.e. "fonte de fibras", "rico em cálcio", "baixo teor de sódio"...
52. See Regulation (EC) No 1334/2008 on flavourings and certain food ingredients with flavouring properties for use in/on foods (OJ L 354, 31.12.2008, p. 34).

laboratories; or natural, of vegetable, animal or microbiological origin), Brazil has a third category: 'flavourings (synthetic) identical to natural flavourings.'[53] Currently, the majority of flavourings used are 'identical to natural'.

The difference between an identical and a natural flavouring is the method of production of its molecules. Whereas the molecules in natural flavourings are obtained from products of animal or plant origin, by physical processes, the molecules in an identical flavouring are created by chemical synthesis in laboratories. But given that "identical flavourings" are "synthetic flavourings" that have the same aromatic molecules as natural flavourings, there can be no justification for a different name. *Qui prodest*? Certainly not for consumers' clarity.

In the EU, the presence of allergens in food has been regulated since 2000[54]. Discussion on food allergens labelling in Brazil started in 2008. Blocked by difficulties in finding a harmonised approach in MERCOSUL, the legislator finally adopted a text in July 2015.[55] The labelling of 18 allergenic foods and/or their derivatives entered into force in July 2016, after a one-year transitional period. Until then, certain food companies were providing allergen information on labels on a voluntary basis. Due to the absence of scientific evidence on the main allergens affecting the Brazilian population, the list of the Codex Alimentarius for allergens was used as a reference.[56] The legislation does not allow for any derogation for food that may not contain allergens by nature. It is thus possible to find at the supermarket fruits or sugar or salt labelled "gluten free". By contrast, over-cautious manufacturers may label their egg packages "allergens: it may contain eggs". And what else?

It would not be appropriate to complete this outline of Brazilian food legislation, without mentioning genetically modified organisms (GMOs). Brazil is the second biggest producer of GMO crops in the world, with an area of more than 40 million hectares dedicated to the planting of GMOs. It comes only behind the United States.[57] As of 1 November 2016, there are

---

53. "Aromas (sintéticos) idênticos aos naturais".
54. See Directive 2000/13/EC.
55. See Resolution no 26 from December 2nd 2015. Report on requirements for mandatory labelling of major foods that cause food allergies. https://www.legisweb.com.br/legislacao/?id=286510
56. The list contains 22 allergens against 14 for the EU (Regulation (UE) n. 1169/2011) and 9 for the USA (Food Allergen Labeling and Consumer Protection Act of 2004).
57. https://gain.fas.usda.gov/Recent%20GAIN%20Publications/Agricultural%20Biotechnology%20Annual_Brasilia_Brazil_11-22-2016.pdf

58 GMOs approved for commercial cultivation in Brazil (compared to one in Europe), of which 34 are for corn, 12 for cotton, 10 for soybeans, one for dry edible beans and, most recently, one for eucalyptus.

GMOs are governed by the Biosafety Law of 2005,[58] which regulates principles established by the Constitution regarding the preservation of the environment and the country's genetic patrimony, as well as the super-vision of entities dedicated to research and the manipulation of genetic material. As far as labelling is concerned, a decree was issued in 2003 to regulate the right to information, as guaranteed by federal law, on food and food ingredients intended for human consumption and animal feed when they contain or are produced from GMOs.[59] Pursuant to the decree, the Ministry of Justice issued the Administrative Act[60] which defines and de-picts the "transgenic symbol" (a yellow triangle with a black T inside) to be used in the marketing of foods and food ingredients containing or produced from GMOs.

In spite of 15 years of application,[61] the labelling of GMOs is still ques-tioned. There are new bill proposals currently being discussed at the na-tional congress that seek to alter the GMO labelling rules, with some even questioning their existence.[62]

How could Brazil benefit from nutritional labelling experience?

Brazilian nutritional labelling has many similarities with the EU mod-el[63] including its apparent complexity for unaware consumers who simply

58. Lei No. 11.105, de 24 de Março de 2005, art. 1, http://www.planalto.gov.br/ccivil_03/_Ato2004-2006/2005/Lei/ L11105.htm#art42

59. Decreto No. 4.680, de 24 de Abril de 2003, art. 1, http://www.planalto.gov.br/ccivil_03/decreto/2003/ D4680.htm#art8.

60. Portaria No. 2.658, de 22 de Dezembro de 2003, available on the website of the Ministry of Justice, at http://portal.mj.gov.br/main.asp?View={4521CE7B-732B-40EB-B529-F-9200C365E93}

61. See de Castro, Biancca Scarpeline, "15 Years of GMOs in Brazil: risks, labelling and public opinion," *Agroalimentaria* [en linea] 2016, 22 (Enero-Junio), available at http://www.redalyc.org/articulo.oa?id=199245407006.

62. For instance, Bill Proposal n. 4148/2008 approved on April 29, 2015 by Brazil's House of Representatives by 320 to 135 to amend the current labelling legislation Executive Order 4,680/2003. The new Draft Bill establishes that only products which have more than one percent of GMOs in their final composition must be labelled. Another impor-tant change is the decision to withdraw the requirement for the "T" label. The Bill is now at the Senate.

63. Currently contained in the FIC regulation, firstly introduced by Council Directive 90/496/EEC of 24 September 1990 on nutrition labelling for foodstuffs (OJ L 276,

do not have any knowledge of basic nutritional recommendations. But this lack of knowledge is not linked to education (or the lack of it). If Brazil is the country with the second highest consumption per capita of sugar (600 kcal/day), the US has the highest worldwide consumption of sugar per capita (658 kcal per day).[64]

Other South American countries are developing similar models.[65] In Brazil, the indication of the excessive presence of some nutrients is under consideration, as already happens in the Chilean model. Anvisa is leading discussions on the choice of model between that of Chile, pushed by consumers' associations[66], and that of the UK, pushed by the industry.[67] A proposal to adopt the traffic lights system was lodged previously but never adopted.[68] The perspective of general elections in October 2018 and the well-known links between the agro-industry ("bancada ruralista") and the current government are certainly unlikely to help the acceleration of the process of adopting a new front-of-package nutritional information model.

The Brazilian health situation is dramatic. According to the Brazilian Ministry of Health, 3 out of 4 deaths are due to diseases linked to lifestyle. According to recent research from the National Cancer Institute and the Ministry of Health, more than 600,000 new cases of cancer arise in Brazil each year. But what is more disturbing and at the same time challenging is that one third of cancer cases could be avoided with a healthier lifestyle.

6.10.1990, p. 40).

64. The estimated average for sugar consumption in Brazil is 30.1 kg per year: see ABIA (Brazilian Association of Food Industries), Cenário do consumo de açúcar no Brasil. Estudo baseado em dados do Instituto Brasileiro de Geografia e Estatística. http://www.abia.org.br/vsn/temp/z201747infograficoabiaacucar.pdf.

65. In South America, Ecuador is testing a variation of the UK traffic lights system and Uruguay is doing public consultations on a model based on the Chilean experience. This latter could have an impact as Uruguay is part of MERCOSUL where nutritional labelling is among the harmonised rules inside the group. Canada and Israel are both studying the Chilean model.

66. Aliança pela Alimentação Saudável e Adequada supported by 32 organisations among which the Instituto Brasileiro de Defesa do Consumidor (Idec) ; http://alimentacaosaudavel.org.br/; see V.Prates, B. Ribeiro, "Rotulagem de alimentos: entenda o debate e suas repercussões," Dec. 2017, *Boletim BMJ*. The Aliança's proposal is supported also by a worldwide group of nutritionists and scientists, see Carta do 14 Março 2018 on their website.

67. Rede de Rotulagem da Industria, in particular Confederaçao Nacional da Industria (CNI) and Associaçao Brasileira das Industrias de Alimentacao (ABIA).

68. Projeto de Lei do Senado (PLS) n° 489/2008 by C. Buarque; Projeto de Lei (PL) n°5522/2016 by V. Macris.

The recommendations of the "Guia Alimentar para a População Brasileira" are no longer enough. The recommendations of international bodies, including the World Health Organization (WHO) and the Pan American Health Organization (OPAS), that the adoption of appropriate food labelling rules contribute to improved food choices and consequently to the prevention of obesity, hypertension, diabetes and other chronic diseases[69] should be implemented in an effective way by national governments.

On one hand, it is a basic right of consumers to be given "adequate and clear information on the different products and services, with the quantity, characteristics, composition, quality, price and risks they present", as provided for in the Consumer Code (CRC). On the other hand, surveys conducted both by Anvisa and by consumers' associations[70] show that the existing rules on nutrition information on food labels in Brazil do not guarantee the right to information on the composition and nutritional quality of food, due to various problems and comprehension of the content and display of contradictory messages on the front of packaging.

Doing nothing is not an option, given the serious health situation of the Brazilian population. It was the same dramatic reasons that pushed Chile to adopt its rules.

Brazil has the opportunity to adopt the Chilean model. However, Anvisa hides its reluctance to do this behind the fact that no data exist proving the efficacy of one mode over another. The time span of current experience is quite limited and if we consider the limits of the models (their voluntary nature and a semi-illiterate consumer target), it is true that this does not help.

Brazil could also opt for a revised traffic lights system based on the model suggested in above, which uses the NOVA system of Brazilian Professor Monteiro. This would be less stigmatising than the Chilean model but would still target ultra-processed food in a more direct way than the soft European traffic lights systems.

Conclusions

All these initiatives are justified by public health considerations. Apart from a few specificities, obesity, diabetes and cardiovascular diseases are

---

69. See in particular WHO, Global Status Report on non-communicable diseases, 2014.
70. See Revista do Idec n°208, Sept-Oct 2016, p. 16.

issues that know no borders. According to recent studies from the WHO, the whole world will face a crisis of huge proportions of obesity by 2030, with many countries at risk of having over half their adults overweight.

Faced with the development of national initiatives, it may be questioned whether it would not be more appropriate, on the one hand, for the European legislator to take back the pen, and on the other hand, for those countries that still do not have any legislation, to take action.

In Europe, the main drawback of the models tested is that they do not impose mandatory nutrition labelling across the country. Secondly, nutritional labelling, as we have seen, only partly meets the needs of "uninformed" consumers as it provides for only partial or ambiguous information.

Law-makers worldwide should do more than merely make recommendations. Ongoing experience rather speaks in favour of regulatory measures in order to be more effective.

The legislator should go back to basic principles. What is food?[71] If we confine ourselves to its definition in EU law, which can be summed up by saying that it is anything that may be ingested by humans, on the basis of this definition, without any quality benchmark, any activity of the food industry could be justified. There is no longer any need to mention a food recipe; it is simpler to call it by its real name: formulation. In this respect, the Brazilian definition of food is more qualitative oriented which could help setting a legal framework that favours natural and less processed food compared to ultra-processed, as food should contribute to the nutrition of the human organism and is not simply reduced to something that can be ingested.[72]

From the point of view of informing consumers, any model should try to obtain the correct balance by referring to the dosage of all proteins and nutrients contributing to a healthy diet. The main limit of the simplified models currently being tested is that they are simply built around the respect of a colour code applied to individual products that are artificially manipulated. It is not therefore only the legal compatibility of a partial

---

71. See Article 2 of reg. n° 178/2002: "food" (or "foodstuff") means any substance or product, whether processed, partially processed or unprocessed, intended to be, or reasonably expected to be ingested by humans.
72. See Capitulo 1, artigo 2, I do decreto-lei n° 986, 21 Oct. 1969. "Alimento: tôda substância ou mistura de substâncias, no estado sólido, líquido, pastoso ou qualquer outra forma adequada, destinadas a fornecer ao organismo humano os elementos normais à sua formação, manutenção e desenvolvimento".

information tool with the fundamental principle of consumer protection that can be called into question, but also the true logic of the models. A balanced diet is based on eating varied food and reasonable quantities of it. The balance is acquired with education.[73]

Education requires good information. This is the real battle for consumers and the benchmark for any information system. That is why consumers should require their respective law makers to enable them to distinguish between the 'natural' ingredients (that are expected to be found in the basic foodstuff by tradition or simple logic) and the "industrial" or "artificial" ingredients.[74]

The protection of public health and of consumers is a universal principle. The solutions already found in one country can be shared in order to guide the reasonable choices of national legislators more in the interest of the consumer. The food industry's influence is strong both in Brazil and in Europe. Brazil could opt for the European sophisticated (and less effective) model or make its legislation more revolutionary by adopting the Chilean model.

Brazil could also build on experience on ultra-processed food to opt for a revised traffic lights system that is less stigmatising than the Chilean model but that will still target ultra-processed food in a more direct way than the soft European traffic lights systems. This cannot be seen as a back-to-the-past battle to preserve tastes that have disappeared, nor can it be seen as an anti-globalisation fight against industrial-capitalism. Nobody denies the food industry's contribution to feeding a growing population, and to improving the distribution, conservation and production of food for the emancipation of women. However, industrial processes have quickly diverted from simple food production on an industrial scale to become almost mass production of 'chemical' products that have nothing to do with the original food, other than their name and appearance. Food has become a tool for industry and not vice versa.

Adopting a revised traffic light system would be a way to protect Brazilian consumers and, at the same time, to strengthen the country's economy in this time of crisis and on the eve of negotiating free-trade agreements.

---

73. See Souza, Sônia & Lima, Kenio & do Socorro Costa Feitosa Alves, Maria, "Promoting public health through nutrition labeling - a study in Brazil". *Archives of Public Health*. 74 (2016).
74. See D.Bianchi, *Comment lire l'étiquette…*, op.cit., p. 25.

Brazil is a major agricultural country, with the potential for developing an agricultural production of high quality on the basis of international standards, not only huge quantities for export. Typical Brazilian food has characteristics of the Mediterranean diet. The Portuguese, Italian, Spanish presence makes Brazil a kind of far west border of Europe on the other side of the Atlantic Ocean. The addition of Japanese and Asian influence has allowed the indigenous tradition to be expanded thanks to these culinary ingredients and the handcraft of African slaves.

All this can contribute to making the Brazilian diet a model of healthy food, but today unhealthy lifestyles and habits put it at risk.

In Brazil, where the consumption of processed foods has greatly increased, the reduction of saturated and 'trans' fats, sodium, and sugar in these foods seems an effective strategy for reducing the intake of these compounds by the population. The goals established by international health agencies should be effectively achieved through partnerships between government agencies, industry, and non-governmental organisations. In addition, adequate nutrition labelling and consumer education will allow healthier food choices by the population. The appropriate response from the food industry, consumer education, and effective regulatory and enforcement policies will allow changes to dietary habits and improve the population's health.

It is clear that everything has a cost—"except values," as the philosopher Nietzsche said.

There is a false idea that investing in consumer information and providing quality and natural food increases costs that not all consumers would be prepared to pay. One can imagine the interests which are behind those ideas; the myth that food should always be cheaper and cheaper should lead the consumer to reflect. There is a popular proverb that says: "there is free cheese only in a mouse trap".

There is also the widely spread idea that voluntary labelling programs are more efficient. In name of this, part of the food industry in the US is trying to keep Chile's model from being adopted more widely. In the new NAFTA talks, the US administration would try to introduce a clause preventing any warning symbol, shape or colour that "inappropriately" denotes that a hazard exists from consumption of the food or non-alcoholic beverages. If confirmed, the attempt of the Trump administration to limit the ability of NAFTA's members (including the US) to warn consumers about the dangers of junk food in the current ongoing trade talks,[75] proves that lawmakers need to find the courage to put health interest first.

"Let's not eat shit anymore!", the late Jean-Pierre Coffe, the great defender of good and healthy food, said in one of his books.[76] Helpful labelling should shed more light on that "shit" before it passes from your dish into your stomach. Happy reading and bon appétit!

---

75. As reported by *New York Times*, 20 March 2018.
76. S. J.P. Coffe, *Arrêtons de manger de la merde!*, Flammarion, Paris, 2013.

Chapter Nine

China and World Trade

Valdemar Carneiro Leão

Opening words by Professor Renato Flôres

This is a Joint Panel[1] with the Brazilian Centre for International Relations CEBRI, another think tank in the city of Rio. FGV believes in co-operation, we have a close relationship with CEBRI and invited them to share a panel with us.

Ambassador Valdemar Carneiro Leão is an outstanding diplomat, an expert on trade, and an expert on China, where he served as Brazilian Ambassador. We shall entertain -in an informal and provocative way- a conversation bringing to the meeting the theme "China", and we shall end up with consequences (impacts/effects) of China in the Atlantic Basin.

The talk

Thank you for your very kind words. I assume the invitation I received to take part in this panel has to do with my experience as Brazil´s ambassador to China until very recently. So, I suppose the contribution I can give to this debate is to present you with a different perspective, namely by introducing China as an intervening force in the Atlantic dynamics. When I refer to China, I'm not limiting myself to whatever influence China may have on Brazil, as China becomes the largest Brazilian trade partner, but also on Europe itself. In any case, these remarks are more of a provocation than anything close to a scholarly presentation.

I will try to put my thoughts together in a nutshell, by looking at three different aspects: first, China as a trader; second, China as an investor; third—and this is more controversial, China as a rule maker.

---

1. The whole event is available at: https://www.youtube.com/watch?v=yrrnUZST79I&-feature=youtu.be.

China as a trader

This is where everything began. You probably recall that as soon as China acceded to the WTO, in 2001, it embarked upon a process of reform, consisting of a profound transformation of its economy. To the external world the reform's most visible traits consisted of an expansion of China´s trade relations. However, this process evolved in an unprecedented speed, until China, in a matter of less than two decades, became the world´s largest exporter (3 or 4 years ago), and the second largest importer. It was a colossal jump. Suddenly, China could no longer be ignored in whatever international trade topic one would wish to address, either because the country was viewed as a threat, or because it had become an indispensable partner.

In the Atlantic space, China became the elephant in the room.

The case of Brazil is emblematic. Over the past 15 or 20 years, the Brazilian industrial sector went through a "shrinking" process and, today, it accounts for a mere 10% or 12% of the country´s GDP. Of course, the loss of competitiveness is at the root of the phenomenon. But this phenomenon could not be fully understood should one fail to take into consideration the big inroads the Chinese industrial goods made in the Brazilian market. Either as a provider of parts and components at far more competitive prices than those produced locally or as supplier of finished products at unmatchable prices. Conversely, almost simultaneously, Brazil rose to the position of the world´s second exporter of farm products, after the US. And China is also behind this transformation (a positive one in this case), as Chinese demand for food and agricultural commodities used as industrial raw materials skyrocketed. The fact that China became Brazil largest trading partner is of no small significance. Should traditional trade links prevail, this position would be occupied by either the US or Europe, or even Mercosul.

But there is more to it than just China´s primacy. China far outweighs its foreign competitors in the Brazilian foreign trade. The bilateral trade between Brazil and Asia (here taking Asia as a whole, though bearing in mind that China is by far the biggest player) is roughly the same as our trade with Europe and the US combined.

To sum up, Brazil is being pulled into Asian rather than into transatlantic trade routes.

China as an investor

Three years ago, China became a net overseas investor and it remains the second largest overseas investor in the world. These investments go to Europe, the US, Brazil, Australia, less to Africa, a lot to East Asia.

In Europe, China goes after high tech, brands and market access. In the US, real estate, entertainment, transportation, high tech but also through the purchase of stakes in financial services. In Brazil China comes for natural resources (oil and gas) and infrastructure (power generation and transmission, and ports).

Now, the question is: is Chinese investment in countries of the Atlantic basin contributing to an increase in output? And is it contributing to a more dynamic transatlantic trade? I submit that it's not. In the vast majority of cases, Chinese investments are not greenfield. In 2017 nearly 95% of Chinese investments in Europe were acquisitions, apparently with little effect on trade.

The objective of Chinese investments has to do with technology transfer and market access, neither with increase in production capacity nor with foreign trade.

My point here is that, while China has become a major source of FDI, its targets don't add much (indeed probably very little) to transatlantic trade. In other words, the shift to the Pacific basin finds no counterweight as China expands its economic might to the West.

China as rule maker

China is becoming a rule maker (in international trade or in international institutions). Let's focus on what is happening in the WTO. China is strongly attached to the WTO while the US (the Trump administration) doesn't seem to acknowledge its value, to put it mildly.

Now, take two possible scenarios:

i) In an extreme scenario, the US decides to leave the WTO. This would entail, at first, a chaotic situation, as all other countries would have to put something into place in order to organize international trade. In this case, China will take centre stage as the second world trading power and will strongly influence the establishment of a new set of rules that would conform better to its own interests.

ii) Second possibility, Trump decides to remain in the WTO but, then, only in a reformed WTO; a weaker WTO, with a less rule-based and more negotiation-based dispute resolution system, among other reformed features. In such a scenario, even considering all other countries would like to put up resistance, China would inevitably emerge as the strongest voice.

In both cases China is bound to be the key player in the shaping of any multilateral trade framework succeeding the WTO current rules. These were made essentially by Atlantic powers (Japan was always a player of little weight in the GATT/WTO treaty negotiations) for use by Atlantic powers. A future set of rules—if it materializes—will bear China´s fingerprint and the Pacific basin trade will probably be the reality that those new rules will aim to regulate.

Countries around the Atlantic Basin will have to learn how best to cope with this giant that is pulling trade and investments to Eurasia and East-Asia rather than to the Atlantic. And that will gradually make international rules reflect its core interests.

Thank you.

The debate

Professor Renato Flôres: I fully agree that the WTO is a very serious issue, I myself don't see the US quitting the organization (it would be a catastrophe!). Let's assume that this scenario doesn't take place. But your last scenario is rather feasible. There is a movement, not by all, but by some members, to progressively weaken the WTO. It will provoke a reaction from China, and at the same time, US will put barriers to Chinese investment. China will fight the US within the WTO. A kind of fight will start within the WTO, specially within the Atlantic Basin. So, there are two very serious points of attrition.

How would you see this in terms of the future, if this were the scenario? So, there are internal disputes in the WTO, which eventually be damaging anyway, and suddenly, Trump becomes more aggressive with the Chinese presence in the Atlantic. What are your views about this?

Second, it's very understandable why China became so important from trader to rule maker, if you look at the evolution of international trade. Since 2012, it has been decreasing, for many reasons: international deflation after 2008/ 2009 crisis, volatile growth in the US, problems in the Arizona, and so forth. Anyhow, the main cause is the decrease of the Chinese trade.

China is growing at 8% or less. My guess is that they will stabilize around 6% to 8% in terms of GDP growth. This represents a fall in the international trade. With the decrease of China as a trader, in the other hand, they will lose power, dependency of China will decrease, and exporters will be obliged to diversify, in terms of partners.

So, there are two different moves here, one movement of conflict at the WTO, here in the origin, and another of decreasing importance of China, as a trader. And a China that will be needing ever more expertise, as for instance, for creating China brands. Could you exploit a bit this scenario?

Ambassador Carneiro Leão: First of all, I don't necessarily dismiss the possibility that Trump decides to leave the WTO. First because Trump is a very unrepressed man, extremely ignorant of world affairs but convinced he can always win because of his wit and his power. His vision of the world is aligned with the US strategic interests in a very narrow and short-sighted way.

As to China fighting the US within the WTO, my view is that it will do it all the time., particularly when the US decides to act unilaterally. China will try to show the world that it abides the rules, that the US are the one that is trying to destroy the multilateral trading system. "The emerging power likes the rules"—that's the image that China likes to show.

China has a number of tools it can use to cause some damage to US trade interests, basically in agriculture and in aerospace sales. China can use those weapons without infringing the rules; China´s state owned enterprises can simply cancel contracts.

On the decline of China, I agree with you in that China will probably stabilize around 6.5 percent or 7 percent growth rate. It will be unsustainable to go on and on and, as a result, trade will come down. But still, China will continue to be the largest exporter, and the second largest importer, at least. Its importance in trade will continue to be extremely significant, regardless of what it might lose in terms of trade growth rate.

Besides, at the same time, China is increasing investments, offering credit, creating international financial institutions, so its expanding its influence in different fields that will more than compensate possible loss in trade.

Professor Flôres: Just two things, first I'm obliged to come back to Trump, the US is in decline, it's not something that Trump invented. It's a very slow and continuous decline, and it has effects. At the same time, China is becoming more dependent of the world. Particularly as they want to show themselves as a fair rule maker. These two effects imply that it's not in the interest of any partner to create a great damage to the relationship; in the end, there must be a kind of balance. Neither China, nor the US will have an interest to pursue further drastic measures. Maybe, this can create opportunities in this area. In the end, we will live a funny equilibrium, a kind of balance, that will both manage the US decline and the US and the rise of the China dependence.

Ambassador Carneiro Leão: The US is so far ahead, particularly in technology and financial power; it will take a long time to happen.

Answer by the Ambassador to questions from the audience: Brazil doesn't see China as an economic rival. Among East and Southeast Asia countries, China dependency is a reality, but, apart from North Korea, no one looks at China as a model to be followed.

As far as the EU is concerned, what I saw in Beijing was an European complaint that China would always try to divide member countries, while the EU delegation did what it could to avoid this kind of game. But the reality is that China has a number of bilateral commissions with different European countries (Germany being by far the most important).

In the energy sector, I have no doubt that China will increase its efforts to get away from coal and to develop advanced energy technology in different directions. I am not familiar with this topic, but I believe that, among renewables, solar is where they have made more progress. They are now the largest producers of solar panels. They have already an overcapacity. In nuclear, they continue to build reactors at an amazing pace. China needs all the energy it can get: the demand is huge.

Chapter Ten

The Future Prospects and Shape of Trade Agreements in the Atlantic Region: A Round Table

Renato G. Flôres Jr., Moderator (R. Flôres), Carlos Mariani Bittencourt (C. Mariani), Daniel S. Hamilton (D. Hamilton), Renato Baumann (R. Baumann), and Roberto Fendt (R. Fendt)

Opening note

Below is a slightly edited version of the recording of the Round Table which took place on March 23, 2018. In order not to lose the spontaneity of both the interventions and the debate, the text is fairly close to the participants' original words; no improvement or substantial revisions having been made. Blunt repetitions or expressions used in spoken language, mostly to add emphasis, have been deleted.

(R. Flôres) *Bom dia!* This is the last panel of our meeting, the second thematic meeting of the "Jean Monnet Network on Atlantic Studies". We had a very enlightening seminar yesterday, and we close with this outstanding panel. We are supposed to discuss the shape and form of future trade agreements.

As we know, the Atlantic area is famous for its love of integration, so we find several regional integrations here, we find the EU, the sponsor of this project and a model of integration; it wants to spread its experience on regional integrations. We are going to discuss this.

My colleagues here are all honourable and serious men, they surely have wonderful presentations. Let me introduce them, very briefly:

[*the four members of the Roundtable, Carlos Mariani Bittencourt, Dan Hamilton, Roberto Fendt and Renato Bauman are then introduced*]

So, to start, I'll make a kick-off and pass the word to my colleagues.

We have a new reality: to perhaps the great joy of the Chinese, who are not yet number one in the world, the US administration stopped the TTIP negotiations, refused to sign the TPP, and is pursuing a trade policy, which is not unusual by the way, but runs different from what had been done in the past 10 to 15 years. We have new realities also in South America, in Africa (in the beginning of this week, we had a very important event: 44 African countries manifested the will to make a Free Trade Area, which in principle was signed by 21 countries, many of them in the Atlantic coast). Ambassador Cravinho, yesterday, was very enthusiastic about the EU—Mercosul Free Trade Agreement, which is already 22 years old. So, there may be very interesting things that are going to be fixed until the end of April; we have a lot of new realities! And my first question to my friends is: we were in this kind of encompassing trade agreements, TTIP was very ambitious, all kinds of regulations, TPP also with standards, rules… And now, we came back to good old times…

I would like to ask: Do you think that these big encompassing trade agreements, particularly in the Atlantic realm, are over? What do you think are the prospects of a comeback of these kind of trade agreements?

(R. Fendt) I'll start this discussion with the background, if you don't mind. Essentially, Mr. Trump has been in office for almost one year and half. Nothing happened in the trade front. There are many remarks by Mr. Trump about the Chinese, not very kind, by the way. The Americans have a very curious perception of the world economy. The system they created, back in 1944-47, this rules-based system, in multilateral trading and in many other areas, the FMI, World Bank, the GATT, produced 70 years of uninterrupted growth. Americans were the ones who profited more from it. Some people say that Mr. Trump is a kind of a "Mussolini". I guess this is not strictly correct. He seems to be all things, and sometimes he is, but he has a master plan.

The multilateral trading system was a system of co-operation; the rules were for everybody. Americans are particularly scared about the prospects for national security of the rise of China as a major power. They are scared on the military side.

The US administration used to have four basic pillars. The first was the President himself, now difficult to understand, and difficult to predict. The second was the faction of trade falcons (hawks). They are firmly convicted that the United States are losing from the current multilateral system. They rather prefer that the US negotiate in a bilateral basis; which is great, but not well accepted by potential trading partners. The other faction is the National Security hawks. These folks believe that China will surge a civil war against the US. The reaction is well perceived, Chinese students are very monitored, what they do, where they go, to whom they speak… The US are blocking acquisitions of Chinese high-tech firms in the States. They share the same worry with Germany. And there was, in the past, a fourth line in the White House, which was the people who were 'globalists'. They accepted that globalization was good for the States, because it had been good for several decades. Unfortunately, the head of this group was fired. But the biggest nation in the Atlantic still is the US; they are left with less illusions, they want to get out of many of the trade arrangements.

So, I really don't know what the future of the trade agreements in the Atlantic is; the US must be in, because they still are the largest economy in the world, without them it will be difficult to have trade agreements.

(**D. Hamilton**) I would caution you, when looking at the United States today, to say "the Americans." We are having a huge political fight in the US, in which each of our two major parties is fighting a civil war within itself. The traditional notion of Democrats vs. Republicans is becoming quite fluid. It's hard to say what it even means anymore. You have many Republicans opposing the President; many Democrats fighting over the legacy of the election debacle. It's very unclear where things will go. But it's also unclear with that many opposing forces what the President is trying to do, particularly in the Congress (including on trade).

So, when it comes down to final decisions, it's not only the President who's erratic; you don't know where the Congress will come out. There are some particular issues they have blocked the President, on a number of variants, when they simply don't agree with him. They are so far a bit clearer about Russia, Ukraine, military issues but there's also a big push against what he's trying to do on trade. Whether it comes out, I can't tell you. There's also a different kind of force, which you will see through the NAFTA renegotiations: the US governors, the leaders of our 50 States, are all heading to Washington to argue why, what Trump is doing is a disaster for their states. And the governors in a big, continental size country, with a federal republic, really do play a big role. This is important to keep in mind.

So, it's fluid. We should not anticipate that everything the President tweets is becoming US policy, because it isn't. It's a constant fight in Washington, everyday among all these forces. That's why it's unpredictable. The President does not have a master plan. He is a transactional businessman, who is using transactional business tactics to leverage the US position vis-à-vis the other partners. Allies and adversaries, it's all conditional, depending on the advantage you can gain in his view for the US.

With that said, after your question, what we are seeing are different and often contradictory trends going out at the same time. You have the whole multilateral system in crisis at the WTO, for reasons that much have to do with the WTO. In general sense, it has not been producing, because we are not getting any consensus or any breakthroughs in the WTO itself, before Trump, on a whole host of really important trade issues. So, it's not functioning.

What Trump has done is to question the premise of it, and to try to block particularly the appellate body that's important to these trade contestations. Because, as you have said, this is a concern, not a fear. I don't think the word "fear" appears in the American perceptions about China; there is rather a concern that China uses a predatory mercantilist type of approach that enables Beijing to game the system, in ways that those committed to multilateralism just aren't prepared for.

This is a debate, and not just in the United States. How wise was it at the time to admit China into the WTO? Many countries now are rethinking why that was done at that time. What were the premises behind the decision? Should it be reconsidered?

The result is that, as you have said, the country that helped to create this liberal order is now questioning it. It's not trying to destroy it, but it wants different terms. So that's one level.

Then Renato's question is, at the next level, what I would call super-charged bilateralism. That's what we are seeing these days! You see the US renegotiating number of its agreements and pulling out of some.

But you see, the EU is doing the same thing. The EU is even acting more bilaterally in trade than the United States, with a whole host of new negotiations, in a way that is trying to encircle the US with some agreements.

Then the mega-regional agenda that existed, you have the EU trying to create this new deal, you have the revival of the TPP without the United States, you have the Africa Agreement. So, the mega- regional agenda is also moving forward, but not in an even way.

When you have Nigeria saying it's not going to participate in the African agreement, that's also a big, big issue. What we are discovering is that other deeper trends are underway that are influencing trade perceptions. One is the digital world. The digital economy, in many ways, is becoming the economy; we don't have any good data about data. Governments really don't know how to measure these flows, or these interactions, in good ways. We don't know the extent to which we are becoming dependent on these digital connections. We know we are, but we don't yet know how. We have to think harder about the digital world, how is it interacting with the traditional trade world. That's a driving force right now, and we don't have good rules about it.

Second, changes in technology are affecting how trade is conducted and breaking it up in terms of trade and tasks. New kinds of technology allow companies to bring things back home that they used to outsource.

The third big trend is energy. A whole new paradigm of energy is unfolding before our eyes. This is particularly important to the Atlantic, because many of the new energy flows are emanating from the Atlantic Basin. This too will affect how we think about trade in the future.

(C. Mariani) The day before yesterday I visited my fellows at the National Confederation of Industry. All negotiations with the EU, and at Mercosul, are conducted by the National Confederation of Industry, since the last 22 years. I witnessed the first years of negotiations inside the members of Mercosul. And then, finally, when we received the visit of a very important German businessman, who suggested, in 1997 or 1998, that we should work together, four countries in Mercosul, and four in the EU. So, we started this, it was not very easy, but it was comfortable to negotiate or to suggest. The first meetings were in early 2000. The negotiations proceeded very well, very friendly, with very qualified people from both sides, and finally we reached, in Lisbon, the date of a possible signature of a preliminary document. And for our surprise, for the South American team, the Europeans changed. Just as always, agriculture doesn't accept what's being discussed by industry. So, negotiations were officially cut. The resuming of the negotiations was in 2010, with a meeting in Madrid, and with the presence of the Presidents of most countries in Europe and South America. And everything started again, just three years ago, we entered in something. Finally, the 31st of December 2017, was supposed to be the date of the signature. The President of the EU was in Brasilia, but there was no signature. And we started everything again.

I met some people at the National Confederation of Industry, yesterday morning, and we wrote something intelligent:

[*reads a set of questions*]

(R. Flôres) Thank you! Just a few points: you remember yesterday what Ambassador Carneiro Leão said about China and the WTO: "China loved

WTO". And you heard what Professor Hamilton said today. So, you see that things start to match! Also, Professor Hamilton raised new points, which is the digital world, the retreat of fragmentation, something very interesting, with deep consequences. I will pass the word to Professor Bauman, to hear his views on the original questions, but I will add another question, related to the first one. An important point in these agreements was the discussion of standards and rules. So, let us suppose that we are not going to have anymore these encompassing talks, although Dan said that Europe is trying to negotiate them to a certain extent. TPP is trying to keep the encompassing character. I think that, without the US, the game is different. I would add: Do you think that, even if we don't have more these mega-agreements, the issue of standards and rules is here to stay, will it be present even in more modest agreements?

(R. Baumann) I will focus on the Atlantic area, as such, not the broad Atlantic area that comprises Indian countries, African countries .... Those at the Atlantic coast. When you see the South part of the Atlantic, us and Africa, it is of course very poor. Few things going on, in terms of trade and investment; it's not the most brilliant part of the world. Most of it takes part in the Northern Hemisphere, the US and the EU. The question is: Are we about to see further agreements or negotiations? And the answer is, definitely yes. At the NAFTA level, two things were brought to table: A) The varying waiver of steel and aluminium tariffs (if you behave yourself, we won't negotiate and we'll treat you differently); B) Then the corporate ex-rate adopted by the US, which is damaging a number of other countries. On the EU side, don't forget we have the perspective of Brexit. Almost half of the value of US exports into EU gets via the UK. So, if the UK leaves the EU, that imposes two things: a very needed bilateral negotiation US-UK, by definition, but then the market value of the EU for the US, comes down, because it is a very important partner, and hence it is bound to be new negotiations US-EU, without the UK, and then you have the 5 years-old Canadian agreement with the EU, and Canada is a member of the Commonwealth.

We, of course, have a very strong hope, not only from the EU ambassador, but I can assure you, from the Brazilian government we are bound to finally have some agreement by late April or early May, and I presume there is a concrete margin for that hope. There are three elements to take into account:

1) TPP minus one: countries have signed that. It is not as ambitious as originally, but it's there, and it gives a very strong signal of what, from now

on, the negotiators must take into account. It provides a bottom line for further negotiations, comprising those countries.

2) China: the turning point of the presence of China is 2001. China is overwhelming, its figures are so important. But this is a very recent thing. And it was trade. What is new? The increasing intensity of China trade with emerging economies. If you plot a chart of the relative weight of low and medium-income countries in China exports, it comes flat and, in 2001, increases.

The unprecedented thing is investment. China is flexing its muscles, and increasing its presence everywhere, including in our economies. There is another aspect with regards to trade negotiations: the fact that the first preferential trade agreement by China dates from 2004. China has 12 to 15 trade agreements, so far. And the point is, different from the US and the EU, when you have one size fits all: "These are the conditions, join it or lose it!". In the case of China, it's tailor made. Every single agreement considers the interest of its trading partner. This opens a wide door to the possibility of reducing resistance with negotiating with China. Because they seem to be so clever, they take into account all things you care most, that's the second point.

3) The third aspect, most of the wealth on trade, for the US and for the EU, is not merchandise, it is services. Trading in services implies change in your domestic legislation, norms and practices. Hence, the agreements are bound to take place, and to comprise government procurement, trade in services, norms, the relation between government and private agency, and so on.

(**R. Flôres**) Thank you! Again, you opened another area of investigations, which is the area of services. It is very interesting the TPP-1 view. And the consequence of Brexit is also interesting. It seems that the British didn't do their homework on Brexit. And given the EU-Mercosul agreement, maybe Dr. Mariani can complement.

(**C. Mariani**) I have been optimistic for many years, but there is something we don't understand very clear, the negotiations between EU and Mercosul. The leadership of Brazilian foreign officers, Ambassador Ronaldo Costa Filho, is very cautious in terms of the information he gives, and he doesn't want to force anything.

(**R. Flôres**) Roberto Fendt, would you like to say something about China?

(R. Fendt) There is a very big difficulty here and elsewhere, regarding China's intentions. The first thing to mention, and to complement what Renato Baumann said, China is not rules-based. But when China joined the WTO, there was a big expectation in the West that this rapidly rising middle class in China would put pressure for democratisation, in the Western way, which is different from the Chinese view. The Chinese do not value conflict; they value harmony; that's why they have one single party. They are not rules based! This new silk road project is the way of integrating China in the world economy. It's completely different from the model the US created in the late 40's. It's not a system of rules, it is a system based on transportation, which will develop the Western part of China, and then will take China worldwide, either by sea or by land. Renato Baumann said something really important, China is very flexible, maybe in the future, when China is number one, this will change, but currently, they have agreements with everybody, not just the small countries, but also the big ones (Australia, New Zealand, South Korea). This should be kept in mind. They will continue expanding this silk and road project, it's a political project. But the main drive is the competitive insertion of China in the world economy.

(R. Flôres) Thank you! I will pass to Dan, but I would like to add a further question: you mentioned a "flowery" of agreements in the Atlantic area; also mentioned the question of Africa, Nigeria… How do you see with this 'certain confusion', an increase in South- South agreements in the Atlantic? Does this imply that nothing is going to happen?

(D. Hamilton) Let me just make a couple of basic points. I think the point about services is also really very important, especially because that's where the jobs are. Trade is just the means, it's not the goal. Maybe we lost track on that in all our narratives. I think the goal for domestic leaders and the public is: "Do I have job?" and "Will I have a job in the future?", "How is trade related to that?" or, "Is our economy growing because of this or not?" I think the narrative supporting the mega-regional agenda got that all mixed up. And many members of the public began to think that the trade negotiator is going to trade off domestically determined standards, because they wanted better market access. That's why it all started to collapse.

So, regarding services, that takes you into the agenda beyond trade and it is about standards and norms and deep intrusion into domestic ways of doing things. And that was put to its limits in the TTIP negotiation, which was between two continental economies that in many ways are very similar. We have to derive some lessons from that.

The second point is that we talk about trade, but trade is not the driver, at least at the North Atlantic economy. And I don't believe it is the driver with the South American-North American or South American-European economies. It's investment!

Investment is absolutely the driver of jobs and growth across much of the Atlantic. Trade follows investment, it doesn't lead it. The real world of Atlantic commerce is the reverse of what you may have been taught in economics 101. When we talk about Brexit, for instance, it's not US trade with the UK that is important, actually US trade with EU is much more important. But US companies based in the UK export as much to the rest of the EU as US companies based in China export to the rest of the world. The really important commercial bond between the US and the UK, the US and the EU, and also the UK in the EU, is the deep linkages of mutual investment. Over 2 million people in the US and the UK directly owe their jobs to these bilateral investment ties. It's a huge relationship. Mutual investments between the EU and the US are even larger. Investment is what matters, much more than trade—although trade is also significant. One must keep this underlying factor in mind when thinking about trade agreements; you want to make sure that you don't do anything that stops the investments flows.

The next difficulty, which one saw again in the TTIP but also in the EU-Canada negotiations, has to do with dispute settlement mechanisms. The traditional approach is that you must have some mechanism by which investor's rights are protected vis-à-vis the state. This is coming undone. There's no more consensus for that, and within the EU there's actually a legal decision that says you have to push that out, that it's more competence of member states than the Commission. The Trump administration interestingly also opposes investor-state dispute settlement mechanisms—a reversal of traditional US approaches. That's why I caution you when one says "the Americans," because the Trump administration in some areas is reversing traditional US approaches, such on this issue, and in this case the business community vehemently opposes the Trump administration. One has to think about a new model, in terms of what we should think about (I'll come back to that later).

Another point important to understand about the EU is that the coming battles will be about the digital world, about privacy. The EU stance is that "privacy rights are human rights." It's a fundamental approach. Any trade partner that negotiates now with the EU has to certify, or the EU has to certify, that it has equivalent protections for privacy to those of the EU itself. That's a very high standard, if you think about what the EU is doing. And even under the EU- Japan deal, it's not done, because there is no adequacy determination yet on this issue. They must finalise that, before there will be a deal with Japan. And the same will be with every other bilateral deal; which makes it hard for the EU to be a multilateral partner -frankly, because they'll have to have every bilateral deal done on the privacy issue. That's why the EU is turning into a bilateral negotiator rather than a plurilateral one, because of its own internal conditions. I think that is going to be an issue that will only become more important in the future. We'll have to understand it much better.

The third point, on the EU dimension here, is Brexit. It's important to understand, at least from the US perspective, back to my point about investment, that the value chain map of Europe is not the same for American companies as the institutional map of Europe. And it's becoming less the same. The role of the UK, the role of Turkey, Norway, Switzerland (which is incredibly tied into the US economy), are all becoming more important. So, non-EU Europe is becoming much more important to the US, relative to the EU. Any type of new kinds of agreements has to encompass the broader European value chains, and not just the EU "qua" EU.

I come back to my final point, at least to your question, Renato. The deep freeze of the TTIP that you mentioned is the road to nowhere. In fact, is the road to trade wars. Both sides have agreed that the obstacles are far too high, and the incentives too low, to do anything except freeze things. Without any framework across the North Atlantic, it is a mess, and it's going to get worse. Because the US has a framework with Nafta, and with South Korea, the Trump administration argued: "Well, we have these frameworks so let's consider maybe some exceptions for those partners". The EU then had to scramble: "What about us too?" But there's no mechanism in which we can mediate these disputes. It's the daily chaos in Washington.... I think this only ends up in a bad place.

One option is to revive what is called the Transatlantic Economic Council. It was created during the George W. Bush administration, but it was a European idea. It's about "cherry picking" agreements. It's not about a big trade deal, but about very small deals, some of which are not about trade but about aligning domestic regulations. Unfortunately, this idea also did not fare well under the Bush Administration. It's a little better than a trade war, better than the Deep Freeze, but it's not much.

The idea of a revival of TTIP, or TTIP 2.0, is distant now. But I will come to my point, which is: the purpose of any of these agreements should be jobs and growth. The group that recommended the TTIP was actually called the High-Level Working Group on Jobs and Growth. If you talk to people, they worry about their job. I think speaking to that agenda, and using trade as an instrument, not as the goal, would be a far better approach in today's climate. So maybe you don't have trade agreements, if you focus on the other things that start to unite you:

1) at least across the North Atlantic, it's about how to better align the education system with the needs of the economy. It's about how workers can be trained and retrained so their skills match those needed by companies in a quickly-changing economy. The whole notion of vocational training is actually very popular in the US, drawing on European lessons. Even the Trump administration likes this. There's a big agenda there, that could be good;

2) split out the investor-state dispute settlement mechanism from "trade agreements," and deal with it on its own, to make sure investments continue to flow. But what are the terms upon which we might agree?

3) one of the original motivations for the TTIP was: "What about third countries? "Can they be part of these things?" or "Are they excluded?" The impression that was left by the US and the EU, because they didn't accept the promise that TTIP would be open to others, was of a closed shop. And this was about high standards, maintaining the high standards for people, and those standards should be the goal, not let those standards erode. That's the point about China. Either we are going to work together, and maintain the standards we believe in, or those standards will start to be eroded by countries that do not share those same views. It's not an anti-China coalition; but it is about one's own social preferences and the standards by which people should live in this economy. That could be a very good part of what I would call Job and Growth Agreements rather than trade agreements. Something different! These types of agreements could also be bilateral.

The basic point is that we can advance commercial interconnections across and around the Atlantic without reducing the issue to that of trade agreements. A focus on jobs and growth would have some resonance in the US and parts of Europe. It helps us deal with Brexit and broader European value chain issues, and is a way for us to engage with certain partners in a different way. And it doesn't hold up progress due to difficult negotiations on trade agreements.

I suggest that this focus on jobs and growth is also worth exploring across the Atlantic South. Instead of thinking about institutional big trade agreements between blocs in the South, which sounds difficult to me, why not think about the areas, beyond trade, in which both sides could profit? Brazil invests considerably in Africa, for instance, and in lots of areas in which there is Brazilian expertise there is considerable African receptivity. Why not expand more of that agenda and find other complementary areas to promote commerce, including investment. Just think differently!

(**R. Flôres**) Thank you very much, Dan! Very interesting points! I would ask my friends here, if they want to add something. Or, should I pass the word to the floor?!

(**R. Baumann**) I fully agree there is lot of Brazilian initiatives in Africa to the point that there is a feeling we are losing ground to the Chinese. This should be our natural counterpart. But the point is, there is no other continent in the world with so many trade agreements as Africa, and yet, the percentage of regional trade is less than two digits. So, I'm sceptical about the initiative of the 40 plus African countries. And the traditional formal way of making agreements, I fully agree with you: specific initiatives, in this case in particular, provide more results than the formal agreements.

(**R. Fendt**) I couldn't agree more with you! I lived for 2 years in Africa, and things deteriorated very much since I left. There's a whole region that is getting worse and worse. You cannot have trade, or big trade, among the African countries with respect to trade agreements. Simply because the economy is too much equal, and then you have the communications/transportations problems. People look at the ways of growth of the African countries; it's the area of the world which is growing faster. But the base is so small. It doesn't matter if you grow very fast. It is not creating too many trading opportunities.

(**C. Mariani**) I will mention the problem of investment. We have been discussing with the Brazilian government for years and years, to have a model of contract with other countries, and finally we got it one year ago. So, this is moving on, and with the South American countries they are moving as well, in both directions; they are accepting the model of Brazilian contracts.

(**R. Flôres**) Wonderful news! Thank you! Well, we open to the floor!

Questions

(Eloy Alvarez) It's a question to Dan Hamilton: You raised many issues, but three of them were related to: investments as a driver, not trade; second, the matter of jobs and growth, and, in your first intervention, you talked about energy as an important issue related to the Atlantic basin. So, my question is: can you detail which is the interrelation, or the connection between these three issues: energy; jobs creation and investments in the Atlantic basin?

(Rafael Almeida) I would like to know if we are heading to a moment of redefining alliances in the South Atlantic, specially related to Brazil and Africa.

The second question is: How can we take advantage of collecting more investments between US and China? Do we have a strategy to bring investments from either side, Chinese or the Americans?

(Anna Ayuso) It's about the optimism or pessimism of the EU and Mercosul agreement. I want to ask you about the possible scenarios. If the agreement is not achieved; what is the scenario after that? It will continue with an un-ended negotiation or there will be some consequences, even internal in Mercosul? And, if the agreement is achieved, which are the consequences? Not only for the trade partners (Mercosul and EU), but the other actors in the Atlantic (for example, the US?)? Because it will be the first time that the EU will sign an agreement with Latin America before the US and other actors like China.

(Kirstyn) One question to Carlos about "investor dispute settlement"? It's that what you said?

[**C. Mariani:** Yes, it's a format.]

(Kimberly Garcia) My question is for Dan: I wanted to get your sense of: ow far does this attrition in the US and the Congress, in terms of trade policy, fall? And specifically, do you see that there's any sense of a fight coming in Congress? Or rather, will there be trade promotion authority?

Answers

(R. Baumann) Regarding the issue of investment attraction; there has been a debate on signing investment protection agreements or not. After a few decades, we do have six or seven investment protection agreements, with a few African countries. But, at least in Brazil right now, it's hard to see a real concern in attracting investment. Because we are receiving 60 plus billion US dollars a year, of course, a good deal of it is on non-tradables, so this raises an issue on itself. But, right now, we do have an institution, APEX, which is the one that you would address potential investors to look for and see what's going on. And, as a small footnote for "merchandising": we at the Ministry of Planning, together with the Inter-American Bank and APEX, organized last year a Brazilian Investment Forum, an experience we are renewing in May 29 and 30, in São Paulo. A number of business opportunities are raised in this type of exercise. So, these are the mechanisms that we have to attract and orient investment. Having said that, we envy the US, UK, Australia, Germany, and so on, because they have the faculty of saying "Not here" to an investor, "You cannot buy this port", "You cannot do that" … We, in Brazil, do not have the means to do that. Except for CADE, which is the institution that forbids monopoly behaviour. It's an institution of the Ministry of Justice that deals with ensuring competition in every market. But that's the only tool we have right now, and this is an increasing concern in Brasília.

(R. Flôres) Thank you very much! I must say that foreign investment in Brazil is still a great success; what I heard from everybody last year, and I hope this year will be the same.

(R. Fendt) A small footnote on what Renato just said, there is an interesting case of the Brazilian government interfering in a particular firm. Probably many of you heard about the negative for Boeing to buy Embraer. Apparently, the Brazilian government is excluding the military division of Embraer. Just to provoke all of you, these 20 years of negotiations with EU, this is due to the fact that Mercosul is negotiating with the EU. Some people believe that we could proceed ourselves: Brazil x EU; Paraguay x EU; Uruguay x EU…. I don't buy it! Because the Argentines and Uruguayans are not disturbing very much these negotiations. The culprits are the EU and us. The decision of the Mercosul council was never published in Brazil, so it's not an official law. So, technically and legally, it cannot negotiate directly with the EU; this of course would kill Mercosul or whatever remains of Mercosul. But, just a point to 'complicate' your thoughts about this subject.

(R. Baumann) Another footnote: I said that there's no mechanism. We have constitutional constraints for investors in some areas (airlines, press, and banking sector). It must be formally approved. And in the case of the banking sector, it has to be authorised by the President himself. The case of Embraer is a bit different, because the government has the golden share, hence, it is one of the partners involved in the negotiations. And, of course, Embraer has the military branch, and there are other issues involved.

(C. Mariani) I should remind that, in South America, we had this "integration" that started much earlier than Mercosul: it had headquarters in Montevideo, and 25 years have already passed. So, all the original agreements, between the 16 countries in South America have already reached tariff zero. Nobody talks about this. It's an improvement in the Brazilian trade here in the South America. And the Colombians had very positive behaviour, Chile also; the only "bad cat" is Venezuela. It's something sizable already, and for this type of operation Mercosul is not needed.

(D. Hamilton) I have two questions directly to me. On Brazilian investments, just to provoke my Brazilian colleagues, the problem of investments flows in Brazil is not that they might stop, instead all the rules governing them make it hard for investors. There may well be a lot of investment currently, but it could be so much more if it was made easier for investors to come here. If you couple that with law that prohibits some investments due to national security concerns. We have a process in the United States that does that. Europeans don't have anything like that, but they are debating it.

On the EU-Mercosul issue, we have a Summit of the Americas coming up, the President said he's coming (so, stay tuned!). Under the US Constitution, trade authority is invested with the US Congress, not with the President. What the Congress has done in the last few decades is to delegate that "trade promotion authority" to the executive branch, to negotiate trade deals, and then the executive comes back to the Congress with the deal and says "take it or leave it", "yes or no". Otherwise, the Congress would be in charge and you could imagine that there would be 500 amendments to any possible deal. And so, this is not workable. But the Congress must delegate this "trade promotion authority" every few years. And it's coming up again now. The Trump administration has just applied to the Congress for a delegation of trade "promotion authority" before June (this year). It puts the Congress in a considerable position on how to monitor the administration's trade policy. And there will be a lot of debates about this issue, over the next few months. So, coming back to my point, I can't predict it, but this is an election year and it affects different stakeholders differently. The entire U.S. House of Representatives and one-third of the U.S. Senate is being re-elected in November. The primaries influence the debate about trade. Candidates cater to their constituencies. It's very hard to predict. There is really a big debate. The President's popularity is down here. But I think there is a worthy debate on trade and there will be many more tweaks to US policies than one might get from the President's tweets.

Eloy asked about the intersection between investments, jobs and trade, and energy. Actually, you are the expert on this! I would just start again with energy; it is affected by price. The prices right now don't underscore the most ambitious scenario that we have been advancing the last few years. Nevertheless, you could argue that, if you look at all sorts of energy: renewables, biofuels, fossil fuels, … the centre of innovation, the centre of gravity on the margin is becoming the Atlantic Basin, not the Middle East, not Russia, but the Atlantic Basin. If you go all the way down through, from Canada, down through the Gulf, through Brazil, and over to West Africa and up, you see all sorts of new types of energy sources, either coming online or, given price issues again, potentially coming online. You couple that with the bio-fuels giant of Brazil (the only other real biofuels country in the world is the US).

The biggest flow of energy from Brazil to the EU is biofuels. And if you couple that with the revolution in energy that's happening in the US, in terms of all sources and kinds of energy, the US is now not only importing but also exporting certain kinds of energy, it is changing the dynamics everywhere, and will continue. And should prices change, it will even be more. But at the moment this is the underlying fundamental that's developing, and it's not really being discussed or understood. I think that translates into investment implications, again, based on price, you could see new kinds of investment flowing in different areas. Because of the energy economy that's developing, you see a lot of European investment in the US (in Texas, European investment is amazing, because of the energy economy). The US ability now to export liquefied natural gas to Europe has forced the Russians to lower their price; Europeans are building new types of terminals in different European ports, because they want to break the dependence on Russian energy.

That's going to start to develop everywhere. The timeframe is a long one, but it is dynamic, and it will influence energy investments as well, which, of course, then turn into jobs. You will see all sorts of job opportunities in many different parts of the energy sector. We see that tremendously in the US, in areas that haven't been traditionally part of the energy economy. This is transforming a lot of state economies in ways they wouldn't think about, and not just Texas; we have a whole book on energy and transportation in the Atlantic Basin,[1] and I think it's worth to read it.

(**R. Flôres**) Thank you, Dan! Well, we started late, but we shall stop in time. I would like to thank my colleagues at the roundtable very much: you did a wonderful job!

---

1. P. Isbell and E. Álvarez Pelegry, eds., *Energy and Transportation in the Atlantic Basin*, Washington, DC: Center for Transatlantic Relations; distributed and available through Brookings Institution Press: the first publication by the present Jean Monnet Project (*Editors' Note*).

Closing Speech By His Excellency the
EU Ambassador to Brazil

João Titterington Gomes Cravinho

Ladies and gentlemen,

I would like to thank Mr. Carlos Ivan Simonsen Leal and Mr. Renato Flôres, for the kind introduction, and for inviting me. It is a pleasure and an honour to participate, and after your extensive day of discussions today I hope that I am able to keep you awake and interested rather than thinking of the caipirinha that is possibly waiting for you at the end of this session.

Let me also say at the outset that I am delighted to be here at the Fundação Getúlio Vargas. This is an institution that carries with it a seal of quality in everything that it does, and I am very pleased that the FGV is addressing a theme which is of such importance for the European Union, and, I would say, for Brazil.

And it is equally satisfying for me to participate in an activity of the Jean Monnet Network on Atlantic Studies. The Jean Monnet programme here in Brazil has seven chairs, each of them carrying out important but very differentiated work related to the EU, and I think that there are great benefits in working together as a network, as indeed the Chairs here in Brazil are beginning to do.

Picking up on the themes of this meeting, I would like to talk about three aspects that relate closely to the three topics discussed in today's session. First, I want to talk about the wider principles behind the trade policy of the trade policy *(relates to Session 1 –Broad Views on Atlantic Trade)*. Second, I will present some current realities about the EU's trade relationship with Mercosul and Brazil *(relates to Session 2—The EU as a main trade actor in the Atlantic)*. Finally, I would like to give you all a few insights about the ongoing negotiations with our partners here in Mercosul *(relates to Session 3—Regional Perceptions and Integrations)*. (Actually, I will confess that a couple of months ago, when I received the invitation to speak on this occasion, I thought that it was a great opportunity because it would allow me to discuss the final shape of the EU-Mercosul agreement, after 19 years of negotiations. I believed that for sure by 22 March we would have the final result. Unfortunately, that is not the case, and so what I say about the negotiations is going to have to be a bit different from what I imagined...)

Regarding the first point on European trade policy. The essential elements are laid out in the strategic document "Trade for all", which was issued in late 2015. It is far too simplistic to imagine that EU trade policy is just about free trade. Over the years we have learnt a lot about globalization, and one of the things that we have learnt is that we must create new rules so that the benefits of globalization can reach all sectors of our societies. It is not so much simple free trade that we are pursuing, it is much more rules-based international trade that we want. And when we engage with partners what we are doing is jointly establishing the rules that we need for our societies to have the widest and deepest benefits from trade. The keywords in the strategy are that trade should be effective, transparent and value based.

Effectiveness means that trade policy must deliver on its promises. For instance, we need to make sure that the benefits of trade reach workers, consumers and small companies. EU trade policy seeks to support the creation of new jobs. Around 31 million jobs in Europe depend on exports. These represent 1 in 7 jobs across 28 EU Member States. About 19 million jobs outside the EU depend on EU exports as well. More importantly, all these jobs tend to be high-skilled and on average better paid.

For EU trade policy to be effective it needs also to benefit consumers. EU consumers enjoy currently duty-free access for around 76 percent of all EU imports. It is estimated that the overall, EU households save annually around 60 billion euros on tariff savings because of EU trade policies. EU trade policy also has the priority objective of facilitating the internationalization of small companies. Only 25 percent of EU-based small and medium-sized enterprises export at all, and an even smaller portion export beyond the EU. A trade policy that helps improving these numbers is crucial as 99 percent of all enterprises in the EU are SMEs. So, these are the issues that concern us when we talk about effectiveness.

The second principle of the strategy is transparency. This is a priority taken very seriously by the EU because a lack of transparency undermines the legitimacy of the EU trade policy and public trust. By transparency we mean that we need to work more closely with all EU stakeholders and to have a more open trade policymaking process. For instance, the EU has opened negotiations to more public scrutiny by publishing key negotiating texts from all negotiations, including of course, texts related to the current negotiations with Mercosul. You could all now access and read texts proposals of the EU in this negotiation in the EU Commission DG Trade website. This is unprecedented, and I think that I am right in saying that it is unique anywhere in the world. For obvious reasons it does not make sense to carry our trade negotiations as a public spectacle; this would make it extremely difficult to achieve anything. But we do believe that the public has the right to know the essential contours of what we are working on, and they have the right to contribute to shaping our approach to negotiations by debating our approach in the public sphere.

Finally, trade for all means value-based trade. EU's trade policy is not just about economic interests. It is also about promoting and defending shared values like sustainable development, human rights, fair and ethical trade, responsible business conduct and the fight against corruption. The trade agreements that the EU negotiates include a chapter on trade and sustainable development. For example, the text proposal of the trade sustainable and development chapter that the EU tabled with Mercosul in the current negotiations—which, as mentioned, anyone could find on the DG Trade website—includes rules intended to promote the implementation of provisions on core labour standards, on the effective implementation of multilateral environmental agreements, the enforcement of domestic labour and environmental laws—the level of protection of which should never be lowered to attract trade and investment—and the promotion of responsible management of supply chains.

Based on this trade policy view, the EU has constructed its trade and investment relationship with Mercosul and Brazil. Let me now provide you with a general view of how our relationship is with these partners.

The EU has a long-lasting trade and investment relationship with Mercosul and with Brazil.

In 2016, the EU was its biggest trading partner, accounting for 21.8 percent of the bloc's total trade (*data for 2017 on how the EU relates to other trade partners of MCS is not yet available, but there are indications that we may have been overtaken by China*). The EU's exports to the four Mercosul countries totalled €44 billion in 2017; their exports to the EU were €42 billion in 2017. This made Mercosul the 9th biggest trading partner of the EU, accounting for 2.3 percent of the EU's total trade. In 2016 the EU exported €20 billion of services to Mercosul and imported €11 billion. The EU is the biggest foreign investor in Mercosul, rising from a stock of €253 billion in 2010 to €447 billion in 2016. What is less well known is that Mercosul is also a major investor in the EU, with stocks of €104 billion in 2016.

Looking specifically at Brazil, this country is the EU's eleventh trading partner accounting for 1.7 percent of total EU trade in 2017: around €63 billion. In 2017 EU exports to Brazil reached €32 billion, making Brazil the 17th biggest exporting market. EU imports from Brazil in 2017 were of €31 billion, becoming the 12th biggest import origin for the EU. In 2016 the EU exported €13 billion of services to Brazil and Brazil exported around €8 billion to the EU.

Perhaps most importantly, Brazil is the EU's third main destination of foreign direct investment, only behind the US and Switzerland; there is greater EU investment in Brazil than in China and India together: Brazil holds 48.5 percent of the entire EU investment stock in Latin America and represents 81 percent of EU investment in Mercosul. It is estimated that the investment announced by EU companies between 2006 and 2015 created more than 278,000 jobs in the Brazilian economy. These jobs accounted for half of all estimates of jobs generated by greenfield investments announced by foreign companies in Brazil. But this investment is not only one-way. Brazilian companies have also invested in the EU. Over in 2006-2015 period, Brazilian companies announced 115 greenfield investment projects, totalling € 2.1 billion, distributed among 15 countries of the EU. The estimated generation of jobs linked to these announced investments was of 6,405 new openings.

All these numbers illustrate the increasing economic interdependence between the EU, Mercosul and Brazil and the importance of trade for all our economies. They also remind us of the importance of finding new ways to further develop the economic benefits of our relationship. On that front, the most important current initiative to make the most of the economic potential of our partnership is undoubtedly the conclusion of an ambitious Association Agreement between the EU and Mercosul.

The EU-Mercosul agreement has been a long time coming. The negotiations were launched in the last century of the past millennium, 19 years ago. Back then, Brazil was only *tetracampeão do Mundo*; Mark Zuckerberg, the creator of Facebook, was a 15-year-old kid completing freshman year in high school; and, most importantly, the world was going to end because of the Y2K problem and the millennium bug. The political and economic context back then was also drastically different. For example, the EU was composed by only 15 countries and the German mark, French franc, Italian lira coexisted for three more years with the new euro.

Negotiations between Mercosul and the EU have not been the swiftest, nor the easiest. There have been a lot of stumbling blocks on the way. However, parties have shown that negotiations have gained a new momentum in the past couple of years. In May 2016, offers were exchanged for the first time in 12 years and, since then, talks have intensified significantly. Several negotiations rounds have taken place with significant progress reported. These technical talks have been backed up by a strong political will, as demonstrated by the recent Ministerial meetings in December in Buenos Aires and in January of this year in Brussels.

Of course, the closer the negotiations get to the end, the harder the challenges. Parties are moving forward now by tackling the most difficult issues. The most recent round of negotiations in Asunción in the end of February reported good and steady progress. Now both sides are in touch to continue the work to bridge outstanding gaps.

After so many years of negotiations and now that we are seemingly in the last stretch, it is important to remind why this agreement is so important for the EU and for Mercosul.

The Association Agreement will generate increased flows of goods and services for the benefit of all. EU and Mercosul companies will both get new market opportunities. The world economy today is made up of integrated global value chains. Our economies are highly inter-connected, and the great majority of companies need to buy inputs or sell their products internationally. Products are no longer made simply in any one place. And services have an increasingly important role, including in the production of goods that are traded. Parts, components, raw materials and services from many different countries come together in a planetary production line. By opening up to each other, our companies will pay lower prices for inputs and reach new clients.

We will both be able to produce more and better by participating in larger markets. We will also benefit from the complementarity of our economies. Consumers on both sides of the Atlantic will get better choices and lower prices; and trade agreements bring more confidence to investors, benefiting everyone. Already now, the Mercosul region represents one euro in twenty of the foreign investment our companies make. Across this region, over 5000 affiliates of EU companies employ more than 1.5 million people.

In Brazil alone, Spanish company Telefonica supplies nearly one hundred million people with access to phones, mobiles, TV and the internet.

The Volkswagen plant in Pacheco, near Buenos Aires, sells its Amarok model in almost 70 markets all over the world. Greater access to global markets offers a great opportunity for products and businesses from Mercosul, which is still relatively closed in on itself. Opening more to the world means new and greater opportunities to attract new investment, and export more.

Particularly in Brazil, several studies have quantified the benefits that an agreement would create. A study by FIESP (2014) showed that the agreement would have the potential to increase Brazilian exports by 12 percent. It further highlights that due to the ambitious scope of the agreement, it could boost the transfer of technology and technical cooperation with Brazil. A study of the FGV indicated that an agreement could increase Brazilian GDP by 2.7 percent. This study also found that agribusiness exports from Brazil would increase 60.8 percent by 2030.

If compared to other EU agreements in the region, these numbers seem even more realistic. For example, in the first four years from the entry into force of the agreement between the EU and Chile, exports from Chile to the EU quadrupled. In the case of the agreement between the EU and Mexico, Mexican exports to the EU have increased 15 percent. The benefits are so clear for both parties, that recently the EU and these partners launched negotiations to modernize these two agreements.

An ambitious agreement could also create positive dynamic effects in the economy. Recent studies of the World Bank and of OECD (2018) point that Brazil can seize greater benefits from greater global and regional integration. Brazil's integration into global trade is much lower than in other emerging economies, as tariff and non-tariff barriers in Brazil shield enterprises from global opportunities and foreign competition. More exposure to trade will allow companies to source the best inputs and capital goods from international markets and will also raise productivity among domestic producers as they improve efficiency and seize new export opportunities. According to these studies, this would create new jobs, especially for those in lower skills and incomes. Consumers will also benefit from more competitive prices, with strong effects on low-income households.

A recent study made by the Secretary of the Presidency for Strategic Affairs reached a similar conclusion. According to this study in a scenario of full tariff liberalization over a period of 20 years, Brazil would increase productivity and Brazilians would benefit of a reduction of 5 percent on consumers prices. More importantly, the study finds that in 48 out of 57 economic sectors in Brazil, employment levels would increase or at least would be maintained—while the decrease in the remaining 9 sectors would be limited ranging from 0.5 to 2 percent maximum.

In sum, all these numbers point to the fact that the conclusion of an ambitious Association Agreement between the EU and Mercosul will benefit both sides. Nowadays we are seeing that voices of protectionism and indeed advocates of trade wars, are spreading fast and are unfortunately materialising. The agreement would be a clear signal to the world that, rather than closing markets, the way to move forward is to find better instruments to integrate our economies in an effective, transparent and value-based way.

In other words, we not only have the opportunity to benefit our own citizens, we also have the opportunity of sending an important message to the world.

Thank you.